LABORING FOR FREEDOM

LABORING FOR FREEDOM

A NEW LOOK AT THE HISTORY OF LABOR IN AMERICA

DANIEL JACOBY

M.E. Sharpe
ARMONK, NEW YORK
LONDON, ENGLAND

Library of Congress Cataloging-in-Publication Data

Jacoby, Daniel, 1951–
Laboring for Freedom : a new look at the history of labor in America / Daniel Jacoby.
p.   cm.
Includes bibliographical references and index.
ISBN 0–7656–0251–2 (alk. paper). — ISBN 0–7656–0252–0 (pbk. : alk. paper)
1. Labor—United States—History.   2. Labor movement—United States—History.
3. Labor policy—United States—History.   4. Labor laws and legislation—United
States—History.   I. Title.
HD8066.J33 1998
331′.0973—dc21
97–31985
CIP

Printed in the United States of America

The paper used in this publication meets the minimum requirements of
American National Standard for Information Sciences—
Permanence of Paper for Printed Library Materials,
ANSI Z 39.48-1984.

BM (c)   10   9   8   7   6   5   4   3   2   1
BM (p)   10   9   8   7   6   5   4   3   2

For my mother Dorothy and my daughter Corianna,

Though I am sad neither of you can read this now, I am thankful we have had these times together.

My love and affection.

Contents

Acknowledgments   ix

Prologue   3

Part I: Independence or Contract   **11**

1. Republican Soil   13
2. Contracting Liberties   33

Part II: Illusory Freedoms   **53**

3. The Properties of Labor   55
4. A Skillful Control: Managing the Labor Process   68
5. Incorporating Paternalism   84
6. Free Education   98

Part III: New Deals and Old Ideals   **115**

7. Union Compromise   117
8. "Rights" of Passage   130
9. Playing the Global Piano   149

Epilogue: Memories and Challenges   166

Notes   169
Bibliography   185
Index   195
About the Author   211

Acknowledgments

It is a pleasure to acknowledge the assistance and encouragement I received from others during the course of this book. Foremost, I want to thank Bruce Kochis, who scrutinized both the structure and content of my work. Not only did he read my manuscript carefully, but he also knew how to provide feedback that my delicate ego could process. I also want to thank the students, particularly Priscilla Holcomb, Tobin Dale, and Angie Douglas, who, after struggling through relatively unedited copies, commented on those early versions of this manuscript. Melvyn Dubofsky deserves two thanks, one for being the extraordinary undergraduate teacher who interested me in my subject, and the second, for his helpful suggestions in reviewing the manuscript for M.E. Sharpe. Upon their readings, Michael Honey and Alan Wood each provided ideas as well as moral support. Elinore Appel provided constructive and painstaking editorial assistance. My program director, Jane Decker, made it possible for me to find time to write despite a new baby and ever pressing departmental needs. The University of Washington generously provided financial support during the summer of 1994. I also wish to express appreciation to Marc Stern, Phillip Cushman, Constantin Behler, John Braeman, and C. Patrick Morris, all of whom have contributed to the making of this book. Finally, I want to thank my wife, Nancy Beaudet, who, over the years, has kept me a whole human being.

LABORING FOR FREEDOM

Prologue

People labored out of necessity, out of poverty, and that necessity and poverty bred the contempt in which laboring people had been held for centuries. Freedom was always valued because it was freedom from the necessity to labor.

—Gordon S. Wood,
The Radicalism of the American Revolution

Freedom means work.

—General Oliver O. Howard,
Freedman's Bureau, 1865

I would be hard-pressed to define the character of the United States without emphasizing the word freedom. Expressions such as "home of the free," "beacon of liberty," and "crucible of freedom" have been indelibly etched onto the American psyche. Despite widespread recognition that freedom is in some way linked to the American soul, accord extends little further. Even the nation's two founding documents reveal tensions at the heart of our self-proclaimed virtue. From the time of the Declaration of Independence to the ratification of the Constitution, the term "freedom" was used to bridge a wide chasm separating competing conceptions. Under one conception, a person's freedom rested on self-evident and inalienable rights, while integral to the other, freedom was synonymous with an individual's liberty of contract. Blind faith appears the most promising way to span the chasm between these alternatives, but where faith fails, ambiguity has succeeded. Freedom has become a slogan full of sound and fury, which, rather than signifying nothing, may now, perhaps, signify everything.

One of freedom's allures is that it promises the impossible: a world without constraints holding us back from our desires. However, we cannot seriously begin to discuss freedom without placing limits upon it. Although this does violence to freedom's promise, we know freedom can never be absolute. The laws of nature pull us toward our death against our will. Likewise, the laws of man pull us toward our 1040 forms each April 15.

3

As if it were not enough that gravity limits our leaps, civil ordinances keep us from scaling city buildings with climbing gear. In addition to nature and law, social taboos keep us from thinking the unthinkable or, at least, make most of us feel guilty when we do. We do not expect to be able to do everything, but we cannot stop ourselves from wishing to expand the range of the possible. When we are lucky, we can increase our power to do what we wish with little or no cost; more frequently there are trade-offs. So, what is left of our freedom?

That is precisely the crux of this book. It does little good to answer such a question in the abstract. It is better to think about the problems that freedom poses in a particular context. For our purposes that context is labor. One reason for starting here is that labor is central to the problem of freedom. After all, slavery—the antithesis of freedom—is a specific condition of labor. More broadly, our personal knowledge of many labor contexts enables us to better understand the issues at stake. However, by placing freedom into this familiar context, we may be tempted to think we already know it all. One aim of this book is to liberate us from accustomed ways of thinking so that we can reconsider labor and the conditions of our liberty in a historical context. Only when we understand that the words we use today are rooted in circumstances quite different from those to which we presently apply them will we slowly gain mastery or "freedom" over our own thoughts.

Different Kinds of Freedom

There are three big issues that we will need to confront to gain a firm grasp on labor freedom. First, we must distinguish between the concepts "freedom from" and "freedom to." This is an old distinction that few of us explicitly recognize in conversation. On one hand, it is the distinction between being free from governmental constraints, like not having to obtain a license before we hang up a shingle calling ourselves a doctor, and on the other, being free to achieve power, say, to turn our raw talents into the skilled practice of medicine. In the first case, we ask society not to stop us from doing something, while in the second case, we ask society to make available to us the means to accomplish our purposes or to exert our will. Laws, rules, and social inhibitions are the impediments from which we seek negative freedom or *freedom from*. Production, education, and civilization itself are the tools that empower positive freedom or *freedom to*. In this sense, the meanings of freedom constitute a battle between restraint and facilitation. *Freedom from* pits the individual against society, while *freedom to* lifts the individual, like a rider, onto the back of society.

The second issue involves the relationship between property and freedom. Property is actually a very complicated concept. It is not enough to say this is mine and that is yours. In most instances what is yours is yours only under certain conditions. For example, if you drive for Domino's Pizza, even if you drive your own car, you may not exceed the speed limit to deliver pizzas within the thirty-minute delivery time the store guarantees. Domino's right to run its own business as it pleases and your right to drive for whom you want in the manner you want are not guaranteed through property ownership.

Instead of thinking of property as a thing, we must think of property as expressing our rights to that thing. These include the rights to sell, to restrict use by others, or rights to enjoy what you own as you see fit. Even a thing that has no physical substance, like a song, has property rights attached. However, it is the incomplete nature of ownership rights by songwriters that allows you to sing their songs without payment for the privilege. The greater the rights of property, the more power owners have to do as they please. In this way, property rights draw zones of protection between you, as owner, and those who would tell you how you have to behave with respect to your "property." It is the boss's claim to own his store that gives him the right to tell you how to behave on the job. Of course, his or her property rights may not be absolute. For example, the law *may* protect you if, while at your place of work, your boss believes you have misbehaved and punishes you unjustly. Property is the legal device that defines your rights to subject things to your will and power and, consequently, defines the limits to owners' liberties. However, the expansion of private property is not equivalent to the expansion of freedom. Slavery, for example, allows one person to own another person as property, which is to say that one person's rights in property may deny freedom to others. The protection of freedom, therefore, requires limits upon property rights. Those limits might usefully be thought of as human rights—inalienable rights—rights which if sold or surrendered, as distinct from property rights, would jeopardize human freedom. But which rights are "inalienable" is, unfortunately, not always as self-evident as the Declaration of Independence suggests.

The third issue we must confront in discussing freedom is power. Power, too, is a double-edged sword. It may be used to liberate and transform, or it may be used to subjugate. Power is legally conveyed by property or human rights. Rights—whether property or human—are only claims unless they can be enforced. Usually we call upon governments to protect our rights, although sometimes individuals or groups, like labor unions, define and defend their own rights. In the United States, only government has the legal power to secure rights by force. Obviously, that does not mean government alone uses force, only that government alone uses force lawfully (and that, conveniently, is because government alone defines what is legal). But power is more subtle than this. Power rests in numerous conditions that are the subject of the various chapters in this book. Technology provides power to create in new ways. In so doing it extends the realm of the possible. As planes make it possible to thumb our noses at gravity, so machines in general have opened the rest of nature's niggardly cupboards to produce a seemingly magic cornucopia of material wealth. At the same time, however, as George Orwell envisioned in his book *1984,* technology also opens up possibilities for control and human domination, as in the use of electric cattle prods for torture. Our freedom is conditioned by our powers to exploit the possibilities before us, and the advantages and disadvantages those possibilities yield.

Because the world keeps changing, the conditions of freedom are in constant flux. Old maxims about freedom too often fail to reflect the situations that confront us today. Yet the past is not without its uses. We will not recognize the conditions of freedom before us today if we cannot discern how they differ from the conditions of freedom that confronted our predecessors. To forget the past and focus solely upon the present foists freedom up as an empty platitude behind which a naked emperor stands.

A Few Words about Labor

Before proceeding to our subject, a few words of caution must be interjected. Labor is not used here as a synonym for unions. Although unions play an unmistakably important role in discussions of labor and freedom, most labor in the United States has always been conducted outside the supervision or control of such organizations. To appreciate both unions and the activities of the non-unionized worker, it is best to place labor organization in its proper context. Historians who place unions center stage ask a set of questions that are not central to our investigation. They want to know why it is that organized American workers have been so weak relative to their European counterparts. They want to know why, in this respect, America is "exceptional." In consequence they find themselves examining the conditions of labor organization as if this were the goal to which all men and women aspired.[1] The history presented in these pages instead places freedom center stage, and examines the various conditions that defined workers' evolving liberties. Though it would be as incorrect to assert that all workers actively seek freedom as it would be to assert that all workers seek organization, in many respects the legacy of freedom in the United States is more central to labor history than is the legacy of unionization.

Any real history of labor that does more than chronicle unionization in the United States must take account of the fact that factory or industrial workers, in the traditional sense, have never dominated the labor landscape. Industrial workers in the United States never exceeded one-third of the labor force, so to define them as the measure of labor is grossly inaccurate. Not only would this exclude the unpaid but crucial labor of household family members, it would also exclude agricultural labor as well. There can be no basis for such a rejection other than theoretical concepts that seek to characterize the modern world as an opposition between capital and labor. While that opposition surely exists, such a division of society blinds us to other important realities. Not only has the history of women and farmers, until recently, typically been left out of accounts of labor, but so too has that of the increasingly important middle and professional classes. By shifting the thesis from organization to freedom, we see that many issues concerning the greater part of the laboring classes have not been adequately attended to.

To write a complete history of all these groups would be an immense undertaking far beyond the scope of the present work. Instead, we will explore key issues that define work and the conditions of liberty in the United States. We must take account, however briefly, of the early forms of labor that existed in colonial life and persisted to the Civil War. Many of these forms, such as indentured servitude, craft apprenticeship, the household economy, and the institution of slavery, were transparently discordant with republican conceptions of freedom. In an introductory section, we will briefly survey the challenges these forms of labor posed and the reconciliations that were forged. By 1865, these early labor institutions were either beaten back or so transformed that the antebellum period has been labeled the "triumph of contract."[2] Of course, that triumph was only fully secured with the advent of the Civil War and the Emancipation Proclamation.

The triumph of contract could not secure "absolute" freedom in the United States. Instead, it heightened the tensions between those who proclaimed their "inalienable rights" and those who maintained their rights to contract freely for their own gain. The period after the Civil War revealed the limits inherent in contract. Contract involves voluntary exchange and is presumed to reflect the "will" of free persons. As the outer edges of free exchange were exploited, the question emerged whether one could trade one's freedom to associate, to protest, or to quit, and still be free? Moreover, how much had to be written into a contract before it defined the "will" of an individual? Did free exchange exist when specific wage payments were exchanged for uncertain labor obligations? For many Marxists, the crux of the labor problem lay in the attempt by employers to extract the greatest surplus from workers who surrendered their time, rather than a definite quantity of work. Selling one's time, they would contend, often involved the surrender of one's will. Seen in this light, the classic Marxist formulation of labor exploitation is part of the more general quest by workers in America to secure their freedom.[3]

Contract, control, exploitation, and freedom frequently intersected. Piecework, as opposed to wage labor, was one way employees could avoid the control of employers who bought their time without specifying in contract how hard they had to work or what type of tasks they would have to do. Even here, however, employers often seemed to hold an extra measure of control. In the coalfields the payment per ton of coal seemed a definite wage for a definite amount of work. However, the intensity of work varied according to who weighed the coal. Workers often believed that weigh masters cheated them at the scales. Consequently they sought control over the weight measurements in an attempt to ensure that the contracts they signed had the meaning they intended.[4] Power to define the unit of work often turned some men into masters and others servants. Informed and voluntary consent lay at the heart of the legal definition of contract. However, only if contracts could define all the contingencies that might occur could the signers know what the exchange consisted of. However, no contract could do this and consequently freedom of contract necessitated some system of dispute resolution or "justice" when unidentified contingencies arose.

In the large, three conceptions of labor justice emerged. One relied upon market competition for labor to limit abuse by employers who used their property rights too arbitrarily.[5] The second relied upon collective action by workers in their attempt to enforce their own rights.[6] The third involved state intervention either through recourse to the courts or through legislation.[7] None of these alternatives could be pursued without redefining conditions of freedom. In the period between 1865 and 1933, these alternatives contended with one another. This is the subject of the second section of this book.

The Great Depression broke the impasse. In 1933 President Franklin Delano Roosevelt proposed legislation that redefined the balance of power. Power to enforce worker claims, or establish worker rights, was partially delegated to individuals who organized themselves collectively into labor unions. This involved a new dilemma: The freedom of individual laborers was to be preserved through organizations whose survival depended upon their ability to force members to act collectively when narrow self-interest dictated each act separately on his or her own account. The conditions of this kind of freedom appeared antithetical to the earlier triumph of contract that had relied upon individual rather than collective action. However, an irony arose in that the rise of collective rights was accompanied by legal recognition of new forms of individual rights. From civil rights to pension rights, individuals found that regardless of their ability to use freedom of contract to bargain for improvements, the state now guaranteed specific employment rights. Whether these were, in fact, the inalienable rights the founders believed were self-evident or whether these rights were a new species altogether different, the conditions of freedom had changed once again.

Thus three broad movements define the sections that punctuate this book. The first involves the transformation from republicanism to freedom of contract. The second describes the limits of contract and the quest for alternatives. The third section explains how collective rights, as one of those alternatives, replaced individual freedom of contract only to find that new rights were created protecting individual employment. The movement from period to period has to be bridged with some understanding of the motivating forces. Accordingly, we will see that many of the underlying forces that contributed to change involved technology. As a science both of production and of organization, technology empowered new possibilities and these have changed the conditions of labor. Although a powerful motivating force, it is not possible to rely entirely upon technology to explain the evolution of American society. Most of the technology available here was available elsewhere, and few other countries developed precisely the same rules and institutions as did the United States. Thus, the uniqueness of the American quest for freedom must be lodged in the force of its character, environment, law, history, and leaders.

Ultimately, my hope is that this book assists in our emancipation from the belief that freedom is a well-defined concept. Rather, freedom should be imagined as permanently lying just beyond existing constraints where alternative conditions are either a little more empowering or a little less onerous. Our struggles toward greater freedom depend upon a fruitful dialogue between competing conceptions of freedom. Liberty will always have its conditions and it is up to us not to be swayed by the rhetorical appeal inherent in phrases like "liberty of contract" or "inalienable rights." Our duty, as individuals who would be free, is to think critically about the values that are promoted by one formulation of freedom as opposed to another, and then to act accordingly.

—— PART I ——

INDEPENDENCE OR CONTRACT

—————— Chapter 1 ——————

Republican Soil

Nothing is a due and adequate representation of a state, that does not represent its ability, as well as its property. But as ability is a vigorous and active principle, and as property is sluggish, inert, and timid, it never can be safe from the invasions of ability, unless it [property] be out of all proportion, predominant in the representation. It must be represented too in great masses of accumulation, or it is not rightly protected. The characteristic essence of property, formed out of the combined principles of its acquisition and conservation is to be unequal. The great masses therefore which excite envy, and tempt rapacity, must be put out of the possibility of danger.
—Edmund Burke, *Reflections on the Revolution in France*

It is an underlying theme of this book that there are only two types of workers: those who are struggling to be free and those who are unfree. Although absolute freedom is a fable, the failure to struggle toward it guarantees that conditions will not improve. In revolutionary America, the impulse toward freedom was best captured by the mythic allure of the independent yeoman: The proud homesteading farmer was the central symbol of American life. Our discussion of labor and freedom in America begins by examining this symbol as it has survived through historical memory.

Farmers and Master Craftsmen: At the Heart of Republican Ideals

Today, when labor issues and history are discussed, farmers are seldom mentioned. This was not always so, and why it should be so now requires explanation. Farming is obviously work, but whether it is also labor depends upon the definition one chooses. If we imagine—incorrectly—that farmers always worked their own land, then it might be said of them that they comprised a unique class of workers—one that by virtue of its self-employment was not forced to sell its labor, but instead simply sold the grain or meat that its labor produced. To sell your labor conjures up two immense social, legal, and economic questions: Is it possible to sell labor without also selling yourself? If not, can a person whose survival requires the sale of his or her labor ever be free? The questions flow from the fact that in selling our labor we sell to others the right to direct and control that labor. If labor is not separable from the person, then the sale of labor is the sale of freedom. The farmer, like the independent or master craftsman, stands at one end of the spectrum of labor freedom while the hired hand stands at the other.

It can be argued that this distinction is merely one of appearance, not of substance. After all, if economic need forces the farmer to produce goods demanded by the open market, is it not a chimera to call the sale of goods "independence" and the sale of labor "servility"? The ideas that dominated political thought during the revolutionary era, ideas that are encompassed under the label republicanism, sustained exactly this distinction.[1] Furthermore, although much has changed, this distinction continues to weigh heavily upon conceptions of freedom today.

Although republicanism was an outgrowth of European Enlightenment thinking, its hold over the imagination was nowhere so great as in the United States. In Europe, tradition and status played too great a role to permit common people to constitute themselves as free citizens in an independent republic of their own making. American colonists, however, carried away the seeds of Europe's new thought to their more fertile soil. Human imagination fertilized the crude customs and practices they brought to this land so as to nurture republican ideals; ideals that promised to satisfy the colonists' needs and aspirations. The image of the yeoman farmer, and also of the master artisan, stood at the heart of these republican ideals. Although late colonial and early American life often fell short of realizing its ideals, it provided enough hopeful signs to sustain the emerging republican faith.

The yeoman farmer and master artisan were European, not American, creations. But it was Americans who allowed themselves to believe that the independence they promised was universally achievable. Where such faith was not practical in the old world, their new land-abundant and labor-scarce environment nourished colonists' peculiar hopefulness. The prospect of a homestead was the prospect of independence. By successfully establishing and governing a household enterprise, a man established the rough equality that entitled him to the full rights and privileges of citizenship in a republic. More important than the mere possession of land and property, however, was the ability conveyed by such ownership to act independently without need to curry favor. Only this enabled citizens to exercise their political judgments with integrity. A family household was regarded as its own "little commonwealth." Successful household management and property were in this way linked to the proper governance of a republic. Americans differed from their European forefathers chiefly in their belief that it was reasonable for the common man to aspire to such independence. This republican ideology found anchor in the conditions of labor that the New World offered.

To understand the New World, one must know something of what was left behind in the Old. The first American colonies were planted in the early seventeenth century just as social, intellectual, and commercial revolutions began to jolt Europe's aristocratic society. Feudalism had passed centuries earlier without undoing the formal structures of titled status and privilege. As the Kings of Europe grabbed power for themselves, their increasingly centralized military control established a civil order that, by the thirteenth century, eroded the feudal society. The manorial system that superseded feudalism converted warlords into landlords. The new civil order vitalized commerce and, in turn, expanded the class of merchants and manufacturers. These men of commerce sometimes achieved wealth so great that they could buy the lordly titles that, in centuries past, had been accorded solely through heredity or battle.

In the 1600s the old and new nobility constituted roughly 5 percent of Britain's population. Atop this social hierarchy, Lords of the Realm (dukes, earls, marquees, viscounts, and barons) and Lords Spiritual (archbishops and bishops) comprised the peerage that was entitled to sit in the House of Lords.[2] By the colonial period, however, the value of this privilege was reduced, and would subsequently be reduced still further, by the increasing importance of the less aristocratic House of Commons.

Although the formal power of Britain's landed lords diminished substantially, their influence remained much greater than that of the rent collectors we call landlords today. Since antiquity these lords had enforced the customs of their manors and exercised personal dominion over the land upon which peasants were bound. Ancient lords had exacted payments from their tenants for everything from their marriages to their burial rights, not to mention the simple tilling of their soil. In the Middle Ages those payments customarily involved labor services. Such obligations to their lords defined the peasant's servile condition. By the thirteenth and fourteenth centuries labor obligations had generally been commuted to monetary rents.[3] By the seventeenth century, the most visible legacy of the past lay in the deference common people owed to their titled gentlemen. In the colonies, however, only a few untempered remnants of the old order survived. Along the Hudson River in New York, for example, Dutch Patroons continued to command the fealty and services of their tenants. More often, however, the hereditary transfer of noble land, titles, and status were not easily reestablished in a fresh land. Although crown land grants to men like William Penn and Lord Baltimore raised the possibility of resurrecting a titled nobility upon American shores, in actuality this did not happen.

Colonization was simply a dimension of the ongoing commercial revolution that had earlier conspired to convert servile labor dues into the freedom of cash payments. Colonization similarly advanced the spread of freer, more contractually oriented relationships by increasing the demand for labor at precisely the moment when commercial life endowed money with new possibilities. Money gave master and servant alike the freedom to pursue more options than did custom-defined service payments. This new freedom was important because it enabled both to pursue self-defined best interests. Economic and personal incentives, not custom, would govern individual behavior.

Not too much should be made of these tentative movements as not all people were equally affected. Hired peasants, for instance, were not completely exempt from all customary obligations. For example, agricultural workers were often obliged to render a year's service ending at harvest time. Failure to perform their contractual labor obligations was a imprisonable offense.[4] As legal historians like Robert Steinfeld point out, the ability to use the law to enforce labor contracts was what distinguished early English labor markets from latter-day "free" labor markets.[5] That is, during colonial times, failure to fulfill a contract to work was a criminal offense whereas today, at worst, it would only constitute grounds for a suit to recover damages. Among common country folk, only the yeoman farmer, the man who had used his release from custom to sizably increase the land he held in *fee simple*—free of obligation—was considered an independent man. Aside from religious tolerance, the principle attraction stirring American settlement lay in the greater prospects the new land afforded for such independence.

Ironically, in order to attain independence, many British emigrants to America submitted to lengthy servitudes called indentures.[6] Merchant Companies, like the Virginia Company, sought to people their commercial plantations in the New World by dangling inducements, particularly the prospect of landed independence. As before, trade continued to expand the freedoms that one's labor might achieve. In the seventeenth and eighteenth centuries close to three-quarters of the immigrants to British Atlantic coast colonies were indentured servants. Indenture contracts detailed the terms of the transaction. To ensure its validity, the contract was ripped in two, one part for each party, so that its validity was guaranteed only when the teeth of the two halves fit together. The indenture system was a colonial innovation, adapted from the European tradition of guild apprenticeship. Under English guild practice, youngsters were bound to artisan masters— usually until age twenty-four—in exchange for being taught the "mysteries" of their craft. Apprenticed boys exchanged labor for training, whereas indentured servants, on the other hand, received transportation instead. Such service enabled men, women, and children to borrow the payment for their passage to America in exchange for a number of years of labor.

Indentured servitude may be distinguished from apprenticeship in a second way. Overlooking the young orphans of London who periodically were forcibly shanghaied to the Chesapeake, indentured servitude was, at least in principle, a matter of choice. By contrast, the English Statute of Artificers required children to be bound by apprenticeship unless parents could ensure that their children would not become public burdens requiring poor relief. This 1563 law was intended to buttress the English guild system, then already in decline. Prior to this law, the guilds, not the government, were responsible for regulating their own crafts and apprenticeship systems.

In their time, the guilds too had converted commercial opportunities into freedom, two elements of which were central to British liberty. As commerce initially expanded, serfs who ran away from manorial lords found protection under town guilds. It was said that, "Town air makes men free." Thus, one element of liberty was freedom from obligatory personal service to a manorial lord. This was not the personal liberty we think of today. In fact, guilds regulated membership through apprenticeship, the conditions of work, and the quality of production; rules that many today would regard as antithetical to freedom. These regulations were frequently stipulated in minute detail. For example, weavers' guilds dictated to their members how many threads each piece of cloth must contain. As the medievalist Stephen Epstein points out, although these regulations deprived members of considerable personal liberty, they were tolerated, if not actually encouraged, because through the maintenance of quality and the suppression of uncontrolled competition and innovation they stabilized their trades.[7] The privilege guild members enjoyed in regulating their own affairs constituted an important second meaning of English freedom. The two freedoms—freedom from personal service, and collective governance—are aspects of liberty that coexist in tension with each other.

The enactment of the Statute of Artificers in 1563 signaled that the power of guilds was waning. The state, aided by bounty-hunting informers, undertook responsibility to regulate countryside infractions that the guilds could no longer enforce on their own. Enacted just forty years prior to the first American settlements, the statute's coercive labor regulations correct any misimpressions that colonial American life was built upon a strong tradition of individual freedom. Although the heritage of British freedom was real, it had not reached so far, or so many, that American citizens today would want to return to those times. Though England was fast removing the yoke of customary personal servitudes, state compulsion, economic desperation, and deference to persons of high status continued to separate common people from meaningful personal freedom.

The Mercantilist System

The Statute of Artificers was a key element in the emerging mercantilist system, the workings of which are important to an understanding of the times. Under that system, aggressive merchants contested the control that landed lords had traditionally exercised over public policy. Mercantilists argued that the protection of commercial interests was prerequisite to the maintenance of national power. In pursuit of this end, nations like England granted merchants protective tariffs and monopolies in exchange for taxes and royalties.[8] This revenue made it possible to levy a royal navy and this, in turn, made it possible for Britain to dominate the sea. Sea power enabled England to plant and secure the colonies that supplied its home workshops with vital raw materials. The symbiotic relationship between industry and state stoked the fires of Nationalism and Empire. What mattered was not the wealth of the individuals who comprised the nation, on whose behalf economist and moral philosopher Adam Smith would later argue, but the wealth of the traders upon whom the state depended. Insofar as the state had concerns about its working people, its regulations were intended to ensure that they not impair Britain's trade position—and that usually meant low wages and minimal economic rights and freedoms. For example, mechanics were denied the right to emigrate, lest they take with them England's trade secrets. Democracy widened only so far as to extend citizen control from those peers who inherited it to those merchants who could pay for it. Mercantilism, insofar as it was a coherent set of ideas, tipped the levers of state toward those commercial interests in whose self-interest ever greater governmental protections and favors were required.

Nonetheless, mercantilism inadvertently seasoned a revolutionary brew in America. Just as mercantilism's quest for trade and profit made America possible, it also stymied many dreams for which colonists had endured numerous hardships and servitudes. Ultimately, it made bedfellows of diverse colonists who, had they remained in Britain, would have been divided by social rank. For merchant, artisan, and farmer alike, mercantilism undermined faith that Britain would rule its empire justly. Crown policies were perceived as partial to domestic interests and harmful to those of its colonists. Not only did mercantilism require sacrifices from colonial traders and manufacturers, it also denied America's would-be gentry the self-rule possessed by their European cousins.

Foremost, it was merchants who defined British policy as intolerable. Had American merchants enjoyed the same sovereignty as their British counterparts, whose consent to taxation was required before policies affecting them were imposed, grievances might have been settled more amicably. Colonial discontent was excited not just by particular policies—policies that seldom exacted from colonists more than the value of services British administration yielded—but by the perception that the crown was usurping privileges that the merchants believed to be rightfully theirs. These colonists told themselves that if they ceded self-government without protest, they could never be sure that England's rule would not regularly sacrifice their interests. Rich and influential colonial merchants opposed the British Navigation Acts that enumerated specific goods and prohibited their direct transport from the colonies to foreign destinations. Such rules gave rise to smuggling by otherwise respected citizens, John Hancock being the most notable example. Hancock and others did well enough until the British began to enforce their laws by seizing the smugglers' vessels. Policies such as this flared passions. Denied direct consultation before the enactment of such rules, colonial merchants came to resent the fact that the rights their brethren had won in Britain did not exist for them. Through a number of ill-thought-out confrontations, the British managed to enrage not only the merchants, but artisans and farmers as well. This, even though British rule often provided the latter with more benefits than burden.

The result was a revolution whose monetary cost has been calculated to have exceeded its immediate gain. However, a revolution fomented by the allure of independence could not be contained by simple cost accounting. Once unleashed, the concept of independence turned colonists' sights inward toward their own customs and practices. The revolution gave them new eyes with which to recognize self-imposed servilities. The politics of liberty penetrated the sinews of daily life and exposed the contradictions between assertions of independence from England and colonists' more everyday subordination. The significance of the revolution, thus, lies not in the drive for national independence, but rather in the way the revolution imploded internal inconsistencies. From the revolution until the present, the rhetoric of freedom has affected everything from welfare to immigration to surrogate parenting. The yardstick of liberty and independence now measures virtually every labor issue with which this book concerns itself.

The Revolution and Its Legacy

The revolution made the ideology of republican independence the nation's unofficial creed. If only because there was so much to be independent of, republicanism became the rallying point for divergent interests. Whether farmers, merchants, artisans, or slave owners, each group presumed republican self-rule more responsive to their aspirations for independence. American republicanism made any individual who was competent to govern his household a stakeholder in the governance of the community. If government defined and protected the people's property and rights, who better than such stalwart citizens to comprise that government? Expanding on an earlier British idea, Thomas Jefferson proclaimed that governments derived their "just Powers from the Consent of the Governed." Any man of property, whether comprised of land, securities, or skill, was a responsible citizen for whom the affairs of state were a source of legitimate concern, and in whose hands the affairs of state could reasonably be entrusted.

As used above, the phrase *man of property* defines the thinking of that age. Although women's labor was vital to colonial life, female participation in its politics was almost completely non-existent. Jefferson is reported to have said that "[O]ur ladies have been too wise to wrinkle their foreheads with politics. They are contented to soothe and calm the minds of husbands ruffled from political debate. They have the good sense to value domestic happiness above all others."[9] Such opinions did not go entirely uncontested—patriot John Adam's wife herself protested the "Tyrannical" nature of men's dominance over women.[10] But, as one Virginian explained, "Nature herself had ... pronounced, on women and children, a sentence of incapacity to exercise political power." That the Constitution had neglected to say this, according to this wag, was simply, "Because to the universal sense of all mankind, these were self-evident truths."[11]

Gender thus defined one limit that republican independence was not designed to breach. Men made the facile assumption that husbands and fathers could adequately represent to the outside world the interests of the households they governed. With hindsight, we may now readily ask why, if consent was required for the exercise of governmental power, was not democracy within households equally important? In answering that divisiveness was avoided by creating a single spokesman for the household, many men relied upon the same argument that justified monarchy. Contemporary thinking aside, when it came to legal rights and the law, gender differentiation was so thoroughly established that logical inconsistencies were readily rebuffed. In practice, however, we will see that marital and household relations often did change even though legal presumptions subordinated women to men.

In addition to gender problems, republicanism faced a more immediately pressing issue involving the question of property. What was property and what rights should be accorded to it? Land created few problems. According to John Locke, he who tilled the land had a natural right to the fruits of his labor. Financial wealth, resting as it did upon claims to tangible entities, caused only slightly more difficult questions. Property in one's skill, on the other hand, posed a more substantial quandary. In England, craft guilds had decided the rights and duties of their artisan members. However, guilds had weakened in England and they were even less successful in its colonies. In their absence, American investments in skill were provided little protection, save the occasional occupation that required practitioners to possess a license. Even in medicine, where this practice was initiated in 1760, it was to be a long time before licenses effectively prevented unlimited competition from quacks and thereby protected the investments doctors made in their craft. More generally, though, only material wealth, like the craft master's shop, was clearly protected as property. Before industrialization took hold, the artisan was able to govern an independent household workshop in which he was his own master. However, with massive new machinery and production changes then afoot, the master craftsman was already, even during the revolutionary era, being challenged.[12]

The vast majority of colonists supported themselves through farming and consequently land occupied a central place within emerging republican traditions. Agriculture, land, and household were the building blocks of colonial independence. Farm households were comprised not only of husbands, wives, and children, but often of servants, slaves, and apprentices as well. Thus, households should not be thought of in familial terms alone. Only the master of the household possessed a freedom that we might still be able to recognize as such today, and even he was subject to supervision from his church, community, and state.

Religion imposed a strong set of moral strictures upon individuals in early colonial society that were enforced by stripping away individual privacy. Crowded within households, people were under constant surveillance; outside them, church busybodies kept up the vigil. According to historian Edmund Morgan, seventeenth-century Massachusetts' Puritan ministers taught a religion designed to instill a fear that would inspire individuals to remember their earthly duties, foremost among which was the obedience owed to one's masters.[13] Of masters, no one, from the top of society on down, was free. Ministers served their lord, husbands served their ministers, and wife, child, servant, and apprentice served the heads of their households. Southern society was not much different. There, solitary persons could be ordered to live in "licensed families" whose masters were charged to observe the "course, carriage, and behavior, of every single person . . . whether he or she walk diligently in a constantly lawful employment."[14] Between fear and community supervision, individuals were expected not to succumb to earthly temptations and indolence.

When religion and ostracism proved insufficient, the community imposed legal strictures to produce a harmonious community safe from the economic forces that threatened it. Together, both God and state legislatures held markets and materialism within bounds. In the assize of bread, for example, the state dictated the weight, price, and ingredients of bread in order to secure cheap and adequate supplies. The various forms of price gouging were anti-Christian offenses.[15] Communities not only told their members what not to do, but also compelled them to fulfill social obligations. Early settlements demanded that citizens contribute their labor in building bridges, roads, and other community necessities. However, as with the older English manorial customs these obligations resembled, wealthier citizens eventually succeeded in buying their release from such servitude. Ultimately, taxes replaced compulsory labor. Our now dormant military draft is a lone reminder of these personal servitudes.

Men found respite from external control as the masters of their households. They alone had legal authority to sign contracts and hold property. While single women held similar rights, unmarried females were pressured by their communities to marry, or remarry, as quickly as possible. Widows were not expected to grieve for long and spinsters were regarded with suspicion. The oath to "love, honor, and obey" defined the basis of the marriage relationship. Although wives might work outside the household, husbands could legally demand that their wages be paid directly to them. In fact, because masters held the right to assign household labor, similar payments could be arranged for work done by slaves, servants, children, and apprentices as well. Husbands had legal latitude to use such force as was deemed necessary to secure domestic harmony—provided that they did not inflict permanent injury. Protected by the sanctum of the household, even transgressions beyond this legal limit were difficult to prosecute.

Control almost always involves the use of both carrots and sticks. It would be too one-sided a discussion to dwell only on punishment when family control was also facilitated through reward, the most important being the land or property that provided households their living. Historian Philip Greven documented how, in Andover, Massachusetts, parents used land to secure obedience from sons.[16] Even after their children had married, parents withheld title to family land while sons provided for them in their old age. Parents secured filial obedience to the very end by dangling the carrot of inheritance before their children until the last moment. With greater difficulty, husbands used land to control their wives. Custom required parents to bestow a dowry at marriage to secure a wife's support when her husband died. Dower protected the community, lest the widowed became destitute, requiring poor relief. During her marriage, the wife's dower was folded in with the husband's property to do with as he pleased—except to sell it. Consequently, control by husbands over their wives relied upon legal and religious prerogatives.

As fathers, men could use dowry to constrain their daughters' freedom to marry. Seventeenth-century parents seldom brokered marriages against their children's will, but their permission was still generally essential to secure matrimony. Boys typically sought their fathers' consent to marry. If the father agreed, the youth would seek out the woman's father to negotiate the new partnership. Only at that point was the daughter's formal consent sought. Parents could withhold, extend, or enhance dower and inheritance in order to secure obedience. Consequently, it was not until the nineteenth century that "romantic marriage," a concept that enabled children to first engage themselves and only afterward seek parental approval, became widespread.[17] Even today, romantic marriage may be stymied if children fear that parental disapproval will result in retribution. As society became less agrarian, the control that parents held over their children's economic future ebbed. Land became less essential to economic success. Its replacement, education, once given, could not be withheld.

The concern parents displayed regarding their children's marriages was neither petty nor spiteful. Colonial parents literally could not afford to be indifferent regarding their children's spouses. Their security and status depended upon their children; matrimony extended the sphere of kinship in a society where kinship was an important asset. Noted historian Gordon Wood points out that in colonial society people needed to "know those with whom they were dealing . . . [and] were immediately conscious of strangers and unattached persons and subjected them either to intense questioning or openmouthed staring."[18] Family and patrons cut through this suspicion. In modern terms, linking one family to another was akin to the merger of two great enterprises so as to achieve greater results. Naturally, parents then—as they often still do—groped for the best available social connections as the means to a better life for themselves and for their children.

Patronage seems a remote and uncertain concept in today's world, filled as it is with impersonal relationships. Today there are nearly 260 million people in the United States tied together through remote forces of supply and demand. Money arrives from cash machines and computers phone us to solicit magazine subscriptions. Before 1740, fewer than one million people had settled themselves sparsely across the Atlantic seaboard. People depended upon one another in very personal ways that inevitably compromised their liberty. Patronage was particularly important for the artisans, shopkeepers, and laborers whose economic existence depended upon wealthy clients. Farmers, too, found their independence compromised by patrons who provided credit, bought their marketable surplus, or extended influence on their behalf in any of a hundred useful ways. Merchants who transacted business over great distances needed partners who would not use distance as an excuse to rob or deceive them. Consequently, they often turned to trusted relatives and in-laws to staff their enterprises. For similar reasons, it never hurt to have local officials who were members of one's extended family. Relations were often helpful friends and patrons in a world where, as Gordon Wood put it, "[s]ociety was held together by intricate networks of personal loyalties, obligations, and quasi-dependencies."[19]

Social connections were complicated by distinctions in rank and status. Despite the absence of a hereditary nobility, the ability to distinguish who was a member of the gentry and who was not was almost innate for members of colonial communities. As in Japan today, where each member of society knows just how deep to bend in deference to another, each person in colonial society knew his or her place. Colonial patriarchy established rank as a tangible phenomenon obliging deference to a hierarchically ordered series of father figures. Rank left no one truly independent.

Yet the produce of a nearly self-sufficient landholding family yielded just enough independence to make the ideal of freedom meaningful in colonial America. Unlike the long settled yeoman in Europe, freedom's most vivid symbol in this new land was the frontiersman, the pioneer who continually pushed outward the boundaries of white civilization by felling trees, clearing land, fencing fields, and building homesteads in relative isolation. These were individuals who appeared to be beholden to no one. Relying upon trade only for the few manufactured items or food staples that they could not make themselves, such men forged their own households' course of action and reaped its rewards.

As noted earlier, often enough the sacrifice to attain freedom was freedom. To gain a freehold over an estate, European emigrants signed indentures surrendering to others control over their labor. The proprietors who stood ready to command this labor were masters whose economic incentives lay in working their servants to the utmost for the entire period of their servitudes. Despite the harsh terms involved in these contracts, the prospect of obtaining one's own homestead provided incentive enough for many to emigrate. If these immigrants did not die first—as large numbers of them did—their indentures promised that, upon fulfilling their term of service, they would be rewarded "freedom dues" that typically included fifty acres of land. In this way, new colonists temporarily surrendered their independence, believing it would buy them land, greater independence, and success. In reality, however, the newly freed servants' independence was almost always compromised. Having gained title to a piece of land, a new farmer encountered the restraints of credit, patronage, and market demands. Lacking the wherewithal to set up their own grub stake, many newly emancipated servants almost immediately had to sell their land, and with it their prospects for independence. While their hard-won freedom was more attractive than servitude, it seldom yielded genuine independence.

The Role of Markets

Markets played two important, albeit opposing, roles in shaping early American freedom.[20] On the one hand, markets helped loosen the servile bonds that tied servants to their masters. Both the master's customary right to command and the servant's duty to obey were reshaped by an emerging market mentality. Trade destroyed custom and replaced it with a more malleable relationship: one in which individuals were free, even expected, to search for their own best alternatives and employment. Where before servants had been subject to their masters' discretion, growing labor markets now created alternatives that enabled servants to contract according to their own desires. Masters who attempted to exercise power in opposition to the will of their servants discovered that rivals, promising better deals, stood ready to lure workers away. Not only servants, but children, wives, and apprentices used this competition to free themselves from custom and find better situations. The active labor (and marriage) markets that arose as trade expanded thus collided with age-old customary obligations. Only when the law was deployed to reinforce customary "rights" to their workers' services could masters prevent their running away to better situations. Not surprisingly, masters frequently sought to insulate themselves from competition by using the state to preserve their "rights." In this way the existence of market alternatives simultaneously helps to account for the decline of indentured servitude and the contradictory attempts to invoke state protection to prevent such results. The expansion of markets thus involved a second tendency that stood in precise opposition to its other more liberating tendency. In America this tendency was most fully realized in the brutal institution of slavery used to secure a labor force when indentured servants could no longer be relied upon.

Economic historian David Galenson showed that the rise and decline of indentured servitude was contoured by credit and transportation markets.[21] In the seventeenth century, when transportation costs were quite high, it was difficult for workers to save enough for passage to the colonies. Many opted for indentured service, the exact terms of which depended upon the skills, age, or other valuable considerations they could offer employers. Many of the first servants were sent to the Caribbean islands where the hard work of sugar production was done by labor gangs. News of the killing conditions awaiting workers spread, and it became more difficult to recruit white servants for such destinations. On the mainland, harsh—though not quite as deadly—conditions prevailed in many southern colonies. By the mid-seventeenth century, servants who had a choice were more attracted to the Middle States such as Pennsylvania and New York.

Failing to secure sufficient white labor, big planters in the colonies seeking to export crops commonly resorted to African workers. Demand was greatest in the Caribbean, where sugar plantations produced horrendous mortality and morbidity rates. The first Africans were brought to Virginia in 1619 where, despite their forcible exile, they labored as servants under legal terms similar to those of white European indentures. Brutal conditions were resented by whites and blacks alike. In 1676 black and white servants—and even small landholders—united in a militant uprising against both the ruling elite and Indians, whose land they coveted. Bacon's Rebellion, as it was known, provided testimony to the extent of southern agricultural servants' frustrations. But among servants those frustrations varied: British citizens were free to enlist for indentures elsewhere, Africans were not. Consequently, the supply of white servants dwindled, exacerbating pressures on southern planters needing labor. Plantation owners responded by coercing black workers more until ultimately their condition degenerated into complete slavery.[22] It was not simply the threat of rebellion that caused the change, because Virginia legally recognized slavery in 1660, well before Bacon's Rebellion. Instead it appears that the difference in supply and demand for white and black workers, not threats of revolt, were more important in separating their destinies. To justify black slavery, planters offered tortured explanations ascribing racial superiority to whites. Once the practice of discrimination on the basis of racial differences was legally instituted, harsher methods of repression proved expedient to prevent slaves from rebelling and running away. In this way, African Americans lost their freedom and legally became a mere commodity within an expanding and evolving market system.

On the contrary, by taking advantage of new labor markets white workers were able to parlay their freedom to contract into economic and social improvement. In England, expanding demand raised workers' wages, which made it less necessary for them to submit to indentures. This was especially so in the early nineteenth century when improvements in transportation reduced the cost of intercontinental voyages. Rather than surrender their liberty for several years merely to secure passage, European workers were finding that could often pay for it themselves.[23]

Human progress is often linked to the expansion of free markets. However, the mere existence of markets could not ensure that labor alone—and not the whole person—was transacted as human fodder for commercial enterprise. Three things saved white workers from the fate that befell black Africans: their traditional rights under British common law to exercise their own will; the expansion of labor markets and options; and the reduction in the relative costs of trans-Atlantic passage. The logic of trade is to find a price at which the owner of a good will part with virtually anything. Just as the King sold the very rights upon which his royal prerogative was founded, so too did impoverished men and women sell their independence. This they did through indentures and apprenticeship. Poor relief itself was often obtained precisely through public auction of desperate individuals. Only a high colonial demand for labor ensured that competition improved general conditions rather than forcing workers to surrender all their rights. As we have seen, however, the improvement of conditions for whites made the transformation of blacks into slave laborers more attractive to many employers.

Colonial life and society were part of European history and economy. As Europe's commerce advanced, it replaced custom and barter with cash exchange. Not surprisingly, even political liberty began more frequently to be sold. Mercantilism, broadly defined as policies designed to foster commercial interests for the benefit of the state, flowed naturally enough from the Crown's sale of rights, privileges, and even rank to merchants in order to keep the ship of state afloat. Behind the slogan, "No taxation without representation!" was the reality that government and royal authority had been placed upon the auction block. As the frontier of commerce, colonial government was typically the outcome of a royal quid pro quo, the heart of which was usually financial and seldom directed toward the well-being of the colonists. Naturally then, despite colonists' unusual ability to obtain elements of personal liberty, much less was forthcoming vis-à-vis their rights to govern their own new commonwealths. However, such a glaring inconsistency could not go unnoticed for long.

In Europe, trade transformed society because men of money, through their investments and innovations, achieved the power to redirect daily life. Compared to the effects on the colonies, however, European commerce merely eroded customary obligations and status. Facing far fewer deep-seated traditions, Americans encountered less resistance in throwing off those oppressive customs that survived the ocean journey. Thus, although commerce and freedom gave rise to Europe's Enlightenment thinking, it was in America that these critics found their most responsive audience. John Locke and Jean-Jacques Rousseau argued that the power of the state emanated from a voluntary exchange of individual autonomy for justice and protection: Government was a "social contract" among the people designed to preserve their rights. Republicans enlisted market and contract to revolutionize not only their economic and social relationships, but politics as well. But they did so without fully comprehending how far the reach of commerce and market forces extended. At one and the same time, the market created and destroyed the equality upon which the democratic republic was based.

The Creation of American Democracy

Too infrequently is it noted that the Declaration of Independence and *The Wealth of Nations* were published in the same year, 1776. Although the first was authored by the American Thomas Jefferson and the second by the Scotsman Adam Smith, both documents shaped the context in which the new republic was formed: Jefferson's by propounding a government based upon equality and natural rights, and Smith's by reconciling the market and property with the general good. Together the thoughts of these two individuals exercised a powerful influence on the meanings and possibilities of freedom.

Smith's influence is significantly less understood than is Jefferson's. This professor of moral philosophy decried the misguided British mercantilism under which the crown favored certain enterprises and merchants with special privileges. Smith wanted policy to be based on the general interests of society, not on those of the commercial classes:

> Merchants and master manufacturers . . . by their wealth draw to themselves the greatest share of the public consideration. . . . To widen the market and to narrow the competition is always the interest of the dealers. To widen the market may frequently be agreeable enough to the interest of the public; but to narrow the competition must always be against it. . . . The proposal of any new law or regulation of commerce which comes from this order, ought always to be listened to with great precaution. . . . It comes from an order of men, whose interest is never exactly the same with that of the public, who have generally an interest to deceive and even to oppress the public, and who accordingly have, upon many occasions, both deceived and oppressed it.[24]

Rather than give grants and privileges to the commercial classes in hopes that they would pursue the public good, Smith asserted that social welfare was best achieved by harnessing the power of avarice in the service of the public good. Only when checked by active competition could self-interest be channeled into productive enterprise. The monopolies, patents, guilds, and apprenticeships that the business classes sought obstructed the free play of markets. Adam Smith forcefully explained that competition alone provided the surest protection against the exploitation of workers and consumers.

Smith's ideas on government varied from those put forward by Jefferson in the Declaration of Independence. Where Smith placed little emphasis upon the political and civil rights of the common man, Thomas Jefferson declared: "We hold these truths to be self-evident, that all Men are created equal, that they are endowed by their Creator with certain unalienable Rights, that among these are Life, Liberty and the Pursuit of Happiness." Although both men were suspicious of government, only Jefferson presumed that the common man could reasonably be expected to pursue the common good if permitted to participate in self-government. Smith drew back from this possibility and contented himself with discourses designed to reveal the proper and most profitable course for government action.

Jefferson sought to make land and education widely accessible to create conditions that would support democracy. In his scheme, the backbone of the new republic would be comprised of the yeoman farmers who had created their own independence. Through the 1785 and 1787 Land Ordinances, Jefferson helped make it possible for individuals to buy government land free and clear. As president, he doubled the acreage available for settlement by purchasing the Louisiana Territory in 1803. Citizens who were economically dependent upon others, Jefferson believed, could not exercise virtuous power on behalf of the general interest. Dependency compromised their will.

Perhaps Adam Smith's reluctance regarding broad-based democracy stemmed from the fact that most lands in Great Britain were largely taken up, most crafts were monopolized, and the prospects for the independence of commoners were remote. Under these circumstances, Smith's preference was for limited government. Rather than expand the number of voters, Smith sought to educate those who exercised political power that they should refrain from regulating enterprise whenever market competition might better obtain the desired ends. Paradoxically, in promoting markets for public ends, Adam Smith, the moralist, made the pursuit of self-interested profit legitimate. Having sanctioned self-interest in market affairs, it became less reasonable to hope that self-interest could be turned off when it came to matters of legislation. Although Smith's principles made it more difficult for politicians to condone blatant special interest legislation, profit made the purchase of government favor more seductive.

Where Smith placed hope in the idea that education would improve the ruling classes' capacity for government, Jefferson promoted institutions that would favor enlightened broad-based democracy. His strategy for attaining the common good rested upon a different view of natural rights. Jeffersonian rhetoric announced "all men are created equal" having "certain unalienable rights." This premise lent itself to arguments that an unequal distribution of property undermined equality and independence. Conservatives sought protections against such fulminations. If such ideas did not inspire outright rebellion, they certainly encouraged democratic institutions under which the propertyless majority might pursue its "unalienable rights" by leveling society through redistribution. Such fears underlaid Edmund Burke's *Reflections on the Revolution in France* (1790). He wrote "those who attempt to level, never equalize" but "only change and pervert the natural order of things . . . setting up in the air what solidity of the structure requires to be on the ground."[25] It was in its opposition to such concerns that Jeffersonian rhetoric was potentially revolutionary.

In the final analysis, however, James Madison, not Thomas Jefferson, became the architect of a conservative American Constitution designed to preserve the "solidity of the structure" that Edmund Burke believed nature "requires to be on the ground." Like Smith and Burke, Madison feared that direct democracy would not respect the rights of property. Madison argued that the economic interests of political factions had to be tamed:

> [T]he most common and durable source of factions has been the various and unequal distribution of property. Those who hold and those who are without property have ever formed distinct interests in society. Those who are creditors, and those who are debtors, fall under a like discrimination. A landed interest, a manufacturing interest, a mercantile interest, a moneyed interest, and many lesser interests, grow up of necessity in civilized nations, and divide them into different classes, actuated by different sentiments and views.[26]

Accordingly, the Constitution subordinated direct democracy in favor of a system of congressional representation designed to make mob "passions" of the moment more difficult to act upon. The prerogatives upon which congressional representatives could act were to be clearly limited, and the remaining few were subjected to presidential and judicial review. In separating governmental powers, Madison and the other framers sought to prevent radical changes and contain the effects that the rhetoric of "self-evident" natural rights inspired.[27]

Politics constituted an essential part of the conditions of freedom under which early Americans labored. It was through their political institutions that eighteenth- and nineteenth-century citizens gave the prevailing labor theory of value its meanings. It was labor that entitled one to the fruits of his property because one's labor was presumed to be the primary, if not the sole, source of value. The contour of private property defined the confines in which individual liberty could be lawfully exercised: What one did with or to one's own property, so long as it did not harm another, was one's own affair. In practice, the fullest expression of individual liberty came not with the exercise of labor, but with the lawful acquisition of property. John Locke, the foremost exponent of property, explained that in a land devoid of owners, the person who worked that resource was also its natural owner. However, in a well-settled land, the privileges of property were often entrusted not to those who worked the land, but to those who inherited or bought it. In obvious and subtle ways, property rights were not then, and are not now, "self-evident." Political power mediated the disputes that pitted natural rights claimants against lawful title holders. Consequently, the boundary of property rights—and therefore of liberty—was opened to question in the very act of creating democracy. Fundamental to our understanding of American freedom is the fact that Madison's Constitution successfully prevented simple majorities from defining rules according to their own rights.

From the beginning of the union to the present, appeals have been made by and to working folk to change the property rights that underlie the distributions of the rewards to, and the choices facing, labor. The difficulties facing post–revolution farmers show how political participation affected the conditions of early American labor. If the revolution was fought in the name of vague "unalienable rights," the Constitution gave conservative definition to those rights by forbidding states to impair the obligations of contract. Most citizens of the new federation were farmers for whom the cash-scarce cycle of harvest and planting made debt relief a subject of common concern. If they borrowed, failure to repay could result in imprisonment or foreclosure on their property—the same property that was the wellspring of their liberty. States sometimes attempted to satisfy debtor demands by issuing paper currency to make repayment easier. However, paper currency often resulted in inflation. When governments attempted to alter the obligations of contracts by enabling debtors to repay what they owed in devalued dollars, the Constitution put an end to that by declaring that states could not coin their own money. When states enacted bankruptcy and insolvency laws to relieve debtors of their burdens, the courts interpreted the contract clause to insist that the only relief the state could grant was prospective, as retroactive relief impaired the obligations of contract. Such constitutional provisions resulted directly from Federalist understandings of the limits to democracy. When every "desperate debtor" held a vote, and when debtors outnumbered creditors, Federalists believed the majority would use the state to undo what they regarded the just and lawful rights of the minority. By proscribing states from impairing contract and coining their own currency, Federalists attempted to ensure that a wiser national government would veto local majorities when they threatened the rights of property. These and other constitutional provisions reflected Madison's understanding that direct democracy would not guarantee the rights of all. Madison believed the federal government, as compared with local constituencies, would be more congenial to the protection of individual rights. At the federal level, factional interests would have be to resolved in favor of more general interests.

Whether intended or not, the contract clause stamped a Puritanical brand upon American liberty such that it involved not only the right of free and mature individuals to make contracts, but perhaps more importantly, the obligation to fulfill those contracts with no expectation of state relief. This construction of liberty, naturally, did nothing to eradicate the fundamental fear that "liberty of contract" would enable the strong to dominate the weak. Those who possessed little with which to pursue their happiness were to be at a disadvantage compared to those who possessed more. After all, would not, and did not, persons facing poverty sell their liberty, their bodies, and perhaps even their souls in order to relieve their destitution?

Why should the community care whether individuals sold off their own liberty? The answer requires an investigation of Adam Smith's premise that market competition promoted the wealth of nations. Was competition truly beneficial when free workers had to secure their livelihoods by underbidding those who were bound? Would not such a scheme compromise the liberty of free workers, forcing them to compete for jobs by relinquishing personal rights? Even if contracts for indentured servitude or apprenticeship could be rationalized as temporary conditions that were warranted because they made longer-term independence possible, still, chattel slavery stood in total opposition to liberty. How could a nation assert the right and responsibility to govern itself without bestowing that right upon each individual? To bestow such a right, did the nation have to protect individuals from the dangers of unfettered contract and competition?

The problem outlined above may be defined as an inherent opposition between inalienable rights and liberty of contract. The tensions in this opposition constitute the warp and woof upon which this book is woven. Before the Civil War, the tension between these two ideas was muted as the struggle for liberty was widely regarded as complementary to the advance of contract. When contract and consent were absent nearly all else was subsumed by the quest for them. After the Civil War, when slavery was abolished, the conditions on freedom that liberty of contract imposed became more readily apparent.

Chapter 2

Contracting Liberties

[B]y equality, we should understand, not that the degrees of
power and riches are to be absolutely identical for everybody,
but that power shall never be great enough for violence, and
shall always be exercised by virtue of rank and law; and that in
respect of riches, no citizen shall ever be wealthy enough to buy
another, and none poor enough to be forced to sell himself.
—Jean-Jacques Rousseau, *The Social Contract*

After the American Revolution, apprentices, servants, and children, among others, found courage to assert themselves anew. If during the colonial period Americans learned to contract for their own benefit, in the post-revolutionary period they refused to recognize accepted authorities. Abetted by an emerging cash economy, they proclaimed their rights and bargained for a better deal. If that deal was not forthcoming, they packed their bags and left. For example, the comments of Ebenezer Fox, an apprentice at the time, reveal how the revolutionary rhetoric became a part of everyday life:

> I, and other boys situated similarly to myself thought we had wrongs to be redressed; rights to be maintained; and, as no one appeared disposed to act the part of a redresser, it was our duty and our privilege to assert our own rights. We made a direct application of the doctrines we daily heard, in relation to the oppression of the mother country, to our own circumstance; and thought that we were more oppressed than our fathers were. I thought that I was doing myself a great injustice by remaining in bondage, when I ought to go free; and that the time was come, when I should liberate myself from the thralldom of others, and set up a government of my own; or, in other words, do what was right in the sight of my own eyes.[1]

If independence and revolution provided the language with which Americans pragmatically dismantled remaining bastions of traditional authority, it was the expansion of markets that gave them the opportunity to do so. Increasing specialization, the extension of trade, independence from British rule, and a rapidly growing domestic population raised the demand for servants, construction workers, artisans, and other assorted hired hands.

The availability of such options meant fewer individuals were willing to suffer bad situations quietly.[2]

Even before the revolution there had always been some need for wage workers, but it was during the early nineteenth century that this need became more acute. Not only did Americans hasten the pace at which they created internal improvements such as turnpikes and canals, they also began to increase the number of mines, workshops, and factories that depended upon hired help. The agricultural labor force, which at the turn of the century was estimated between 75 to 80 percent of the population, fell to roughly 70 percent in 1830 and nearly 50 percent in 1860. More people came to reside in urban places of at least 2,500 people: only 5 percent of the population in 1790, but 20 percent in 1860.[3] These statistics make it clear that not everyone who left the farm went to work in the city. The weak correspondence between the expansion of urbanization and the decline of agriculture highlights the extremely small scale of most early industrial pursuits. Manufacturing and craftsmanship frequently remained rural affairs, often located near the rivers and falls that drove their works. The initial impetus toward urbanization depended, instead, upon the growth of commercial centers spurred on by improvements in transportation. For example, when the Erie Canal linked New York City to the frontier grain belt in 1825, New York became a bustling metropolis. By 1830 it had 200,000 people, and by 1850 it had exploded to 700,000 people.

These post-revolutionary developments provided workers with new choices, choices that chipped away at traditional society. The family was one of the first institutions to bear the brunt of this change. Even before the revolution, parental control was slipping. Parents' ability to determine their children's marriages and work weakened as the mechanisms they used to enforce their will lost effectiveness. Many large families found their land holdings inadequate to provide for their children. Parents found it necessary to bind them out as apprentices. Once domiciled outside their parents' household, children had a freer hand as well as less reason to submit to parental authority.

Those children who stayed on farms with their parents faced increasing temptations to set off on their own rather than to dutifully await their inheritance. Such possibilities could not help but make sons and daughters more headstrong. Where once the farmer's eldest son expected a bequest that would enable him to marry into a more prosperous family, already by the second century of colonial life fewer first sons found it possible to do this. That younger females began to marry out of turn more frequently suggests that daughters, too, less willingly submitted to parental dictates.

After the revolution, wider markets accelerated social change. Control over family members weakened severely when children moved away from the household to find work. A child who earned his or her own money without constant parental supervision was freer to make his or her own decisions. The early textile factories in New England provide a case study. Girls flooded into Lowell, Massachusetts, and other factory towns in response to entrepreneurs' carefully constructed enticements. Females often came to these first American factories because they could earn their own wages to provide a marriage dowry. The value of their labor in the mills was significantly higher than it was on their family farms. Factory owners, in turn, provided clean, wholesome, and chaperoned dormitory facilities. Or, at least, they did so initially—until competition, immigration, and a depression decreased mill earnings in the 1830s and 1840s. The women employed within these early American mills used the labor market to wrest greater control over themselves from their parents. Although young women exchanged one master for another, family for mill, most did so because they believed the change improved their condition.[4]

The growth of markets should not be thought of as an event separate from the social changes it entailed: instead, it embodied these changes. Markets consisted of individuals who bargained with one another over food, clothing, shelter, art, entertainment, employment, and, increasingly, over almost any conceivable aspect of life. This bargaining transformed passivity into power. Individuals were no longer willing simply to take what custom dictated; within the limits of their means, they chose what they wanted. Bargaining extended personal liberty, enabling workers to rearrange more of the environment within which they lived.[5]

Markets and the Triumph of Contract

Market and contract affected the ways people thought and acted and this altered work relations. Employment was no longer a social status to which fate and birth required submission, but instead a contract voluntarily chosen and, perhaps more importantly, a contract voluntarily left.[6] In short, servants were not slaves; peasants were not sold and tied to their land as serfs; children were not so easily assigned to masters as apprentices; and workers were not prohibited from seeking the employments enjoyed by the more genteel classes. To the extent one followed the logic of contract it also implied that debtors ought not to be compelled to perform services when they failed to pay off loans, nor wives be bound to husbands and left without a legal will of their own; nor should seamen be impressed into navies or compelled to stay on board their ships.[7] In such ways, men and women valued the choices generated by an active market for employment.

The market, not status, law, or custom, was to parcel out workers to their various tasks.

This transformation of American society reflected the country's democratic impulse: all were equal and none had the right to command another except when true consent was given. No one captured this new thinking better than a young Frenchman named Alexis de Tocqueville, whose visit to the United States resulted in the classic masterpiece, *Democracy in America*. After nine months of observing Americans in 1831 and 1832, Tocqueville wrote:

> In democracies servants are not only equal among themselves, but it may be said that they are, in some sort, the equals of their masters. This requires explanation in order to be rightly understood. At any moment a servant may become a master, and he aspires to rise to that condition; the servant is therefore not a different man from the master. Why, then, has the former a right to command, and what compels the latter to obey except the free and temporary consent of both their wills? Neither of them is by nature inferior to the other; they only become so for a time, by covenant. Within the terms of this consent the one is a servant, the other a master; beyond it they are two citizens of the commonwealth, two men . . . the master holds the contract of service to be the only source of his power, and the servant regards it as the only cause of his obedience. They do not quarrel about their reciprocal situation, but each knows his own and keeps it.[8]

This passage describes the triumph of contractual relations. Society had turned itself into commerce. Authority, security, and, if one takes the social contract theory of government seriously, then government itself was a matter of consensual exchange.[9] The triumph of contract fulfilled the economic program articulated by Adam Smith. The complete liberation of self-interest would have enabled society's course to meander wherever the convenience of private arrangements among individuals took it. The only limiting proviso was that individuals not interfere with the rights of others, a proviso easier to articulate than to implement.

Although America was the nation most able to take advantage of contract in the early nineteenth century, it nonetheless contained within itself three contradictions that fouled its own conception of individual liberty. The most obvious was the grinding institution of slavery that forced some individuals to relinquish their liberty by becoming the property of others. As important as this institution was, there was a second, more vexing issue that also troubled American workers, and that was the question of debt. Finally, there was the still more insidious worry that, through contract, workers cast off the very independence they sought. Without the coexistence of slavery and debt, this last contradiction might not have been important. However, always omnipresent, these involuntary servitudes held in check the demands of freer workers. This chapter examines the important relationships between free contract, on the one hand, and slavery and debt, on the other, and leaves aside, until later, more subtle methods of self-enslavement.

Slavery

In the same year Tocqueville spent admiring American freedom and democracy, an event took place that demonstrated the frailties of the new society. On August 22, 1831, Nat Turner, a Baptist preacher, exhorted his fellow enslaved African Americans to revolt. For two days they rampaged through Southampton County, Virginia, and killed nearly sixty white people. The uprising stirred fears among slave masters throughout the South. In retribution the white community cracked down on African Americans with terrible vengeance.

If the passions of white society were easily roused against tyranny, then slaves who faced a more brutal denial of their rights could hardly be expected to behave differently. To subdue their passions required force, more even than would have been necessary in a society where bondage was the norm. The ownership of human beings in the United States required a vast array of devices to help slave masters sleep securely at night. By eliminating opportunities for meetings, by refusing permission to carry fire arms, by keeping slaves illiterate, by teaching a censored version of the Bible designed to promote justice in the hereafter and obedience here on earth, Southerners even attempted, in addition to shackling their bodies, to shackle the hopes slaves nurtured.[10]

Many Northerners believed that, if contained geographically, slavery would die of its own weight because of its inefficiency. Tocqueville, for example, argued that "the colonies in which there were no slaves became more populous and more prosperous than those in which slavery flourished. The farther they went, the more was it shown that slavery, which is so cruel to the slave, is prejudicial to the master."[11] Anti-slave zealots jotted down all indications that slavery killed the zest for labor. Of these there were, of course, many; field slaves had little reason to work to their capacity. When not watched, they ceased working. Resentful slaves, observers noted, sabotaged their masters in any way they could, whether by breaking their hoes or by running away. Additionally, the relative decline of the Old South in Maryland, Virginia, and the Carolinas convinced Northerners that without fresh new land, slavery depleted soils and exhausted the South's opportunities.

As if these difficulties were insufficient, Northerners argued that slavery undermined the South's entire culture by denigrating the work ethic.[12] Hard work became slaves' work. Although not all bondsmen worked as field hands and servants—many were employed as mill workers, skilled craftsmen, and even as managers or drivers of other slaves—most were employed in the distasteful jobs for which it was difficult or costly to recruit free white labor. White Southerners, rich and poor alike, held themselves superior to those who performed degrading manual labor. Plantation owners mimicked the British aristocracy whose station in life was defined by the absence of physical work. By denying any nobility to simple physical labor, Southerners gave credence to Northern conclusions that slave societies lacked industriousness.

More than its demise, Northerners sought to contain slavery. Even though slavery existed throughout the colonies, it was not so engrained into the fiber of northern society. Yet the presence of slaves in northern states diminished prospects for the constitutional abolition of slavery. The only real progress on the issue achieved under the Constitution involved the federal power to ban the importation of slaves after 1808. Though Northerners saw this as a step toward the elimination of slavery, some Southerners, specifically Virginians, had earlier supported such a ban so as to raise the price of their products. Moreover, the South was well aware that ending the international slave trade in no way abolished the institution.[13]

After the revolution, the northern states that had the least dependence upon slavery were the first to pass laws emancipating their slaves. Eventually even New York, whose slave holdings matched those in some southern states, officially discarded the institution. It is worth noting, however, that most northern states chose to abolish slavery gradually so as to protect the interests of slave owners. Owners were generally permitted to retain their slaves for years—if not until their death—and slave children had at least to reach the age of adulthood before they were freed. In the interim owners could, and often did, sell their slaves to buyers in states where slavery remained legal. Nonetheless, the North slowly succeeded in purging itself of chattel slavery.

As the North dealt with its internal slave problems, the vibrancy of the South caused slave owners to look after their interests beyond their own borders. Hardly had the ink dried on the Constitution when Eli Whitney's cotton gin turned short staple cotton into a major commercial crop. Within ten years of Whitney's invention of the cotton gin, production expanded more than one hundred fold. The South was put to work feeding the English textile industry's colossal appetite. King Cotton, as the export came to be known, dramatically swelled the South's demand for slave labor. To accommodate the rising demand for cotton, southern planters shifted production from the Old South to more fertile soils in Alabama, Mississippi,

Arkansas, Louisiana, and Texas. As both North and South believed their destinies were linked to expansion, the westward movement increased sectional conflict. The South pressed its right to continue slavery in the new territories, whereas the North feared large slave plantations would foreclose the opportunity free whites had to achieve economic independence.[14]

Both sides recognized that settlement of new territories altered national politics. Legislative representation for the new western states threatened to tip the balance of federal power regarding free and slave labor institutions. If either side achieved control over the new states it would have been able to dictate the property rights it desired. That was the significance of political wrangling over Missouri, Texas, the lands from the Mexican Cession, California, Kansas, and Nebraska. Political power, not economic prowess, was going to determine the rules governing property in human beings.

At first blush, one might ask, "Why could not a nation exist half slave and half free?" Indeed, many Northerners were content to let slavery exist in the South so long as it did not affect their free institutions. Such insulation, however, was impossible. But the question resurfaced each time African Americans crossed state borders. Whose laws were to prevail when slave owners from the South went North with their "property"? If free states respected the property in slave states, then they opened the door to all sorts of abuses including temporary—perhaps even permanent—northern enclaves in which slavery could be employed. However, for a state to refuse to recognize "foreign" property was contrary to the constitutional powers that gave the federal government, not the states, authority over interstate commerce. In their own way, northern states, as much as those in the South, sought sovereignty over their own territory. The North did this by refusing to recognize the rights of slaveholders over persons residing within their jurisdiction. The problem grew as increasing numbers of slaves escaped north seeking asylum. In requiring the return of fugitive persons to their owners, Southerners argued, with some justification, that the U.S. Constitution explicitly recognized and protected slave property. To resolve any doubt on this score, they secured The Compromise of 1850, which, in exchange for California's entry into the union as a free state, reinforced provisions for fugitive slave return. Regardless of Congress's intentions, northern courts had earlier recorded precedents opposing extradition.

The issue came to a head in 1857 when the U.S. Supreme Court denied Dred Scott, a slave transported by his master from Missouri to the North, his personal freedom. The Court thereby secured slave owners' property rights in the North as well as the South. In requiring free states to recognize property in men, the court denied self-rule to northern states. Whereas a contrary holding would have required Southerners to think twice before taking slaves north, under the Scott decision Northerners were required not only to tolerate a repugnant institution within their own domain, but to contribute to its perpetuation.[15]

The slave issue was not settled by the Dred Scott decision. Although Northerners were unwilling to accept the court's decree as final, they were equally unwilling to offer compensation to Southerners to induce them to manumit their slaves peaceably. It has been estimated that such a policy would have cost vastly less than did the Civil War.[16] Except for the stalwart abolitionists among them, Northerners were less interested in emancipation than they were in containing slavery. As Tocqueville observed, Northerners were principally concerned over slavery's effects on their own society: "It is not for the good of the Negroes, but for that of the whites, that measures are taken to abolish slavery in the United States."[17] Once the few black workers in the North had been freed, a policy of southern containment ensured that western land remained open for homesteading by free labor. Further emancipations, on the other hand, could intensify competition between white and black workers.

Regarding the viability of slavery, Tocqueville and others told themselves that, "As soon as competition began between the free laborer and the slave, the inferiority of the latter became manifest and slavery was attacked in its fundamental principle, which is the interest of the master."[18] Like Tocqueville, many Northerners preferred to believe that the inefficiency of slavery would spell its own demise. Recent research, however, contradicts this view.

Although the viability of slavery in the South has been frequently questioned, the most exhaustive research on the subject, particularly that by Robert Fogel and Stanley Engerman, has found exactly what the naive bystander might expect: Slavery was an extremely efficient and profitable enterprise.[19] Indeed, it would have been quite surprising to find that masters, who held virtually unlimited powers over their laborers, could not extract enough work from slaves to render them profitable. Only the wishful (and occasionally racist) views advanced by slavery's opponents, were responsible for delusions that the southern slavocracy was incompetent and about to crumble. These opponents constructed a picture of a system so irrationally in love with the status of holding slaves that it was willing to sacrifice its own profitability; a system so bent on self-destruction that it was incapable of adjusting. However, research findings simply do not support such pictures.

One problem commonly laid at slavery's doorstep concerned rapid soil depletion in the South. Observers contended that slave labor could only be used in the production of cash crops requiring gang labor that performed routine work. According to this view, crop rotations necessary to restore the fertility of the land were abandoned to accommodate the existing slave system. Conservation measures were, allegedly, omitted. The truth, however, was that the South, like the North, simply responded to the reality of cheap land. When land was inexpensive, growers acted as though they could exploit their soils without regard for the future. Only as land became more scarce did soil depletion become an issue; when this happened it was the large plantation owners in the South who led the way in innovating conservation techniques.[20]

Another criticism of slavery involved its physical brutality. It was not generally true that owners relished sadism so much that they willingly jeopardized their profits. Certainly, each master and overseer found his or her own approach in managing slaves and indeed some, like cash-poor northern capitalists, skimped on care that would increase the long-run value of their investments. For bondsmen, this meant punitive treatment and short rations. On the other hand, the most far-seeing owners mixed harsh techniques with positive rewards associated with freer forms of labor. Masters often granted slaves rights to till private plots for their own benefit. Slaves could even be offered rewards, like cash bonuses or the opportunity to advance to better jobs. Masters occasionally let slaves hire themselves out. In these circumstances slaves paid their masters for their time, as though they were renting their own bodies, and kept any difference between their earnings and their payments for themselves. With their proceeds, slaves could buy goods on their own account. A small profit earned this way could lead slaves to drive themselves harder than free workers. Incentives like these increased slave productivity. It did not always take brutal physical treatment to drive slaves; there was brutality enough in being compelled to accept conditions denying their humanity. When slaves forgot these fundamental relations, then overseers deliberately reminded them by meting out those punishments to which free labor simply refused to submit. Slavery, it seems, operated with an oversized tool box at its disposal, one that, in addition to reward systems, was also filled with prods, whips, and assorted other devices designed to fit any situation a master could anticipate.[21]

It is not necessary to find that slavery was devoid of rational self-interest to conclude that it was a system bereft of morality.[22] On the contrary, rational self-interest involved an amoral, pragmatic use of labor; whatever technique seemed expedient—kindness or cruelty—was utilized to improve work. The slave was an asset to his owner, an expensive one at that. To punish too severely, to starve too greatly, or to work too unmercifully made management unnecessarily costly and inefficient. It should not therefore be surprising that although whippings, rapes, and forced family separations occurred with distressing frequency, they were not the everyday norm.

Slavery did not merely earn profits; it earned returns as good as or better than those of northern industrial activities. Southerners even found it possible to use slavery in urban employments. Although city work was controversial because it mingled free with bound workers and because it put slaves into urban areas offering better opportunities for their evasion, the returns from this enterprise were generally positive. The primary reason this practice did not spread rapidly was that the profits on farming, particularly in cotton and sugar, were greater than those in southern factory work.[23] These findings refute the common assertion that free labor alone was suitable for the emerging industrial conditions. The example of Nazi Germany's profitable slave labor factories, composed of Jewish and other prison workers, provides a similar negation that emancipation and industrialization were causally linked. It is true, however, that urban employment of slaves required special efforts and expenditures in order to monitor and enforce slave masters' property rights. Such policies were so inconsistent with the culture of freedom, that special blindness and indoctrination were required for them to survive in a democratic nation.

Why, given the previous discussion, was there ever a presumption that free labor and industrial efficiency went hand in hand? Two major advantages of contract labor are suggested. The first is that the free worker had to support him or herself during non-productive periods, or as Tocqueville put it, "the white man sells his services, but only when they may be useful."[24] Slavery, on the other hand, was a total system; in owning their workers, masters became responsible for their lives. Only the most despotic masters risked an environment in which slaves believed they would be turned out when old or infirm, their children sold off at birth, or their most desperate adversities met with flat refusals of assistance. Masters understood that if their slaves had nothing to lose, they also had nothing to lose from rebelling. The complete responsibility for the lives of their slaves added costs to slave ownership that were not borne by employers of free labor. In practice, however, this was offset by a labor force participation rate twice that which was extracted from the free white population.

A second advantage was not so easily overcome. As with the case of urban slaves, the costs to masters and employers of enforcing their rights to the labor of workers was significant. The fact that the free laborer was not owned reduced expenditures to prevent his or her running away. Investments in free and slave labor had to be protected. Employers who trained workers often feared they would run off before they maximized the return on their investment. Free laborers often had to invest in themselves through education or through apprenticeships if they wanted to learn skills. They did this through reduced wages and long terms of indenture. Investing in slave skills posed significant risks as well. Because it was assumed that literacy would increase access to ideas that increased rebelliousness and discontent, masters were loathe to invest too much in training slaves.[25] Nonetheless, having already created an environment from which escape was difficult, a master may have found investments in his property worthwhile. While there are some advantages to free labor in a regime of industrial capitalism, the benefit is not so obvious as appears at first blush. [26]

The appeal of the proposition seems to rest instead upon the pleasing idea that freedom and industrial progress are inextricably linked.[27] Advocates of capitalism like to suggest that this system alone ensures individual freedom and economic efficiency at the same time. However, slavery was a form of capitalism in which human rights were alienable; it was, so to speak, a free market in people. Slave auctions have been touted as a highly efficient method of pricing slaves so that human assets were allocated to their most efficient uses. Robert Fogel explains that even a slave's potential for rebelliousness was capitalized into the prices bidders were willing to pay.

No one should look to account books to find slavery despicable. That higher accounting must depend, instead, upon the daily abuses entailed by the absence of personal freedom. Slaves were so robbed of their autonomy that complete, even cheerful, submission was expected. Slaves had no recourse to an impartial source of law and justice in the face of such assaults upon their spirit. After the Civil War, one woman who left slavery behind is reported to have commented on her new-found freedom saying, "I am now my own mistress, and need not work when I am sick. I can do my own thinkings, without having any to think for me,—to tell me when to come, what to do, and to sell me when they get ready."[28]

Ultimately it was only force that could halt slavery in America. If any economic inefficiency was going to lead to slavery's demise it was going to take many, many years. Without force, slavery appears to have been fully capable of competing with more mature forms of capitalism.

Slavery and Free Labor

During the antebellum period, slavery stood in stark opposition to the otherwise complete triumph of contract. Ultimately, however, slavery proved so incompatible with liberty of contract that it ensnared North and South in a devastating conflict. Because the new republic saw independence in terms of land or property, the rapid ascendance of wage labor posed a new problem.[29] Bad as slavery was, its defenders could justify it by showing that it provided workers with some relief against old age, infirmity, and unemployment in ways that the free labor market did not. Wage labor was a marginal institution held in low regard until well after the industrial revolution took hold. At its best it was viewed as a temporary situation until an individual could stand on his or her own feet. Consequently, the comparison between slave and wage labor generally seemed less important than that between slavery and family farming. As wage labor began to play a more important role in society, becoming for many a permanent condition, its relationship to slavery became the subject of greater discussion. The labor question, like the slave question, became a serious issue.

In 1831, the same year that Nat Turner led Virginia bondsmen in their revolt, New York shoemakers, Philadelphia tailors, and factory girls in Lowell, Massachusetts, also asserted their rights militantly. Unlike the slaves, these free workers were able do this by striking. However, even when their walkouts succeeded, workers could still face a difficult time in the courts. Workers who struck were subject to the legal charge of criminal conspiracy. In 1836, when Judge Ogden Edwards imposed fines upon striking tailors, New York City workers compared their plight to that of slaves:

> Mechanics and workingmen! A deadly blow has been struck at your LIBERTY! The prize for which your fathers fought has been robbed from you! The freemen of the North are now on a level with the slaves of the South— with no other privileges than laboring that drones may fatten on your lifeblood. Twenty of your brethren have been found guilty for presuming to resist a reduction in their wages![30]

This protest was distributed in a leaflet called the "coffin hand-bill," which mourned the passing of equality.

Judge Edwards's decision followed an important precedent established a year earlier in *People v. Fisher,* a case involving a Geneva, New York, shoemakers' strike. This case illustrates how burgeoning new labor markets affected workers. Glued together through the turnpikes and canals that proliferated, small towns grew by buying and selling goods in distant markets. As these towns expanded, the possibilities for greater specialization, additional machinery, and factory labor increased. An intensification of competition required artisans to hone their skills to a particular task rather than engage in the complete craft for which they had been trained.[31] The output of one worker became input for another. Increasingly supplies were transferred impersonally, without direct communication between the different producers at the different stages of production. As work became specialized, employers found it desirable to substitute relatively unskilled workers for skilled artisans in order to trim labor costs. This enabled them to meet the competition that increased trade foisted upon them. In 1823, Auburn, a town neighboring the Geneva shoemakers, even injected prison labor into the production process for boots. Free workers naturally found it difficult to compete with cheap prison labor. In this competitive environment, Geneva bootmaker Daniel Lum sought cost reductions any way he could. He hired a worker who agreed to sell his boots for substantially less than other artisans. Seeing this as an assault upon their standard of living, Geneva bootmakers struck Lum. When brought to trial under New York State law, Judge John Savage directed the jury to find their strike an illegal "conspiracy."[32]

Did, as the authors of the "coffin handbill" protested, the arrest of these shoemakers put them on a level with the slaves? Where slaves had no choice, free labor consisted in having the liberty to choose whether to labor or not. The greatest impediment to the betterment of slaves' condition was their inability to quit work, whether that quitting was to find a better situation or to be relieved from an abusive one. The power to quit work meant that employers had to rent or lease the labor of a free man; they could not own it. This worker was paid for the time or the work performed under contract. The distinction between a rental agreement and a purchase made a world of difference. Individuals who could threaten to quit were able to bring the market to their aid. The costs of replacing workers might cause employers to change by themselves. The fact that slave owners never had to match or better a competitor's offer meant that they were in a position to exploit fully the bondsman's labor. Employers of free labor, on the other hand, were compelled to consider their employees' options. Competition for slaves existed as well, but in slave markets increases in demand resulted in higher prices for the owner rather than higher wages or better working conditions for the slave. The *Geneva Shoemakers* case reveals a condition neither fully slave nor fully free.

The verdict in the *Shoemakers* case indicated that if a worker walked out, he or she could not do so collectively with other workers. Such a move was a strike—a combination—and therefore, according to law, a conspiracy against the public. In common with slaves, therefore, these shoemakers could not express their will collectively. Was this missing right to speak out, this freedom of expression, one of the "inalienable rights" that all men are endowed with? If it was, then the state legislature had taken it away. The decision preserved a narrowly defined right to quit, but emasculated that right by denying collective action when it injured producers pursuing their business interests.

Where previously it seemed that there were only two major conditions constraining the liberty of laborers, slavery or freedom, American law now defined a third. Did it make a difference to preserve workers' individual, but not their collective, right to quit? That depended on the way people thought about liberty. Collective bargaining stood ready to displace individual contract. Arguably, this displacement could affect three separate parties adversely. First, employers would lose some advantages and rights they believed their property justly conferred upon them. For example, the Geneva shoemakers went on strike against Daniel Lum precisely to prevent him from maximizing the value of his property by hiring the worker who offered him the best deal. Second, collective bargaining could restrict the liberty of individuals who were not party to the contract: in this case, the low-wage bootmaker denied employment by his fellow bootmakers. Finally, collective action fostered a "tyranny of the majority" upon those within any combination who did not agree with its goals. In this light, collective action and liberty were mutually exclusive.

This conception of liberty, which found in collective action an unfair and deliberate hurt, grew directly out of the market-oriented thinking then shaping the American psyche. Adam Smith had earlier articulated the limits of fair competition so as to exclude collective action. "In the race for wealth, and honors, and preferment," said Smith, "[an individual] may run as hard as he can, and strain every nerve and every muscle, in order to outstrip all his competitors. But if he should jostle, or throw down any of them, the indulgence of the spectators is entirely at an end. It is a violation of fair play, which they cannot admit of."[33] When workers consorted with each other for their own advantage, it was seen as a violent act against another runner. Moreover, American judges told themselves that such actions were unnecessary. In his 1836 conviction of New York's striking tailors, Judge Edwards rationalized his finding by arguing that "the road to advancement is open to all."[34] Free markets, so the argument went, preserved those opportunities.

How then could workers justify their actions? In many ways. First, contrary to Judge Edwards's assertions regarding advancement, the route to independence was increasingly unsure. Machines made the cost of opening a small shop more prohibitive at the same time that it undermined apprenticeship investments artisans had made in their skills. The intensity of competition and the prospect of remaining dependent upon wages convinced many workers that advancement was not "open." In the increasingly competitive struggle for survival, they found that wages were one element that could beneficially be influenced through collective action.

The independent household central to republican ideology was increasingly at odds with the reality faced by working people. More importantly, Tocqueville's republican assumption that competition between free and slave labor would result in victory of the former was by no means as firmly held by those actually so engaged. In Geneva, competition between shoemakers and prison labor put downward pressure on wages. A worse example occurred in 1842 when the Tredegar Iron Company of Richmond, Virginia, cut its labor costs by employing slaves. In contradiction to Tocqueville's triumphant free workers, historian Kenneth Stampp reminds us,

> In 1847, the increasing use of slaves caused the remaining free laborers to go out on strike, until they were threatened with prosecution for forming an illegal combination. After this protest failed, [Tredegar manager] Anderson vowed to show his workers that they could not dictate his labor policies: he refused to re-employ any of the strikers. Thereafter, as Anderson noted, Tredegar used "almost exclusively slave labor except as the Boss men. This enables me, of course, to compete with other manufacturers."[35]

When the cost of replacing a worker was high, the market worked to labor's advantage. Conversely, however, if the costs of replacing workers were low, then the situation was reversed. In the early American republic, the general trend was toward freedom and contract. However, that trend could not have taken place without vigilant resistance. The existence of unfree and semi-free labor threatened individual workers and called into question the viability of a Jeffersonian republic composed of independent citizens. For workers, the War for Independence was still being fought. From that war, workers constructed their own legacy in which liberty was purchased through solidarity and struggle.

Workers invoked the tradition of the revolution's colonial merchants and artisans. They too had asserted their rights in a way that New York's judges would have defined a criminal conspiracy. Protesting tariffs under the British Townshend Acts, colonial merchants boycotted British manufacturers *as well as* colonial merchants who continued the import trade in disregard of their compatriots wishes. "Sons of Liberty" assisted the boycott with threats and occasional violence against non-cooperators. Later, another gang of vigilantes would destroy private property during the Boston Tea Party. Such actions were justified in the name of liberty. Still, one merchant faced with militant coercion from the Sons of Liberty incredulously wondered how colonists could "still pretend to talk of LIBERTY, PROPERTY and RIGHTS without a blush?"[36] The point is that revolutions fought for freedom and for rights that are as yet unrecognized by law can seldom be waged without collective action or coercion. Where others saw a violation of liberty, strikers, like the colonial protesters before them, instead saw a defense of liberties threatened by tyranny.

There will always be someone who will justify force in opposition to any oppression. Who is to determine what oppression is sufficient to require violence? While humanity may be endowed with "certain unalienable rights," contrary to Jefferson's declaration, what they are is not exactly "self-evident." Jefferson's appeal to natural rights was an inspired rhetorical device, but when it came down to the business of running a nation, the founders abandoned his brilliant justification in declaring independence and wrote a Constitution that was exceedingly careful not to encourage citizens to define their own rights independently. Americans thus had two traditions of liberty from which to choose: a revolutionary tradition justifying militant resistance against tyrannical abuses, and a second, the constitutional framework, which gave citizens a definite, but cautious and cumbersome, democratic mechanism through which to protect and define their liberty.

When workers walked out on strike, they invoked America's revolutionary tradition of liberty. When the courts condemned their actions, workers invoked that tradition more loudly. The legal system gave ground. Because trials in the early nineteenth century gave juries considerable latitude on matters of law, it often proved difficult to obtain criminal convictions against workers. More importantly, freedom of association was increasingly viewed as a significant component of liberty itself. In 1842 in *Hunt v. Commonwealth,* the Massachusetts court exempted mere participation in collective action by union members from criminal prosecution.[37] It replaced the conspiracy doctrine with two specifications concerning union conduct: unions must pursue lawful objectives and use legal means to obtain them. The decision left undefined which objectives were lawful and what means were legal. In practice, courts found that seeking an advance in wages or improvement in conditions might be lawful, but strikes that relied upon pickets and boycotts were often considered illegal means of obtaining those ends.

Public sympathy for aggressive collective action was not particularly strong as long as citizens believed the path toward advancement and independence was open. In the early 1800s small farmers, who still formed the largest class of employment, found it possible to believe property and opportunity survived. It was a long time before solidarity between workers and farmers could realistically be imagined. Workers unionized to assert their rights against property, while farmers saw in property not oppression, but their liberty. Still, one factor posed a common threat to both groups. That factor was debt.

Debt

By the mid-1800s the self-sufficient farmer was largely a remnant of the past. To succeed, one had to produce for the market. Cash crops and livestock provided a far better living than did the attempt to provide all of one's own food, clothing, and shelter. There was, however, a trade-off. In producing for the market, farmers lost control over the costs of their inputs and the prices of their production. There were too many farmers to unionize and consequently, relief, when it was sought, was through an easing of land purchases and credit. Government attempted to do this with an increasingly easy homestead policy that reduced both the purchase price of frontier lands and the minimum size of the farms to be purchased. Unfortunately, the major cost in setting up a farm was not the price of land, but the costs of clearing, fencing, and building a homestead. Such costs restricted ownership of the open western lands to those with money or credit.[38] Others became tenant farmers, once again trading independence for a livelihood. All this suggests that the West, even though its opportunities were real enough, was not the vent for surplus population that was commonly depicted. That so many immigrants, like many of the famine-driven Irish, remained in dirty, slum-infested eastern cities makes it clear that farming was not universally regarded as feasible.

However, for those who did move west to take on homesteads, as well as for anyone else who borrowed, debt constituted a powerful threat to independence. Legally, failure to pay one's debts constituted breach of contract. Lenders seldom cared whether the default was due to bad intentions or bad luck; they simply sought relief. In the case of farmers, creditors typically secured their investments by putting a lien upon the borrower's property. Debt kept many farmers from being their own masters. Their property was theirs in name only when the uncontrollable risks they bore cascaded into financial disaster. If the creditor did not take over the estate and evict the tenant, at a minimum he or she could dictate key decisions. Under the pinch of distress, debt felt at least as degrading to farmers as wage work.

Debt was still worse for those who did not own property. Many unsuccessful borrowers languished in prisons or repaid their debts through forced labor. Through contract we have come full circle: Individuals may have had inalienable rights to life, liberty, and property, but so long as debt was legally punishable by imprisonment, free men gambled their liberty every time they borrowed money. Some may not find this paradoxical at all, believing instead that liberty cannot be taken lightly; that the promises of a free person must be kept; and that those who rely upon those promises must be protected. After all, if a borrower faced no ill consequences, then debt might be incurred too freely. However, at least three practical factors suggest that imprisonment and compulsory servitude were poor remedies for breach of contract. First, imprisonment too seldom improved the creditor's chances for complete recovery. How could a large debtor repay a debt while deprived of his or her occupation?[39] Second, if creditors were unwilling to lend without security, onerous remedies might as easily deter debtors from borrowing as creditors from lending.[40]

This, in the commercial environment of the nineteenth century would have deprived society of benefits derived from the free flow of capital. The third factor was that imprisonment for debt was increasingly at odds with republican values. Particularly when violent business cycles depressed the prices of the output borrowers used to repay creditors, any honest person could be reduced to penury and thus compulsory servitude.

Debt, more than anything else, revealed the contradiction between the inalienability of rights and the freedom of individuals to contract. Could rights really be inalienable if people put their freedoms on the auction block daily? On the other hand, how could individuals be free if they were unable to sell what they needed to secure their own happiness? Neither inalienability nor alienability could go unqualified. Most rights had to be alienable, but limits upon the contracts through which they were transacted had also to be imposed. Courts and legislatures attempted to thread this needle. Between 1812 and 1819 Pennsylvania, New York, and Massachusetts attempted to provide relief for debtors, but the Supreme Court limited their actions on the grounds that the Constitution prohibited states from impairing contractual obligations, including contracts of indebtedness. Finally, in 1827, the Court explained in *Ogden v. Saunders* that although states could not provide debt relief for existing contracts, they could enact legislation denying imprisonment or other remedies for the breach of *future* contracts.[41] State regulation of contract could now secure free labor from the paradox-free contract created.

One writer has declared that abandonment of imprisonment for debt smashed the "legal rock upon which indentured servitude rested."[42] This may overstate the case. Economic historian David Galenson argues that the decline of indentures owed less to abolition of debtors' imprisonment and more to the joint impact of falling transportation costs and rising European wages—conditions that made it less necessary to sell one's freedom for passage to the States.[43] Farley Grubb argues an even more powerful explanation was that improved communication enabled kinship networks to replace indentures with cash remittances enabling would-be immigrants to pay their own way and then to repay their debt after their arrival.[44] Nonetheless, the importation of European indentures dried up rather suddenly in 1819, the very moment when debt issues were hotly debated.

Although a few cases of northern servitude continued, an 1856 Connecticut Court verdict describes how the attitude toward servitude and contract had changed. In *Trask v. Parson* a young women came to America in exchange for five years' service. The Court held the contract a violation of public policy: "It is, in substance and effect, a contract for servitude, with no limitation but that of time, leaving the master to determine what the service should be, and the place where, and the person to whom it should be rendered."[45] In effect, the Court was arguing that before one could sell his or her personal freedom, at a minimum the exact limits of that sale must be described in the bargain. Without such delineation, the principles of contract were violated. In this, the law clung closely to economic theory. In any exchange, each party must believe that they receive at least as much value as they give. However, under lengthy and indefinite servitude, a person cannot know how much they will be asked to give. In such a case, it cannot be presumed that absolute freedom of contract benefits each trader.

Enduring Tensions

In the years preceding the Civil War, the conditions of freedom changed substantially. The market yielded choices that empowered individuals to defy traditional authority. Social status could not counteract the power that the market conferred upon underlings to pursue their own will. The market meant that people came together freely to contract in order to improve their own situation. Only among slaves was this freedom completely denied. However, it is unrealistic to suggest that people were either free or slave. Between these two extremes rested several degrees of dependency. One was that workers who sought the freedom to act collectively found the state blocking their course. Even though unions were found legal, their ability to exercise power was limited by judicial doctrines that favored individual freedom. A second was that personal sovereignty challenged the very conception of the obligation of contract. Any freedom of contract that was enforced through state compulsion begged the meaning of liberty. Attempts to grapple with these issues created improvements and fixes, but the fundamental issues did not go away. Instead, they returned to haunt society after the Civil War, when all men, supposedly, were free.

PART II

ILLUSORY FREEDOMS

—————— **Chapter 3** ——————

The Properties of Labor

The property which every man has in his own labor, as it is the original foundation of all other property, so it is the most sacred and inviolable.

—Adam Smith, *The Wealth of Nations*

In ending slavery, the Civil War closed one chapter in American life. The struggle against slavery was a black and white issue in two senses. Not only was slavery vilified as a backward and immoral institution, but slavery also placed color consciousness at the center of American culture.[1] Officially sanctioning separate treatment for black and white Americans, national law promoted exactly the kind of group, as opposed to individual, rights that it rejected when the issue turned on the collective action of workers. Unfortunately, the Civil War did not end this inconsistency.

Federal law aimed at nothing less than the transformation of the country from a loose federation of separate states possessing vastly different cultures and values, into a nation united under a single legal commitment to equal rights. An impressive series of federal enactments mandated this change: the Emancipation Proclamation (1863) first declared slaves in unoccupied territories free; the Thirteenth Constitutional Amendment (1865) then abolished involuntary servitude; the Civil Rights Act (1866) and the Fourteenth Amendment (1868) accorded all blacks citizenship and equal protection under the law; and, finally, the Fifteenth Amendment (1869) established a right to vote for black males. Despite, or perhaps even because of these acts, the legal issues involving labor became grayer. Overt bondage was eliminated, but the ideal of republican independence appeared more remote than ever and the strategies used to achieve it gave expression to unresolved tensions involving property, contract, and individualism.

Black and White Workers After Slavery

Only property, not merely the freedom to contract it, yielded an adequate basis for real independence. On this score, however, the federal government did little. Freedmen received only their liberty from a federal government unwilling to redistribute property from the vanquished slave owners. In their propertyless condition, southern black workers joined large numbers of northern laborers, some native but most immigrants, for whom the prospect of holding property or of becoming a master artisan was dim.

Matters were made worse when the defeated southern planter class allied itself with poorer whites to impose a race-based caste system. Several southern states enacted "black codes" stipulating differential treatment for black workers. These codes often restricted blacks to agricultural labor and criminalized vagrancy. Workers who broke the codes frequently ended up shackled to chain gangs forced to work on public projects or auctioned off to private employers. Because these laws virtually reimposed slavery, the federal government was compelled to oversee southern reconstruction.[2]

One of the most important tests of national law pitted white against black butchers in the famous Slaughterhouse Cases.[3] The Supreme Court weighed the arguments, which involved, as well, the right of local authorities to abate a health hazard. Slaughterhouse waste dumped into the Mississippi River caused epidemics of water-borne diseases. Yellow fever killed over 9,000 people in one outbreak. When another 3,000 people died in 1867, a commission was set up to study the problem. New Orleans sought relief but lacked jurisdiction to regulate the slaughterhouses to its north. To avoid future problems stemming from state regulation, 400 of the city's most established butchers organized a benevolent society and raised capital to start a "super slaughterhouse" south of the city. Their giant new wharf, railroad facilities, loading docks, and sheltering pens loomed ominously as a potential means to achieve exclusive control over the slaughtering business. To this point, butchering had been a relatively easy trade to enter—a few knives and a floor were all that was needed. It was, therefore, an occupation that attracted black freedmen, particularly as many had gained experience slaughtering animals when they were enslaved. Thus, the Butcher's Benevolent Association was reasonably viewed as a threat to the opportunity of free black workers to pursue their livelihood.

Black citizens, exercising their voting rights, gained substantial influence over the Louisiana legislature. The state decided to charter its own Crescent City Slaughterhouse. Unlike the Benevolent Butcher's facility, this slaughterhouse was to be regulated as a public utility and open to anyone who paid the minimal fees it imposed. Simultaneously, the state required that older establishments either close down or operate within the new public premises. The state justified its legal monopoly on the basis of the existing health hazard. Although the Butcher's Benevolent Association protested, in 1873 the Supreme Court upheld the state's actions.

Although the Fourteenth Amendment had been designed to extend equal protection of the laws to the South's newly enfranchised black citizens, perversely it was the white butchers' Benevolent Association that used its provisions to bring suit. In a dissent that eventually had greater weight than the Court's actual finding, Supreme Court Justice Stephen Field supported the Benevolent Association's contentions. Field argued that the Constitutional Amendment meant that states could make no law that denied *any* individual of his fundamental rights to *life, liberty, or property.*[4] This reading of the amendment would expand the latitude federal courts possessed to strike down state laws, particularly if they interfered with the "privileges and immunities" of citizens as Justice Field enumerated them. Field's analysis held that members of the Butcher's Association had been denied equality under the law because the substance of their property, their callings, had been stripped away by the state's monopoly.[5]

To make his case, Field relied upon a version of the labor theory of value that reduced all property to labor. Consequently, any law that impaired individuals from pursuing legitimate callings involved a taking of private property without due process of law. Field's dissent became the root of the new legal doctrine known as Substantive Due Process.[6] The significance of the doctrine lay in its ability to establish a formal equivalence between freedom of contract and effective republican independence. Where previously it had been land, not mere freedom of contract, that was thought necessary to achieve real independence, the law now equated ownership of one's own labor with the ownership of tangible property. Field's minority opinion eventually became reigning legal doctrine and remained so until the Great Depression and the New Deal spelled its demise.[7]

Skill, Specialization, and Technology

The equivalence between freedom of contract and property ownership could never be more than a formal relationship. Property in labor confronted different conditions from those encountered by the holders of real property. The value of property increased through investment. Without protection such investment was risky. To promote investment, corporate stockholders were given the special legal privilege called limited liability. Skill, too, takes an investment involving costly training, experience, and education. Artisans believed they needed protection of their trades—protection from unlimited entry, which would devalue their investments. Such protection was exactly opposite to the property right in one's labor that Justice Field's substantive due process doctrine allowed. Field specifically argued that the attempt to control entry into a skilled trade denied individuals rights to their labor and liberty of contract.

In medieval times, entry into various trades was legally restricted either by guilds or by royal patents. As time passed, it became more evident that it was impossible to restrict competition without restricting technological progress. Each new invention competed with the skills of some ancient trade. To protect skill completely one had to freeze technology. Assuming one wanted to step in on behalf of working men, the more problematic question would have been, *who* should be protected? For every skilled artisan enriched through the practice of his or her trade, there stood some wretched pauper constrained by protectionism from pursuing a similarly lucrative calling. Substantive due process sacrificed the former while extending to the latter freedom to compete.

The rising industrial order placed workers in nearly constant competition with one another. This competition played an essential role in the destruction of the community and the continuity that defined the earlier, status-based world. Workers' conceptions of themselves seemed incapable of changing as fast as the world around them. They sought the stability of a stronger sense of identity and security. Increasingly, workers turned to the solidarity of combination, vainly attempting to revive the independence of guild organizations. Collective governance of artisan crafts provided protection, community, and identity.

The conflict between the free labor ideology advocated by the courts and the artisan's demand for collective craft governance is strikingly illustrated by the experience of journeymen cordwainers.[8] Even before the Civil War the economic lives of Geneva, New York bootmakers had been disrupted by the expanding market. By mid-century, Massachusetts workers faced an even more powerful threat stemming from the industrial revolution. In the 1820s and 1830s expanding markets had already divided the work of cordwainers. Workers were divided by the quality of the goods they produced, some making custom-fitted goods and others producing cheaply for the rack. They were also subdivided within the trade itself. The work of stitching the upper portion of the shoe frequently became women's work, while men worked as skilled cutters and bottomers. Further divisions of labor only made sense as the market expanded. By 1885 over 200 new machines and gadgets assisted in the breakdown of the shoemakers' craft. Each device spurred on the specialization of workers. One old-time shoemaker from the period described how the single process of heeling changed. At first, "[a] man working exclusively at this branch of the craft soon became an expert, even though he knew nothing else of the art of shoemaking. The 'heeling' was afterward subdivided into 'nailing,' 'shaving,' 'blacking,' and 'polishing;' and from this gradually came that minute division which is now the marked feature in this business, distinguishing the new order of things from the old."[9]

The most fundamental changes involved the adaptation of the sewing machine to shoemaking. Invented in 1846, it was first applied to the binder's work in 1852. Women binders, who at first worked at home, increasingly found employment in factories. Gordon McKay developed a bottom-stitching machine in 1862 that greatly accelerated the destruction of cordwainer skills. Male artisans found it impossible to maintain their traditional workshops, known as "10 footers," and were, like the women before them, forced to apply to the factory for work. McKay's shoe machine company expanded, and within twenty years was able to outfit an entire shoe company with the promise that they would also train the factory's entire work force in two days. This constituted the virtual destruction of the cordwainers' craft, which fifty years earlier took five or six years for its practitioners to master.[10]

Cordwainers had a long tradition of asserting themselves. Sean Wilentz tells the story of New York City cordwainers who, as early as 1808, led a general walkout to protect their craft against the hiring of non-society men and illegal apprentices.[11] Workers worried that their trade would degenerate if improperly trained workers set up on their own. They feared these green hands would either end up producing shoddy goods or begin to compete with "all around" shoemakers by specializing in one branch of production for which they accepted lower wages. Like the disaster that befell farmers who specialized in a single crop only to find its price collapsed, overspecialization in detail work posed similar hazards. Thorough trade knowledge helped abort financial catastrophe. Even when they did not employ their trade knowledge in its entirety, broadly skilled artisans were protected in the event demand for any one part of their field dried up. Craft was as much a part of workers' independence as it was a way of coping with change. However, the legal difficulty of collective action pursued under the name of craft is best discussed in the context of the campaigns of the Knights of St. Crispin between 1868 and 1871.[12]

Worker Organization

In the wake of a massive defeat for Lynn, Massachusetts, shoemakers in 1860, cordwainers gradually went about the business of putting their lives back together. After the Civil War, the Knights of St. Crispin attempted to organize shoemakers on a national basis. Within three years, the organization claimed over 50,000 workers. The Crispins defended what remained of their craft in the wake of the destructive technological changes in shoemaking. The preamble to their organizational charter seemed almost to echo the words of Justice Field's *Slaughterhouse* dissent:

The objects of this organization are to protect its members from injurious competition and secure thorough unity of action among all workers on boots or shoes in every section of the country; claiming, as we do, that labor is capital, and the only capital that possesses power to reproduce itself, or, in other words, to create capital; that labor is the interest underlying every other interest, and therefore is entitled to and should receive from society and government, protection and encouragement.

Recognizing the right of the manufacture or capitalist to control his capital, we also claim and shall exercise the right to control our labor, and to be consulted in determining the price paid for it—a right hitherto denied us; and believe an international organization, embracing all workers on boots or shoes in the United States and provinces of North America is the only way in which this right can be successfully vindicated.[13]

To further their ends, the organization required that "No member . . . teach or aid in teaching any part or parts of boot or shoe making, unless this Lodge shall give permission."[14] There is in these words a puzzle that historians have hotly debated. Early accounts saw in the Crispins the final resistance by craftsmen against the invasion of the incoming shoe manufacturing system. Why else would they vehemently battle against the employment of green hands, good for operating machinery but not much more. More recently, however, Alan Dawley and others have convincingly shown that most of the members of the Knights of St. Crispin were not craftsmen, but were the very factory workers who were previously thought to represent the corruption of the cordwainers.[15] Moreover, the organization's strikes were over wages, not training. But if all of this is correct, what sense can we make of the union's prohibition against the employment of green hands?

The argument here is that the rule helped overcome the legal and economic difficulties inherent in organizing workers at that time. As the Crispins noted, the manufacturer's right to control his capital was protected by law, but workers could only achieve similar control over their labor through collective bargaining. If the state could not or would not protect them, they had to seek whatever means they might seize, the most promising of which appeared to be mutual solidarity in combination. Despite the 1842 *Hunt v. Commonwealth* finding that labor unions were legal, it was still quite difficult to act collectively without stepping on the law's toes, as *Walker v. Cronin,* a case involving the Crispins, showed.[16]

In Milford, Massachusetts, the Crispins organized pickets in a successful effort to get workers to strike. Skilled workers, who received work from the factory to complete at home, refused to finish the shoes and boots consigned to them. Under law, these facts allowed the manufacturer to argue that the union infringed upon its rights. Picketers were accused of "obstructing and molesting" factory employees for the "unlawful purpose of keeping plaintiffs from carrying on their said business." Allegedly, the organizers also "coerced" skilled workers to refuse to perform their work. The firm, as a result, had to endure significant extra expenses. Because one skilled out-worker had been under contract, the Court found the Crispins' organizer guilty of enticing him to break a lawful contract. The union argued that it had the right to persuade workers to act in their own interest, that workers had the right to quit, and that even if a worker was under legal contract—an allegation they denied—a free man still had the right not to perform a contract. However, the Court did not agree, holding, "Every one has a right to enjoy the fruits and advantages of his own enterprise, industry, skill and credit. He has no right to be protected against competition; but he has a right to be free from malicious and wanton interference, disturbance or annoyance."[17]

Given these circumstances, it is easy to see why collective action that inflicted economic damage upon an employer could quickly run afoul of the law. The situation was made more difficult because strikes and pick-ets were commonly accompanied by threats and even by violence. Even if a union pursued lawful ends, the courts would examine whether they had used illegal means, such as force or intimidation, to achieve those ends. This was one reason why trade unions like the Knights of St. Crispin preferred to remain secret, unincorporated associations. Behind the cloak of secrecy, only the individuals actually found guilty of illegal actions could be held accountable. The organization itself could not be sued for damages. In *Walker v. Cronin*, however, even without allega-tions of violence, the activities of the organizers were deemed illegal, and it was against these persons, as individuals apart from their union, that charges of enticement were brought. The 1871 is verdict in *Walker v. Cronin* was a blow to the St. Crispins, as it was to all unions that sought to control their trades.

This case demonstrates how difficult unions found it to secure legal sanction for their activities, particularly if courts were willing to assume that all workers had unbreakable contracts with their employers merely by virtue of their employment. That would make all attempts to organize walk-outs enticements. In actuality, courts were not usually willing to call mere employment an inviolable contract. When workers were hired at will, that is without a definite contract, employers often managed to achieve similar protection from collective action by requiring workers to sign "iron-clad oaths," which later were better known as "yellow dog contracts." Such oaths required workers never to join a union as a condition of their employ-ment. In agreeing to these conditions, workers not only signed away their freedom of association and speech, they opened up the possibility that organizing unions would again be found guilty of enticement. Such was still the situation some fifty years later in the important case of *Hitchman Coal and Coke v. Mitchell.*[18] An almost endless array of legal games were played by employers that made almost all collective action by workers susceptible to legal prohibitions.

The hidden genius in the Crispin stipulation that members not teach green hands was, most likely, not actually an attempt to recreate artisan conditions of old—the industry was too far advanced for that—but to provide a lawful basis upon which collective action could be sustained. Even though their work required little training, in refusing to teach new men without the permission of their lodge, the Crispins could ensure that only their local lodge members gained factory employment. Closed shops of this type made strikes by relatively unskilled workers more potent. Secure in the knowledge that employers would have to train and replace an entire work force, strikes for wages were less risky. The judge's verdict in *Snow v. Wheeler,* another case brought against the Crispins, suggests that this was indeed their purpose. Here the Court noted that "In relations between labor and capital, the attempt by cooperation on the one side to increase wages by diminishing competition, or on the other side to increase capital, is within certain limits lawful and proper. It ceases to be so when unlawful coercion is employed to control the freedom of the individual in disposing of his labor or capital."[19] As owners of their own labor, workers could freely refuse to impart it to others. Accordingly, in this case Judge Colt specifically found the Crispins' purposes lawful.

Because Judge Colt's decision relied upon the activities of the North Brookfield Lodge, the case did not provide an easy precedent for other unions to emulate. Unlike the larger Crispin lodges in Lynn and other factory towns, North Brookfield did make apprenticeship an important issue. Thus, the principle established in this case may have had limited value for unions in which the training of one worker by another was not a vital part of employment. Although the propagation of trade skill was declared a lawful purpose, under the industrial conditions then taking hold this was a purpose that protected an ever-shrinking proportion of workers. In those instances in which apprenticeship continued to play a major role in reproducing skills, employers sought to draw apprentices under their own control by indenturing workers to their associations and not to the craftsmen who trained them. When this left employers vulnerable to the strategy espoused by the Crispins, employers best circumvented the power of skilled workers by creating and supporting trade schools immune from worker boycotts. The trade school movement picked up steam in the late 1880s and continued on through the early 1900s.

Legal Limitations to Labor Organization

Immediately after the Civil War, northern and southern workers, as symbolized by the New Orleans butchers and Massachusetts shoemakers, were forced to recognize that their freedoms were shaped by court rulings that relied upon legal theories not very sympathetic to their causes. Legal rulings in the early 1870s established the principle that these workers had the liberty to sell their labor to whomever they pleased under almost any conditions—save those outlawed by the prohibition on involuntary servitude. What they could not do, however, was to combine when the effect was to injure other persons, whether employers or workers. Combinations designed to create improvements or efficiencies that benefited the larger population were free to compete or withdraw from competition, but combinations that the court believed advanced one group interest at the expense of another were subject to closer scrutiny. Courts allowed injuries resulting from the advance of technology, the recruitment of replacement workers, or the subdivision of skilled crafts, holding that they were within employers' prerogatives as part of a healthful competition that advanced the wealth of society as a whole. To protect workers from the ravages of competition was not, said the courts, liberty, but rather unwarranted class privilege.

The *Slaughterhouse Cases* in New Orleans suggested a second, slightly more hopeful, message to labor. It showed that government could pursue general interests through active intervention in an otherwise private market. Without state intervention, white butchers might well have laid the cement for their private new slaughtering facility and plastered it over with a "Whites Only" sign. When free black citizens used their new ballot rights to support a state slaughterhouse open to all, they demonstrated that government activity might be used to preserve, rather than limit, individual liberty. The curious fact about this case was, however, that the courts allowed the state monopoly only because of the public health hazard from unclean waters. Absent such a concern, courts typically regarded public facilities as a subsidy or as class legislation advancing the interest of one group—in the *Slaughterhouse Cases,* butchers—at public expense. The use of state assistance to advance the cause of labor, as workers would quickly find out, was thus narrowly circumscribed.

Overall, northern white workers and southern blacks learned very different lessons from court involvement in the early 1870s. Southern blacks looked to the courts to protect their rights from the actions of unfriendly whites. Northern white laborers, however, found their efforts for improvement stymied at court doors. By the end of the 1870s, black workers began to experience a similar reality.

Black and White Work in Post-Reconstruction

The end of reconstruction in 1877 changed southern politics.[20] The with-drawal of the federal troops that had overseen the submission and readmis-sion of southern states to the Union returned political control in the South to racist elements. Southern states enacted legislation reminiscent of their ear-lier black codes. In the face of constitutional amendments guaranteeing equality under the law, these states used race-neutral language to design legislation that nonetheless had a disproportionately negative effect upon African Americans. Post-reconstruction contract, enticement, vagrancy, and prison labor laws worked to the detriment of black workers.[21] For example, the practice of hiring agricultural labor for a year with a small prior cash advance effectively trapped workers who disliked their employers on their farms. If they quit, they could be tried for breach of contract and forced to return. Worse still, state legislatures began to identify workers who ran away as having taken their advances with criminal intent. Convicted for such offenses, black laborers were frequently placed in jail and then bound out in chain gangs or auctioned off to landlords. Laws and practices such as these were designed to reduce competition for labor, reduce wages, and to make the ex-slave more docile. Increasingly, as the post-reconstruction pe-riod progressed, the race-neutral veneer of many laws was dropped and blatant Jim Crow laws were adopted to restrict minority access to public facilities. The Supreme Court in *Plessy v. Ferguson* (1896)[22] found such laws legal under the Fourteenth Amendment, unbelievably holding that they created "separate but equal" conditions.

The South was an unusual labor environment. It succumbed to the worst tendencies of democracy—tendencies that were exacerbated by what econ-omist Joseph Schumpeter called the "creative destruction" rendered by free markets. Unlike many economists, Schumpeter was aware of the price that economic development exacted. Competition undermined stability in favor of material improvement. In the South, however, three factors combined to weaken the resolve of those who would let the market redistribute gains and losses. First and foremost, wartime destruction created a massive disruption in the economy that lowered productivity and income throughout the re-gion. Besides the physical destruction rent by northern generals like Sher-man, the war also disrupted the South's highly productive slave gang agriculture. That led to two additional tensions. First, planters who sought to recreate a labor system that would be nearly as productive as the old quickly discovered that the war had created labor shortages making it virtu-ally impossible for them to unilaterally impose their own conditions on black workers. If it were not for a second factor, their Jim Crow laws could not have been enacted. As it was, however, the emancipation of slaves potentially put free blacks on the same social and economic footing as free whites. In a South already enduring extreme losses in income, white workers were ready to make an unholy alliance with the large landholding class to preserve their social status and economic position. Together, they formed a democratic majority that was willing to shunt aside, as legal niceties, respect for the civil rights of the South's most visible minority community. Although control over the democratic machinery of government gave whites significant power, this did not stop the most militant from using illegal methods of harassment and coercion as well. Thus, where law did not work, the Ku Klux Klan developed its own vigilante justice to intimidate whites and blacks alike whenever they threatened "southern ways."

Despite the hostile environment in which freedmen worked, several researchers have concluded that the economic position of the freedmen improved substantially over the next forty years. In part this was because freedmen simply refused to allow family members to work as much as they had in the past.[23] Moreover, their improvement depended upon their willingness to get up and leave. Although threatened and cowed, blacks changed employers and locations when they could, gradually making small economic advances without state help and despite state impediments. Says Robert Higgs, "As a joint result of migration, education, training, and property accumulation the level of black income per capita in 1900 was probably more than double what it had been in the late 1860s." Of course it is useful to remember that in the late 1860s, as Higgs puts it, "destitution was typical."[24]

To sum up, after reconstruction the South exempted itself wherever it could from the intent of federal Civil Rights reforms. Although the South could not recreate slavery in its old form, it enforced legal contracts in such harsh ways that southern blacks would have been hard-pressed to see much liberty in their new-found contractual rights. When southern planters, workers, and citizens banded together in the most "malicious" way to deny black countrymen their basic rights, courts and local officials looked the other way, if not actually encouraging them. Racial prejudice in the South marred collective action so as to give vivid meaning to Tocqueville's phrase "tyranny of the majority."

Labor in the North

The peculiar southern conditions that fused race, collective action, and state power into a monolithic beast did not exist in the North. There was instead greater legal continuity between the immediate post-war period and the populist years of the 1880s and 1890s. Although workers continued in their struggles to organize collectively, their organizations usually failed to win bread-and-butter disputes. Only when workers' skills were difficult to replace did their organizations achieve significant bargaining power. Consequently, during this period labor organizations oscillated back and forth between entities seeking political reform and bread-and-butter craft unions. The former sought conditions that would recapture the spirit of republicanism. The latter abandoned general reforms as utopian and concentrated, instead, upon serving the immediate interests of their members.

The major labor organization in those years was the Knights of Labor. Although some of its local assemblies were organized by trade so as to resemble craft unions, many more existed as general assemblies combining all types of producers, including small businessmen and skilled and unskilled workers. Only the most "parasitic" classes, such as lawyers and bankers, were unwelcome. Although local assemblies could and did engage in strikes, they also pursued political reforms to boost the dignity and independence of labor. They sought access to easy money and lower interest rates to make it easier for small producers to set up their own shops. When economies of scale dictated large enterprise, they advocated cooperatives run by owner–workers. Such initiatives, they believed, would not be blocked by the courts as class legislation.

Perhaps their most important fight was for the eight-hour day.[25] At the time, ten to twelve hours' toil per day was the norm. Workers believed a shorter day was necessary for a true republic. The argument, according to David Montgomery, was that "shorter working hours would make the worker a more active and effective citizen of a democracy and would induce him to spend his free time at lectures and concerts instead of saloons." Long work days were equated with slavery. One trade journal inscribed upon its mast: "Eight Hours, A Legal Day's Work for Freemen."[26] The logic inherent in liberty of contract, however, punctured this argument. A worker, so legalist thinking went, had to be free to sell labor on whatever conditions he or she thought necessary. If long hours reduced workers' capacity for active citizenship, that did not justify a legal mandate to reduce working time. Consequently state legislatures pretended to take meaningful action: Laws were passed pronouncing eight hours as the legal day, except of course if a worker voluntarily signed a contract calling for a longer day. Competition, not state dictates, set the terms of the contract. Courts repeatedly turned back eight-hour legislation as a violation of the Fourteenth Amendment. Not until the twentieth century did public concerns such as health or fertility provide a legally recognized reason to limit the hours of work.[27]

The difficulty in garnering effective protective labor legislation is illustrated by the case *In re Jacobs* (1885).[28] Here, New York cigar workers sought and achieved legislation to protect themselves from the competition of tenement labor. Samuel Gompers, who rose from leader of the cigar workers to the president of the American Federation of Labor (AFL), convinced state legislators that crowded tenements with poor ventilation and ill-plumbed buildings constituted a health risk, not only to the workers employed within them, but to the consuming public at large. Inside these tenements, unskilled Eastern European families worked up to sixteen hours a day and, in so doing, threatened to erode the standards of the more skilled cigar makers that Gompers represented. Even though Theodore Roosevelt, sponsor of the legislation, confirmed the wretched working conditions, the courts argued that his law deprived workers of their "property" and "personal liberty." Thus, even when the courts could reasonably infer that public welfare required some minimal labor standards, the courts chose not to allow any such legislation. Gompers and other unionists learned from this episode not to trust the state for reforms, but rather to trust only in their own power. According to legal historian William Forbath, this case was crucial in turning organized labor away from the reformist movement of the Knights of Labor and toward the bread-and-butter craft unionism of the AFL.[29]

Effects of the Fourteenth Amendment

The Fourteenth Amendment affected northern and southern workers differently. Southern white workers learned to bypass federal requirements for equal protection and secured legislation that preserved their social status and economic advantages by systematically repressing black civil rights. Black laborers came to see their state legislatures as agents of oppression and looked, instead, for relief in true freedom of contract. In the North, workers possessed this liberty in such abundance that they were unable to keep courts from repealing laws setting minimum labor standards. Collective action provided the primary alternative through which to achieve major change. That course of action, however, also frequently led to the doors of the courthouse. The law protected organization most among those skilled workers who needed it least. Curiously, although the law operated differently in the North and the South, in both sections of the country it made unionization difficult: in the North because freedom of contract favored the individual against the group; and in the South because prejudice and discrimination separated whites from blacks.

───── Chapter 4 ─────

A Skillful Control

Managing the Labor Process

*'Day labor,' explained an Eight Hour League handbill issued
in Philadelphia, 'is the only important article of commerce
which has no fixed standard, its length being determined by the
necessities of the seller, or the generosity of the purchaser.' But
if the commodity offered for sale by the worker (his strength
and knowledge) had no fixed limit, and if he could deliver that
commodity to his purchaser (the employer) only by placing himself at the latter's disposal, the worker, had in effect, delivered
himself into a day's bondage for a day's wages. Here lay the
very essence of the concept of "wage-slavery." The remedy proposed by labor reformers was to draw a clear delineation between that part of the workman's day which might be
purchased for wages and that which remained inalienably his
own.*

—David Montgomery, *Beyond Equality*

In the late nineteenth century the courts defended the idea that individuals
should have a nearly absolute liberty of contract. In arguing that legislatures
could not transgress the rights citizens held to their life, liberty, and property, the Supreme Court defined labor as an individual's most precious
property, a property over which the owner exercised the liberty of control.
In the process, the Court enabled workers to alienate other liberties that
were, arguably, intended to remain inalienable. Simply put, when workers
contracted away their labor they entered personal servitudes; employers
gained rights over their persons as well as their labor because the two were
inseparable. Employers exercised their rights to the workers' labor over
long stretches of the day, sometimes for long periods of time, and generally
encountered few precise legal limits.[1] In seeking to consolidate their legal
rights to their workers' labor, management sought new methods to more fully
control the labor process. Many workers naturally resisted management's increasingly exacting governance of their labor.[2]

Liberty of contract assumes that the sale of labor for wages is analogous to other simple transactions. Wage contracts cannot specify the amount of labor sold but must resort instead to measures of time worked or units of output completed. These measures fail to tell us what a worker must do and how much autonomy he or she must surrender. Liberty of contract gives employers the right to direct their workers' activities. Only the constitutional prohibition against involuntary servitude prevents workers from selling themselves into slavery. There is no single standard by which the various servitudes that fall short of slavery may be deemed reasonable or unreasonable. Naturally, concerns were raised when the duration of the labor contract occupied too much of a worker's life or when workers became too dependent upon the master's whim.[3] However, the legal doctrines concerning liberty of contract seldom concerned such niceties. Workers under contract were assumed to have freely surrendered control over their labor power to masters in exchange for a sum that adequately compensated the temporary loss of their freedom. That economic want and misery led many a worker to surrender vital aspects of his or her freedom in exchange for survival was regarded as a lamentable, but unchangeable, feature of life.[4] Workers, however, seldom regarded their situation in the same terms as legal scholars.

Three strategies yielded hope for preserving freedom when economic want drove workers toward unfriendly contracts. The first was to outlaw some contracts as contrary to public policy. Such was the rationale behind the abolition of slavery and legal findings that very long or indefinite contracts of servitude were unwise. Such decisions established minimal conditions under which the freedom of contract could be expected to foster a genuine liberty. Successful as this strategy was, liberty and contract were generally at cross purposes during times of want.

As some reformers argued, when the length of the working day stretched over virtually the whole of an individual's wakeful state, the labor contract essentially produced a wage slave. Implicit, then, in first the ten-hour and then the eight-hour crusade, was a second strategy that involved a division between work and personal time. Personal time—which they sought to expand by law—was that time in which individuals possessed liberty to exercise their inalienable rights. An unfortunate implication, however, was that during work time these liberties could be curtailed. For those who found that reality unacceptable, a third strategy involved direct attempts by workers to check the right of employers to exercise their legal powers. This struggle fixed its aim squarely at employers' right to regard their workplaces as their private property and to use them as they alone saw fit. This chapter therefore examines how direct control over the shop floor conditioned labor freedom.

Skill and the Limits to Employer Authority

How much subservience could an employer reasonably expect from his or her employees? Once workers agree to put the number of hours they worked on the auction block of necessity, they also signaled their willingness to submit to employer discretion the power to direct the pace of their labor, the autonomy with which they worked, and even the degree of loyalty they were expected to show. Years later Aldous Huxley proposed a solution to industrial civilization's cravings for a stable, orderly world. In his novel *Brave New World,* drugs, psychology, and dream therapy enabled social engineers to condition people to accept, even to desire, the status and work to which they were born. To this day, Huxley's novel continues to have pertinence in questioning the nature of freedom when individuals willingly surrender themselves to established authorities.

Although late-nineteenth-century scientists and engineers developed no elixirs to produce spontaneous docility, it was not entirely for lack of effort. Concern over the unruly independence of workers elicited a legion of managerial techniques to help workers behave properly. Among those especially troublesome employees were skilled workers. Skill produced its own kind of freedom. Labor leader Samuel Gompers described the now scarcely recognizable world of the skilled cigar maker that existed in the 1870s. His words help us understand what cigar makers and other skilled workers hoped to protect, and to recognize the poverty of workers who lost what they had:

> The tobacco leaf was prepared by strippers who drew the leaves from the heavy stem and put them in pads of about fifty. The leaves had to be handled carefully to prevent tearing. The craftsmanship of the cigarmaker was shown in this ability to utilize wrappers to the best advantage to shave off the unusable to a hairbreadth, to roll so as to cover holes in the leaf and to use both hands so as to make a perfectly shaped and rolled product. These things a good cigarmaker learned to do more or less mechanically, which left us free to think, talk, listen, or sing. I loved the freedom of that work, for I had earned the mind-freedom that accompanied skill as a craftsman. I was eager to learn from discussion and reading or to pour out my feeling in song. Often we chose someone to read to us who was a particularly good reader, and in payment the rest of us gave him sufficient of our cigars so he was not the loser. The reading was always followed by discussion, so we learned to know each other pretty thoroughly. . . . The fellowship that grew between congenial shopmates was something that lasted a lifetime.[5]

In these ways, artisans who labored ten, twelve, and sometimes more hours per day retained their sense of identity. Though under the eye of the employer, that employer relied upon their skill, knowledge, and discretion. Bosses quickly learned that there was little point in unnecessarily antagonizing such men. As Gompers explained, a worker whose patience was exhausted might get up at any moment to announce he was leaving and that anyone who remained was a "scab."[6] The fellowship between skilled workers produced walkouts that seriously inconvenienced their employers.

Whether apprenticeship or merely long experience served to initiate them into their crafts, skilled workers alone, not management, possessed the necessary knowledge to keep the works going. But their world of "manly" independence depended upon the inability of employers to independently reproduce their workers' craft and skills.[7] Craft workers' independence also depended upon the ease with which they could find alternative employment. It was common for production to take place in small firms—cigar makers were generally employed in factories of ten to twenty men. If one firm did poorly, an artisan could generally turn to another boss in need of skill. However, when business was slack skilled workers found it more costly to assert their independence.

While a worker's skill might offset a cantankerous spirit, employers who had the choice preferred a hand who would not stir things up too much. Although employers competed with one another for labor, they often cooperated as well, passing on employee references and sometimes circulating blacklists against agitators. When employees were too aggressive, employers banded together in trade associations to lock workers out until they came to their senses. Still, employer solidarity, like worker solidarity, was not always a foregone conclusion. When Gompers was blacklisted by the Cigar Manufacturer's Association, one employer, angry that his Association attempted to dictate whom he should employ, hired Gompers on the spot.[8]

Locking out employees imposed costs upon employers as well as workers; with bills to be paid, the manufacturer who stopped his works risked bankruptcy. Employers found numerous devices to foster the necessary solidarity to break their obstinate workmen. For example, in 1887 leather manufacturers in Newark posted a monetary bond to their association that was forfeitable if they re-opened before their lockout was declared over. Losing a five thousand dollar bond was no trifling matter. Making clear that combinations on both sides of the labor question eroded individual freedom, one small employer complained, "[I]f you [the Knights of Labor] call out my men I can not go on with my work, and if I hold out against the order of the association, I will be ruined."[9] This was no isolated instance. At nearly the same time, a Chicago masons' strike was rebuffed by employers who enforced their lockout with the aid of suppliers who stopped delivery to firms that continued production.[10] The point is not that employers' methods were worse than those of their men—both employed coercive boycotts that made victims of neutrals—rather it is that employers abandoned the rhetoric of individual freedom when it was inexpedient.

Employers were most vulnerable to internal disunity when confronted by walkouts of skilled workers, particularly those that controlled trade entry through apprenticeship. In the construction trades, particularly among brick-layers and plumbers, employer associations attempted to control trade in-struction and bind their apprentices more closely to their bosses. In an attempt to better control the supply of their own labor, boys were inden-tured to the association, not to their unions. Apprenticeship itself became one of those gray areas in which the limits of voluntary contract forced questions. Long-term training contracts such as these involved explicit con-trols that many found degrading for a free person. For example, before changing employment, a plumbing apprentice's master required him to se-cure his previous employer's reference. Through this requirement a lad was reminded that the employer unilaterally defined the behavior and disputes that were reasonable and could if he wished block an employee's progress or even his seeking a new situation. Accordingly, it is not surprising that in commenting on the master's rules, plumbers' union delegate Ed Farrell complained, "Oh, it's a servant girl you be wanting."[11]

The independence of skilled workers in small shops often made employ-ers feel that their ownership of property existed in name only. Sometimes this was, indeed, quite true! Occasionally unions set their own rules, unilat-erally fining employers if they broke them. Bosses, however, were not defenseless. In various tests of strength with their hired hands, employers attempted to prove that they were in control. They did this by training their own workmen, by importing cheap replacements, and by displacing skilled workers with machinery.

During the Civil War, the American Emigrant Company was chartered to import workers to the labor scarce North.[12] The firm provided passage in exchange for lengthy service contracts. It sought, in a sense, to revitalize the defunct practice of indentured servitude. The experiment failed because the firm lacked the means to attract workers into long-term contracts and to enforce those contracts once they were signed. Transportation costs, once the primary obstacle to overseas immigrations, had decreased so that Euro-peans could travel to the United States without having to place themselves into bondage sight unseen. Indeed, some, like Samuel Gompers' father, were actually paid to leave Europe. The elder Gompers was sent to America from England, not by the Emigrant Company, but by his union, which found it more expedient to provide traveling money than unemployment relief during periods of labor surplus in England.[13]

Those who were desperate enough to enter into a long-term contract often discovered there was little to stop them from moving on when they found better opportunities.[14] With a war just over that had been brought on, in part, by the South's insistence upon the fugitive return law, the North could scarcely authorize bounty hunters to force fleeing emigrants back to fulfill their labor contracts. The significance of foreign contract labor during the 1870s and 1880s lay in the perception that they could be used to circumvent native or domestic worker demands, particularly at a time when organization by employers made blacklists and lockouts more effective. One example involved New York's employers in the Tile, Grate and Mantel Association. To win their lockout of 1904, the Association advertised in England and Germany "offering tile masons $5 per day for eight hours' labor in the United States." Fifty workmen came. Two weeks later the employers declared their lockout a victory. Interestingly, after being summarily discharged because they were not "familiar with American tools or methods," four of the misused foreign recruits succeeded in prosecuting the Association under an 1885 law prohibiting contract labor.[15]

This federal law prohibiting contract labor was a consequence of worker agitation, particularly by the Knights of Labor. The large-scale recruitment of Chinese labor on the Pacific Coast was a prime stimulus in organized labor's focus on immigration and contract labor. Gompers's cigar workers also alleged that the Chinese workers who sought jobs in their craft competed unfairly because they were willing to settle for a lower standard of living. In more than one instance, West Coast workers took matters into their own hands.[16] They rounded up Chinese laborers and forcibly put them on trains out of their towns. It was a familiar pattern among employers to recruit members of one ethnic group to compete with another. Violent hatreds were exacerbated by competition. This feature of economic life helps account for the frequent inability of American workers to pull together under adversity. Rather than struggle for solidarity, the majority of unions sought rules and laws that excluded minorities. In this instance, heavy lobbying ultimately produced a Chinese Exclusion Act in 1882 and was followed by the law prohibiting the importation of workers on contract.

If contract labor for foreign workers was illegal, the recruitment of workers from one state or region to another was less troublesome. When faced with strong resistance from skilled workers, firms and their associations posted job advertisements across the land. Employers occasionally wrote contracts requiring a year's service under the provision that payroll deductions would cover passage. Occasionally recruits traveled long distances in response to fraudulent solicitations claiming that they would not be used to break a local strike. In such instances, employers might pressure them to cross the picket lines by withholding the tools with which they made a living or their traveling bags. The sad reality, however, was that workers recruited from depressed areas often needed no blackmail to scab. Once they did, strikebreakers faced intimidation and, often enough, real violence from the workers whose jobs they took.

In the 1880s employers also began to use trade schools to increase the number of tradesmen. Unionists, like Gompers, called these schools "breeding grounds for scabs."[17] In 1905, the same year that the Tile, Grate and Mantel Association contracted foreign workers to oppose its union, that same Association approached the New York Trade School to set up a tile-laying program. Trade schools like the one in New York were powerful artillery in the battle between employers and skilled workers. Through them, employers succeeded in using the apprenticeship issue to tar the reputation of trade unions. Organized labor was pictured as an un-American monopoly, which, if it were not for the trade schools, restricted the right of children to pursue the trade of their choice. Labor retorted that trade schools helped sever the sense of obligation and solidarity instilled in learners by their journeymen teachers. Employer-sponsored trade schools promoted their own values. In this battle, neither side was wholly victorious. Although trade schools did widen the narrow union entryways to the trades, big-city trade unions often succeeded, to the dismay of many manufacturers, in shifting trade education to public schools. Public education often tolerated and sometimes even encouraged the union participation that employers tried so hard to avoid.[18]

Enter the Machine

When importation and training did not succeed in giving employers undisputed control over the shop floor, employers reserved one major weapon: the machine. Technology seemingly promised to eliminate the need for skilled labor entirely. Samuel Gompers's battles on behalf of cigar makers and against tenement employers testified to the effectiveness with which science and technology were harnessed by employers to reduce cost and stabilize production. The cigar workers complained that a new mechanical roller ushered in a distressing new labor system. According to Gompers,

> practically unskilled workers could produce cigars, soon they [manufacturers] added the tenement feature which was an entirely different method from the old home worker factory work. The manufacturers bought or rented a block of tenements and subrented the apartments to cigarmakers who with

their families lived and worked in three or four rooms. The cigarmakers paid rent to their employer for living room which was their work space, bought from him their supplies, furnished their own tools, received in return a small wage for completed work sometimes in script or in supplies from the company store on the ground floor. The whole family—old and young, had to work in order to earn a livelihood—work early and late, Sunday as well as Monday. The system was degrading to employer and workman. It killed craft skill and demoralized the industry.[19]

Gompers's story was anything but new. Over and over again, it occurred in labor markets everywhere. What was new was the rapidity with which change came and the degree to which change became systematic. The steam engine, perfected in the first quarter of the 1800s, made it easier to use machine power to replace human labor. Not only did steam power release manufacturers from the constraint of having to locate near rapid water, it also spurred new development in metals. A new machine tools industry was employed shaping and boring cylinders for steam engines. Those who designed machines to make other machines became expert in solving technological problems.[20] Engineering, the systematic application of technology to problem solving, became an important part of the manufacturing process. The high labor costs associated with time-consuming craft processes were identified as just one more technical problem to be solved. In the late 1700s weavers were replaced by automated looms operated by cheap labor. By the early 1800s most gunsmiths were displaced by Eli Whitney and Simeon North's new American System of Manufacture, which used standardized parts. By the 1870s, even the plumber, once considered a fine shop craftsman specializing in lead, was transformed into an installer and repairman working on manufactured pipes and fixtures.[21]

Nowhere did the process of deskilling go further and faster than in the steel industry. Andrew Carnegie, more than anyone else, pressed his management team to innovate new hearths, rolling mills, and conveyances to load and unload raw materials. Many of the techniques eliminated the back-breaking and mind-numbing work of unskilled laborers. However, in time, the work of skilled heaters, rollers, and numerous others was also transformed. The union in Carnegie's works, the Amalgamated Association of Iron and Steel Workers, did not resist technological changes that eliminated large numbers of employees. Instead, as one company executive put it, they "placed a tax upon improvements." In exchange for the union's accommodation to change, the company shared its productivity gains by giving employees better pay. With this understanding workers were willing to tolerate changes that undermined their own bargaining position.[22]

The tacit agreement between union and management was broken in a bloody battle known as the Homestead Strike of 1892. Carnegie's manager, Henry Frick, decided not to share the gains from plant improvements any longer. When the union demanded higher wage rates after substantial new innovations, Frick seized the opportunity to rid Carnegie's works of the Amalgamated Association. Protesting Frick's actions, employees seized the plant. They fired gunshots at Pinkerton agents who rafted down the Monongahela River to dislodge them. Finally, state troops enabled the firm to retake the steel works and crush the union. More than anything else, this situation showed how market forces undermined attempts to accommodate the interests of workers and employers. The workers' skill, upon which the enterprise had been forged, was not protected in the same way as capital investments. Even if the union's tacit agreement with Carnegie regarding technology had been formalized, competition from those who did not face labor's "tax on improvements" likely would have undone their arrangement.

New machines and technologies did not always lead to deskilling. In fact, the rising middle class owed much of its existence to industrial modernization. Among white collar workers there were bankers who analyzed business plans before providing the credit, managers who implemented and guided new works, engineers who designed change, and public servants and social service workers who busily patched up the holes in the social system rent by massive industrial dislocation. Even some blue collar workers found their skills and opportunities upgraded. Machinists and mechanics in particular were needed to superintend the works. Likewise, many production processes were complex and required highly trained workers who no longer worked by rule of thumb, but rather according to the best practice at the time. From accounting to chemistry, academic and technical knowledge became increasingly important. Artisans whose skills were part art, part tradition, or part mystery faced a barrage of attempts to systematize their work. Among the working classes, this actually tended to create a slight upward leveling in talents and rewards. Although skilled workers remained an essential element of production, even in 1910, the churning of skills and the threat of mechanization served to keep the demands among labor's traditional aristocrats in check. Or, as David Brody explained, "mechanization consistently undercut the worker's full relationship to the productive process."[23]

Even small shop owners saw themselves sinking. Having swum toward independence, such businessmen found themselves in deep waters. Large competitors loomed like predatory sharks ready to digest them. From the 1860s to the 1890s, economic waves battered them; the prices of their products marched steadily downward while their workers adamantly resisted offsetting pay decreases. Given their precarious hold on independence, alliance with skilled workers bent on demonstrating their own "manly rights" seemed a dubious proposition.

The Worker–Employer Relationship

The Knights of Labor, however, were not opposed to working with employers. Officially, they embraced all producers regardless of whether they were employees or employers. By the mid-1880s, there was increasing dissent over this policy. Gompers's American Federation of Labor (AFL) attracted workers advocating a program of labor self-reliance. The AFL aimed "To prevent the skilled labor of America from being reduced to beggary and to sustain the standard of American workmanship and skill." The cleavage between the AFL and the Knights came to a head in the late 1880s and early 1890s. When the AFL emerged triumphant, the skilled, the unskilled, and small producer interests increasingly staked out separate paths. Although the Knights' producerist vision never died completely, the commonality in interests between workers and owners seemed increasingly unattainable. Still, manufacturers who identified with their working-class roots found it hard to turn their backs on their own pasts. Even those who sipped from silver spoons professed, publicly at least, that there was no fundamental separation of interests between capital and labor.

The attempt to resolve the labor question even became a theoretical exercise for academic economists like John Bates Clark. He attempted to prove mathematically that labor and capital fairly shared the rewards of their joint production. His proposition followed neatly from the old idea that no party agrees to a contract from which it derives no benefit. Free contracts made it advantageous for workers to submit to their employers for an agreed upon purpose. In competition with other employers to secure labor's service, no master could refuse to give labor that which it was owed: that which Clark identified as the value of the incremental production created by the employment of labor.[24] Clark's timeless theory failed to comprehend workers in their own terms; it failed to understand their quest for independence. True, if born in poverty or living in want, almost any employment contract was an improvement, but it was most certainly not always one that fostered a permanent change in a worker's fundamental condition. As long as work was extended on a daily basis by small firms that themselves feared to look too far into the future, worker security, savings, and advancement would be tenuous at best. Yet to win workers' hearts and minds, employers increasingly realized that they must make workers see their success as their own. Business and psychology merged to search out employment relations that might achieve this.[25]

Some advocated piece rates because they ostensibly made employees their own masters. Under piece-rate systems, employers paid their employees strictly by the work they completed. The system logically followed on the heels of earlier putting out systems. Before factories dominated production in fields like textiles, shoes, and cigar making, merchants usually provided—or put out—materials that their suppliers worked on in their own time. Out from under the supervision of a master, individuals and families worked as slowly or as quickly as they wished. In theory, then, these outworkers were independent artisans. Under this simple contract, workers' pursuit of their own interests led them also to pursue the interests of their masters. However, when rates of pay slipped too low, the system was called sweated labor. Sean Wilentz has described how it worked in clothing manufacture as early as 1830:

> [T]he system invited brutal competition and a successive lowering of outwork piece rates. . . . [S]uccessive bidding by the contractors for manufacturers' orders (as well as the competition between manufacturers) depressed the contractors' income; . . . credit buying by retailers and country dealers prompted postponement of payment to all workers until finished work was done—and, hence chronic shortages of cash. The result: employers steadily reduced the rates they paid their hands and often avoided paying them at all for as long as possible. . . . Hounded by their creditors, hunted by the specter of late payment and bankruptcy, the contractors and garret masters lived an existence in which concern for one's workers was a liability and in which callousness (and, in some recorded cases, outright cruelty) became a way of life.[26]

Outwork continued, but when production shifted to factories, managers disregarded past problems and transplanted piecework as incentive for labor to work hard in its own interest.

Piecework was best applied when each item produced was of identical quality. Craftsmanship was notorious for its variations. Some skilled workers produced consistently high-quality goods while others were only capable of low or erratic quality. When this was the case, paymasters exercised their own discretion in determining how much to pay workers and even in deciding whether to accept delivery at all. This was perpetually irksome for pieceworkers. Factories helped overcome this problem by standardizing the production process, making it possible to achieve more homogeneous output.

Piecework and its variations were used whenever employers thought these would harmonize worker interests with their own. When commission work was employed in selling it made the salesperson more interested in closing deals. In department stores, the system nonetheless caused numerous problems. Sales had several dimensions and when only the commissionable sales total was rewarded, personnel frequently skimped on other important aspects of their jobs, like the provision of reliable information. Overly aggressive salespeople could easily damage a seller's reputation.

In steel mills and iron foundries skilled workers were also frequently paid according to their output. These workers, in turn, divied up their revenue with their journeymen, helpers, and apprentices.[27] In this setting the skilled worker was much like the franchise owner of a food chain. The factory provided materials and space—as, say, Dunkin Donuts does its name and ingredients—and then sub-contracted out its work on the site. In these cases workers became bosses themselves who had to reconcile their interests with those of their assistants.

No contract can perfectly align the interests of workers with their employers because no contract can anticipate all the dimensions of work and all the workplace contingencies that might erupt. Even though iron masters were their own bosses, they still depended upon management to coordinate production and supplies. This mutual interdependence meant that each side's income might vary by virtue of problems created by the other party, as, for example, when works managers failed to properly maintain their site.

Coalworkers experienced a different type of conflict. Although paid by the quantity of coal, workers disputed owners' assertions that only the company had the right to weigh coal. Workers distrusted management because the contract gave owners no incentive to weigh coal accurately. Simple contracts provided simple incentives: incentives that all too frequently discounted the necessity for cooperation between workmen and management. Piecework promoted production but not necessarily quality or cooperation. More complex payment schemes, like restaurants' combination of wages and tips, helped make waiters attentive to the needs of both employer and customer. Yet most jobs have so many dimensions that management finds it difficult to measure and reward each one separately.

Management

Independent management was a relatively new concept in the late 1800s. Previously, the usual practice was for owners to manage their own small works. Oddly enough, modern management was more frequently practiced on large slave plantations than in early industrial shops. When manufacturing firms also became large, they frequently adopted independent management as well. Adam Smith's dictum that the division of labor was limited by the extent of the market underlay the unexpected and extensive divisions of capital's work into owners, financiers, and managers. The economic function of owners was simply to risk their savings by putting it to productive use. The financiers acted as intermediaries seeking lucrative opportunities for owners and securing the credit managers needed to run their business. This tripartite division occurred as growth made it both impossible and undesirable for owners to personally supervise their enterprises. Before the Civil War, large northern businesses were rare and multi-location firms rarer still.[28]

According to business historian Alfred Chandler, railroads were most responsible for developing the management techniques for multi-division industries. Railroads had to develop a structure to coordinate construction, maintenance, and operations including, among other things, the maintenance of safety.[29] The railroads were notoriously dangerous to their workers. Construction crews had incredibly high mortality rates. Even trainmen and passengers faced perils from exploding steam engines, curling metal track, and faulty brakes. Solutions to these problems required the development of a management science that not only planned, supervised, and coordinated business activity, but also developed mechanisms to ensure that management itself was effective. The development of efficient managerial hierarchies that vested authority and accountability for the elements of business under direct control of an appropriate manager took much trial and error.

Labor management took a back seat to other aspects of supervision. Railroads generally delegated the management of immigrant workers to subcontractors. In construction, for example, division heads bargained with recruiter–agents who brought over crews of workers and then supervised them.[30] In exchange for commissions and other fees, these middlemen provided interpretive services, food, lodging, and transportation. In other industries, hiring was reserved for the crew boss, who often selected workers from a shape-up gang that each day lined up outside the gates to the works.[31] Crew bosses operated similarly to skilled workers in the iron works. They hired, fired, and paid men at their own discretion. Responsible for their part of the overall work, bosses exercised personal authority over men and machinery. Naturally, some bosses were good and others wretched. However, in their control of scarce employment and advancement chances, the wretched ones possessed immense opportunities for abuse. Whatever else these men may have been guilty of, they did not hold back in their efforts to increase the productivity of their employees. The result was a system plagued by high absenteeism, favoritism, and the occasional labor rebellion.[32]

Taylorism

Frederick Winslow Taylor seized the moment by applying the principles of science to the management of labor. Taylor saw many problems in the way work was organized. First and foremost, he believed that owners had actually relinquished too much control of their works to skilled laborers. Quelling the resistance of trade unions was only incidental to his primary concern—to give management the ability to improve labor productivity. Taylor believed that management's techniques were too imprecise; by vesting total authority in their plant bosses, owners failed to define exactly what was expected of workers to earn a fair day's pay. Of the method of pay, particularly the piece rate, Taylor argued that it was a source of "antagonism" between the men and the employer. "The employer is soon looked upon as . . . an enemy, and the mutual confidence which should exist between a leader and his men, the enthusiasm, the feeling that they are all working for the same end and will share in the results is lacking."[33]

To reduce reliance upon skilled workers, it was management's duty to monopolize knowledge of production. Scientific managers had to be able to tell workers the best way to do their jobs. As things stood, Taylor believed that workers seldom worked to their full capacity. Taylor called it soldiering when peer pressure was used to discourage anyone who worked too hard. These employees were shunned as rate busters. Workers intentionally concealed their capabilities, and consequently Taylor advocated precise "scientific" studies of the work process. Each movement of hands, arms, or torsos was timed with a stopwatch. The best combinations of movements to accomplish a particular task were determined by efficiency experts. In these ways, management reconstructed the work of the skilled laborer. Craft "mysteries" were reduced to a set of directions through which management dictated the pace of work on the shop floor.[34]

Management, in this way, attempted to defeat its own capriciousness while simultaneously freeing itself from dependence upon the workers it was charged to supervise. The remaining problem was to secure worker adherence to the system. For this, Taylor proposed a dual payment scheme involving piece rates plus bonuses for beating designated quotas. Through this system Taylor sought to make the working man's interest synonymous with the employer's. It was a wage plan designed to encourage a high quality and intensity of work. Under the old piece-rate system, when workers complied by demonstrating how much they could work, management lowered piece rates until workers were no better off than before. Taylor objected. He urged management to share the gains from their increased output by giving disproportionately large bonuses to workers who exceeded their quotas. Because the increases could be paid for out of higher productivity of plant machinery, Taylor believed that management could and would stand by its commitment.

The main problem that plagued Taylor's program was that even if management wanted to commit itself to scientifically determined standards of production and pay, the market would undermine its efforts. If every manufacturer adopted Taylor's methods—as competitors might find it necessary to do if Taylor's system really produced greater efficiency—all workers would be more productive. Greater productivity would force firms to choose between laying off some workers or having excess production depress product prices. Neither event boded well for maintaining Taylor's piece rates and bonuses. Firms that did so would find themselves at a competitive disadvantage. It was only a matter of time before scientific managers broke their own promises, which they did. In the steel industry, tremendous productivity gains did not prevent managers from lowering the tonnage rates they paid their hands; by 1910 very few steelworkers earned more than the average wage in the manufacturing sector.

An even more fundamental problem awaited scientific management in Taylor's firm belief that his methods synchronized the interests of labor and management. Although the management of many enterprises gradually embraced his ideas, workers seldom did. The very presence of the time and motion experts whose studies were designed to squeeze out maximal productivity immediately caused workers to slow their pace. The problem with Taylor's scheme was that it turned the labor contract into a one-sided affair. Although he continuously maintained that management must set reasonable expectations for work, including time for breaks, ultimately scientific management worked on the premise that management exercised its proper role when it unilaterally determined what constituted a "fair day's work for a fair day's pay." It was unrealistic to expect workers to cheerfully sign away their rights in an open-ended contract that permitted efficiency experts to dictate their every move on the job. Free and voluntary consent is impossible if the terms of a bargain are not sufficiently specified. Scientific management required the surrender of the worker's will to a technological elite that claimed to understand the labor process better than the people who actually did the work.

The Adaptations of Henry Ford

Nonetheless, variants of Taylorism were increasingly implemented in factories and assembly plants in the early twentieth century.[35] Henry Ford adapted systematic management to automobile production in 1913 by combining the moving assembly line with a highly specialized labor regimen in which each worker performed a very narrowly defined task. Labor's efficiency under Ford ratcheted up to new highs. Ford had taken the skilled work of carriage makers and machinists and turned most of it into semi-skilled or unskilled work. With simple jobs, foremen found it easy to monitor production and thereby eliminated the bedeviling trade-off between quality and quantity. Standardization of product and standardization of labor were achieved simultaneously. Even more important, the continuously moving assembly line allowed management to set the work pace. When lines were sped up, workers who could not cope were fired. Wasteful setup motions were eliminated by bringing parts and materials to the worker. The time necessary to assemble a Model T dropped from 12 hours and 8 minutes to as little as 1 hour and 33 minutes. The production process was so regularized that hourly or daily wages, rather than piece rates, could ensure high productivity. Although the repetitive work was often dreary and dismal, Ford adhered to Taylor's admonitions to keep his wage rates high. In 1913, when other firms generally paid two dollars per day for unskilled labor, Ford announced a "five-dollar day." Ford believed attractive wages were good for his company as well as his workers. An expanding market and cutting-edge technology gave him a cost advantage over his competitors, which enabled him to sustain high wages. Indeed, the high wages preserved his advantages by reducing both labor turnover and the threat of unionization, and improving the quality of the pool of workers from which he could hire.[36]

Later, when Aldous Huxley wrote his anti-utopian novel, Ford became the deity to which *Brave New World* paid homage. All the great controllers from Lenin to Hitler were lumped into one. The Brave New World was organized via Fordism and not freedom of contract. In that mind-numbing world, the options and conditions of life would be so successfully manipulated that workers would willingly sell the freedom inherent in their own personalities. In exchange, they obtained order and security.

Chapter 5

Incorporating Paternalism

[O]ne of the most serious problems of all modern politics . . . is not how to reconcile freedom and equality but how to reconcile equality and authority.

—Hannah Arendt, *On Revolution*

By the 1920s most Americans had abandoned the prospect of being their own boss. In 1900 only one in three workers over age ten lived on a farm; by 1920 that number had fallen to one in four, and all portents for the future were that the trend would continue. Until 1910 this decline was only in percentage terms, but the 1920 census marked the first time that the actual number of farmers fell. Between 1900 and 1940 the number of workers in other forms of self-employment rose from 3.9 million to 5.6 million, but these, too, did not keep pace with a labor force that increased from 28.4 to 55.9 million. Statistics for all self-employed workers, including those on farms, fell from about one-third to one-quarter of the total.[1] The prospects for achieving independent employment had dimmed notably. The businesses, particularly the larger ones, on which workers came to depend began to perceive and assume responsibility for more than wages. The ways in which they did so form an important chapter in the history of labor freedom.

The Advent of Large Firms

The expansion of big businesses accelerated at the turn of the century. In the late nineteenth century, to create vast industrial empires, a few entrepreneurs seized opportunities opened by the completion of the rail network. John D. Rockefeller, for example, tied his oil refineries to a huge distribution network in order to sell at retail. Rail carriers thanked Rockefeller's Standard Oil for the privilege of hauling his tanker cars by awarding him secret rebates. The resulting cost advantage helped Rockefeller integrate oil drilling, refining, and distribution into one big firm. By the 1890s, Standard Oil's lawyers perfected the modern general purpose corporation, a form of business organization that could legally buy the assets of its competitors and thereby monopolize an industry.[2] Standard Oil set the pattern and others quickly followed. As if to hail the new century, a giant merger mania, the first ever, exploded in 1898. J.P. Morgan became the great financier of large business consolidations that sought to replace cutthroat competition with stability and order. In 1901, he bought out the gigantic Carnegie Steel Corporation and combined it with its competitors to obtain over 60 percent of the market. Other mergers followed, each steadily consolidating a larger proportion of the nation's industrial assets into a smaller number of large corporations.

In 1901, 185 industrial combinations produced about 14 percent of the nation's manufacturing output and employed fully 8 percent of the industrial labor force. Manufacturing employment in large and small firms exploded: where only 75,000 were so employed in 1810 and 1.5 million in 1860, by the end of World War I over 11 million—fully one-quarter of the labor force—were classified this way. However, even such figures do not reveal the extent to which large firms dominated employment. In 1810 very few mills employed over 100 workers. By 1860, one of the largest steel companies employed 6,000 workers. By 1935, however, General Motors, the largest employer in the nation, signed paychecks for over 150,000 workers. GM employed more workers than the population of many cities. Such data are vital to understanding changes in twentieth-century employment relations.[3]

Clearly, not everyone was employed by a large firm. In fact, the majority of Americans continued to work outside manufacturing either for themselves or for small employers. However, the existence of large employers was important for several reasons. First, never before had so many people's well-being been so directly affected by a single non-governmental organization. Whole city and state economies rose and fell with the fortunes of dominant firms. More than that, however, large firms also paid the highest wages and benefits. Big employers, like Ford Motor Company, made it possible for the average citizen to lead a middle-class life. This, not independence in the old sense, defined a new American dream.[4]

Wages and Purchasing Power

There can be little doubt that higher incomes expanded individual freedom. The availability of resources to buy more of what was wanted not only set individuals free from all sorts of drudgery, but empowered workers to attain goals previously believed unreachable. For example, affordable new household appliances eliminated the most physically demanding chores that, by tradition, fell to women. For example, in 1900 no one had an automatic washing machine, but by 1930 nearly a quarter of all American households did. Domestic chores, from sewing to freezing to cooking to washing, were made less onerous by the purchase of specialized household appliances. Reducing household labor enabled married women to claim greater independence in ways they defined for themselves, whether through employment, through volunteer activity, or for the lucky few simply by using free time to indulge their own desires. Automobile purchases grew even more rapidly than washing machines so that by 1930 60 percent of American households took advantage of the new opportunities they created.[5] The power of cheap transportation is perhaps best visualized in the image of the countless depression-era refugees who fled Oklahoma's dust storms to search for work in old jalopies loaded with all their worldly goods. In these ways and many more, typical Americans used their increased consumption power to avail themselves of previously unattainable options.

Between 1860 and 1880 the average income of non-farm employees oscillated up and down, only gradually recovering its pre–Civil War level. The tenuous nature of worker earnings, which stemmed in large measure from frequent unemployment, accounts for some of labor's restiveness at this time. However, between 1880 and 1890 workers' incomes rose consistently, from $395 to $519.[6] Until the Great Depression, there was no turning back. Between 1900 and 1914 wages had increased almost exactly 25 percent. After stagnating during World War I, wages grew again by nearly 30 percent in the ten years between 1920 and 1929.[7] All told, workers' incomes had more than doubled in the fifty years since 1880. These higher incomes flowed from advances in technology and management. The benefits were shared with workers because competition for labor forced managers to do so. Even when competition was weak, managers hoped that giving workers a fair shake would produce a reciprocal response. If nothing else, they hoped workers would not want to risk their good pay by participating in unions.

The Pullman Episode

Many historians have looked back in disbelief that workers in large auto, rubber, electrical, and other prominent manufacturing plants did not unionize. One frequent explanation is that industry simply succeeded in repressing any resistance from workers. The competing alternative is that workers were satisfied.[8] Both ideas are central to the enormously important labor outburst in Pullman, Illinois.[9] The Pullman Palace Car Company attempted to move beyond the confines of "scientific management" and displace the narrow wage relationship with its workers by restoring a sense of community. Had it worked, Pullman's vision might have quenched labor's thirst by creating a business form that produced a satisfying cooperation between labor and capital. Instead, the Pullman episode more clearly exposed the fragile bonds that held workers and employers together. Ultimately, the episode left unskilled workers isolated from the larger labor movement and demonstrated that they had no really effective champions. The American Federation of Labor would not help them, the Knights of Labor could not help them, and alliance with Socialists ill fit the larger American political framework. It is no wonder, then, that despite the failure at Pullman, many corporations redoubled their efforts to restore workers' lost sense of community and independence. They acted in the belief that corporate demonstrations of paternal concern stood a strong chance of winning labor's loyalty. Events in Pullman are important because they illustrate why workers might resist corporate welfarism as an authoritarian infringement on their personal liberty.

George Pullman's great good fortune was to realize how much the American public loved and would pay for luxury. Perhaps his working-class background heightened his sensitivity to the exhilaration that displays of ostentation produced. As early as the 1850s, he had been at work designing and producing sleeping cars that were much more comfortable than the threadbare accommodations railroads hitherto provided. Where train companies spent $5,000 to produce a sleeper, Pullman spent $20,000 to $25,000, and as time passed he was able to produce even plusher cars for English royalty.

His extravagant tastes seem to have rubbed off on his attitudes toward labor relations. He lavishly underwrote a model town in order to secure a reliable labor force. Planned with an eye toward aesthetic appeal and practicality, after four years of construction the town of Pullman was completed in 1884. The main buildings were artfully crafted. The sewage system was linked to a state-of-the-art farm that recycled the town's waste. Though somewhat monotonous, the tenement residences that housed many of the workers were well constructed. On the whole, the town was enthusiastically commended for its "architectural gardening." Recreational, health, and educational facilities were included. Pullman manufactured this environment to support a "distinct type" of labor, one that was "quite forty per cent better in evidence of thrift and refinement and in all the outward indications of a wholesome habit of life."[10]

George Pullman also manufactured an environment in which worker input was neither needed nor sought. He decided to erect one church. Picturesque as this green stone building was, his refusal to allow other churches desired by the town residents stood as a constant reminder of the proprietor's paternalism. Pullman was not designed to be a free township with an independent government, but rather as a paying business proposition. George Pullman owned, not only the place of prayer, but also all of the rest of the town's buildings, which he rented out. As an enterprise, the town performed quite well. As a democracy, however, it was wanting. This was a company town in which political debate was limited to police, taxes, and water rates. In exchange for a clean and healthful village, Pullman workers surrendered even their freedom of public speech.[11]

During the depression of 1893, George Pullman found it expedient to reduce the company's wages by 25 percent while keeping rents on housing fixed. These decisions made it possible to continue paying dividends to the firm's stockholders. Fed up, the workers walked out in 1894 with the help of the newly organized American Railroad Union (ARU). The ARU, under Eugene V. Debs's leadership, called on all train men to boycott Pullman's cars. Despite Debs's misgivings, a huge strike ensued, halting rail traffic nationwide. The attorney general for the United States secured a court injunction ordering the men to cease their boycott. When the workers refused, troops moved in, ostensibly to protect the federal mail. Although the ARU had organized over 150,000 workers, company strikebreakers under protection of federal troops succeeded in getting the rail cars moving again. Debs's ARU appealed to Samuel Gompers's American Federation of Labor to join in a general strike. Gompers, worried about the feasibility of a big strike in the midst of a depression, and dismayed by Debs's break from the older Railroad Brotherhoods, said no. The boycott was crushed and Debs was imprisoned for violating the injunction. The episode is among the most important battles in labor history and its lessons were several.

First, the strike suggested that even if corporate paternalism muted labor resistance, it would not stop workers from the ultimate realization that capital's concern for labor extended only so far as the bottom line of its financial accounts. Second, the very vehemence with which the Pullman strike was fought and the rapidity with which it spread suggests that workers under paternalistic employers stored cumulative resentments, which, like attic combustibles, awaited only a spark. The strike contained yet a third lesson, this one regarding labor organization. While a member of the skilled Brotherhood of Railroad Firemen, Debs reached the conclusion that effective power required solidarity among all workers within an industry. Unlike either the AFL or the Knights of Labor, the ARU attempted to organize an entire industry. However, its crushing defeat suggested that the effort was premature. The loss consolidated labor leadership in Gompers's more conservative federation of trade unions. Finally, labor learned that government was not likely to be neutral. When all was said and done, the law protected property; and strikes that jeopardized property placed the considerable power of the state on the side of capital.

Oddly enough, one lesson that was not drawn from the strike was that corporate paternalism was inadvisable. Where "scientific managers" attempted to control only workers' behavior on the job, paternalism had greater ambitions. Paternalism operated within the interstices of contracts where incentive schemes could not penetrate. In an incessant attempt to instill corporate values, it followed workers back and forth between home and work. Because the millions of dollars invested in large firms could be held hostage by a band of dissatisfied workers, capital searched for ways to create company men and women—individuals who, realizing their aspirations were best fulfilled by the organizations that employed them, contentedly subordinated their own individuality to corporate needs. To do this, however, corporations strove to prove they were entities worthy of such loyalty, entities whose employees would be properly cared for. The failed experiment in Pullman did not put an end to this quest.

Corporate Paternalism

For business leaders, it was George Pullman, not paternalism, that was tragically flawed: Corporations were not inherently evil, rather George Pullman had lost sight of the goal. Other managers believed they could improve using Pullman as an object lesson in the new "welfare movement." A rush to demonstrate corporate concern gained momentum and reached full blossom in the 1920s.[12]

Whether the movement was called "welfarism" or "paternalism" depended upon the value system of the commentator. Welfarism signified an attempt by corporations to fulfill their social responsibility. Welfare work substituted corporate protections for older, community-based mechanisms for security and insurance. Thus, big business attempted to care for its workers and their families in bad times and good using a new battery of devices including pensions, stock and saving plans, unemployment schemes, medical care, company newspapers, and sports teams. Such activities were not strictly necessitated by production, but were instead designed to establish a sense of mutuality within employment relations. One of welfare work's most prominent exponents, Gertrude Beeks, was hired by International Harvester. To the ire of top managers, Beeks investigated every facet of the farm machinery company and made recommendations for improvement that began with the toilet facilities and ended with the protocols for employee advancement.[13]

The term "paternalism," unlike "welfarism," has a derogatory undertone that suggests corporations used public displays of concern not to redress the fundamental social imbalances caused by industrialization, but rather as a palliative. Corporate paternalism compromised the slim measure of independence workers enjoyed. The pensioner at International Harvester who was told that annuity payments were corporate gifts in reward for loyal and continuous service knew the risks of ungrateful behavior. The sick worker visited by a company nurse understood that what was observed in home visits included evidence of sobriety as well as personal health. Even Harvester's seemingly well-intentioned employee stock distribution scheme took on cynical overtones when it was introduced just as workers were deciding to go out on strike. According to Robert Ozanne, "Cash and stock dangling daily before their eyes, plus the systematic dismissal of union leaders had apparently turned the tide" against the walkout. At steel companies, workers buying or renting company housing likewise knew that good housing and jobs were bound together in faithful service to the employer. Such forms of paternalism, one union man complained, had "many really good men tied up."[14]

For organized labor, all company benefits other than a good wage were worrisome. Paternalism undercut the appeal of unions; worker resolve for independent action weakened with each additional attachment extended by the corporation. Strikes and union membership could result in dismissals whose costs would not be counted in wages alone, but also in terms of lost housing, insurance, pensions, and even community. Corporate paternalism was returning society, in this peculiar way, to the pre-revolutionary days when workers were dependent upon patrons. While early society had many benefits, most notably a greater sense of identity and social belonging, it had always undercut the independence of mind that republicans argued was essential for public debate. Too many citizens were compromised by their personal entanglements to speak their true minds. Ownership and independence alone made republican democracy possible. Organized labor saw in corporate welfarism a return to patriarchal habits that undermined the gains of the past century. Labor argued that if workers were paid a good wage, they could make their own decisions about the housing, medical care, and personal consumption they needed. Unions in the AFL believed it was their job, not the employers', to provide those benefits for their members.[15]

State Paternalism

Many in organized labor resisted not only corporate paternalism, but state paternalism as well. It would be far better for labor if the government defined and protected basic labor rights and left labor unions to take care of insurance and pension needs. Government's duty, as these labor leaders saw it, was to eliminate child labor, set maximum hours, dictate employer responsibility to pay for industrial accidents, and assure a minimum wage that prevented the most desperate workers from submitting to degrading work standards. It was not the state's obligation to supervise people's lives; it was government's duty to ensure that the industrial state was not advanced as an end in and of itself, but only as a vehicle to improve workers' lives.

Among labor organizations, it was the AFL that was most wary of extensive state intervention. According to William Forbath it was AFL president Gompers's early experiences with the law that made him wary of dependence upon the government.[16] Having witnessed judicial repeals of labor-sponsored tenement legislation, hours legislation, and a host of other protective reforms, Gompers did not trust the state to protect its weaker citizens. His skepticism increased with the rising number of court-enforced injunctions against organized labor's activities. Consequently, Gompers strongly disagreed with socialists and Marxists who regarded the state as the vehicle that would drive home workers' complete emancipation. The false security of state protection, he feared, would lull workers into a complacency that disarmed them before they had consolidated effective power. At the same time, Gompers and his AFL supporters had come to find state welfare inconsistent with the premises of freedom in the United States.

The Shifting Responsibility for Social Welfare

Between the 1870s and the 1930s there were three broad phases in which primary responsibility for social welfare shifted from individuals or their unions, to government, and then to business. This was not a clean progression, but rather one that involved sporadic backtracking and messy jurisdictional disputes.

During the late nineteenth century, industrialists played hardball with their workers. Big firms used their economies of scale and new technology not to benefit labor, but to leapfrog smaller competitors. Facing dwindling market shares, small producers clawed at each other's throats in fierce competition that made compassion for their employees seem a luxury they could not afford. Thus, from the 1870s to the early 1900s organized labor and workers individually had to look out for their own interests. Organization was most effective among the skilled workers whose unions provided a host of benefits. These benefits often went far beyond the important but humdrum death and disability payments. The Railroad Brotherhoods protected their men from arbitrary layoffs by instituting a seniority system.[17]

Craft unions developed apprenticeship systems that provided training for their members' children. Additionally, many trade unions were knit together by ethnic bonds that were supplemented by diverse events from sports to picnics. The unskilled had fewer resources and often fended for themselves, drawing assistance, where they could, from charitable organizations, from their communities, or from family. Immigrant workers were generally among the least privileged; they either sank or learned to swim on their own.

Organized labor experienced a burst of success in the first years of the twentieth century as membership rose from well under 10 percent to nearly 15 percent of the labor force and practically 2 million members in 1905.[18] However, its gains were ephemeral, coming at precisely the same time that corporate consolidations created mammoth firms. As firms grew larger they often found it possible to take the long view: Where previously labor costs had been the first item to attack to maintain competitiveness, the giant corporate survivors saw value in redirecting some of their investments into their employees. This change arose out of two concerns. One of these was that many firms believed this was a good way to stop the advancing thrusts of organized labor. And second, managers reasoned, small investments on labor sometimes prevented huge losses from labor turnover or turmoil and was money well spent. Thus, in the early twentieth century, many big companies began to take on welfare work. However, many insightful corporate leaders began to recognize that their problems were best solved with a little help from the state.[19]

The Challenges for Welfare Capitalism in the Progressive Era

The period from 1901 to 1919 is usually referred to as the Progressive Era. What made it progressive was its faith that the deployment of scientific knowledge could and would solve problems. Progressive reformers examined the results of unfettered industrialization and saw a system in desperate need of expert repair. Forward-looking professionals staffed a multitude of state commissions in order to investigate and regulate child labor, immigration, health and safety conditions, and vocational training. Some businessmen found these efforts appropriate and relied upon the state to create uniform standards. Standards protected businesses that pursued welfare work from the fly-by-night firms whose competitive advantage lay in chiseling their workers. However, the accumulation of state rules and regulations also made business more vulnerable to public scrutiny. The progressive movement lost steam as business became increasingly uncomfortable with the excesses they believed it engendered. Convulsive labor disruptions that marked the close of World War I proved the death knell of the movement.

War often promotes domestic social change. Not only is this because warring nations must appear sufficiently worthy to woo loyal fighters to their cause, but also because warfare augments the demand for manpower. In addition, labor has the power to interrupt vital war production. President Woodrow Wilson secured the support of organized labor for World War I by creating War Labor Boards to hear and resolve workers' disputes. In 1920, organized labor claimed 5 million workers where just ten years earlier there were only 2 million unionists. Government directives told industry not to hinder workers who sought collective bargaining. As a result, labor unions increased membership in areas of weakness like steel and shipbuilding. In shipping, the unions secured closed shops. In steel, labor rebuilt some of the base it had lost after the 1892 Homestead Strike, but results were slower. At the war's end, disastrous strikes in both industries impeded industrial unionization for years to come.[20]

In the years immediately after the war, labor militancy reached its zenith. In 1919, workers throughout Seattle combined in a general strike that virtually shut down the city. That same year workers almost succeeded in paralyzing the steel industry nationwide. In Boston, even the police went on strike. The militancy of 1919 owed its momentum to conditions that arose during the war.[21] Activists had succeeded in organizing the skilled and unskilled together so that unions enjoyed a power they had never experienced before, and this at a time when workers were frustrated by their wartime sacrifices. Although money wages had risen, inflation had risen even more. Power and frustration created a tinderbox that was heated by the example of successful revolution in Russia. The workers' state in Russia frightened employers at the same time that it enticed many newly radicalized American workers. In response, American business launched a three-pronged counterattack to break the militant unions pounding on their doors. Their offensive included the American Plan (an open-shop campaign), joint coordination by state and federal officials to monitor and repress left-wing agitation, and renewed welfare work on a larger basis than ever before.[22]

In the 1920s, the Supreme Court helped reverse labor's Progressive Era momentum. The signal event was the Supreme Court's 1923 *Adkins v. Children's* decision, which effectively rolled back minimum-wage laws for women and children.[23] As it had in earlier times, the Court held such legislation inconsistent with workers' liberty of contract. In places like Wisconsin and Oregon, similar laws had provided the basis for factory inspections that effectively regulated work, education, and training. As these state protections were dismantled, corporations gained a new reason and opportunity to advance their own welfare work.

Although corporate welfare work in the 1920s was built upon groundwork that had been laid earlier, the new movement went beyond the longstanding pensions, stock sharing, and health programs: The establishment of employee representation plans became the defining element of the paternal era. Without turning management over to the workers involved, these plans gave employees a voice in corporate affairs. Two factors prodded companies toward the establishment of employee representation schemes. The first was a bloody strike and massacre at Ludlow, Colorado, and the second was the democratic rhetoric that World War I fostered.[24]

The strike at Ludlow pitted the United Mineworkers (UMW) against one of America's most powerful families, the Rockefellers.[25] America's mines had been the scene of almost continuous confrontations between workers and companies since the 1860s. Unlike other major unions, the UMW organized on an industrial basis that combined the skilled and unskilled alike. In 1897 and 1898 the UMW achieved an agreement over working conditions in the mines located between the Ohio River and the Great Lakes known as the Central Competitive Field.[26] The agreement, however, did not cover the important coalfields in Alabama, West Virginia, and Colorado. In 1913 the UMW attempted to improve its situation in Colorado by forcing Rockefeller's Colorado Fuel and Iron Company (CFI) to recognize the union. At the time, the CFI had already undertaken welfare initiatives including a hygiene campaign and an effort to train women in home economics. The company's welfare concerns, however, apparently did not sufficiently embrace the priorities set by the miners themselves. The union miners' demands ranged from an eight-hour day to the elimination of compulsory purchases at the company store. In an unusual show of solidarity, the UMW managed to hold together a disparate strike force of 12,000 miners divided not only by skill but by thirty-two different nationalities. The demonstration convinced CFI that stopping industrial unions was essential.

This the Colorado Fuel and Iron Company set out to do using every tool at its disposal. Not only did it hire gunmen to enforce its own rules, but the company offered to pay for state troops as well. It was at times like these that one could see the veneer of corporate welfarism drop and in its place corporate power move forcibly to eliminate any distinction between the public and private spheres. The town was the company and the company was the town.

When the strike was declared, workers who had been evicted from company housing set up a tent camp nearby. Their home economics classes disrupted, women joined the picketing. Although Colorado's governor initially refused to protect strikebreakers, he relented under pressure. Still, the miners continued to resist from their camps. In April, amid music and dancing, guardsmen opened fire upon their tent encampment. The miners returned the fire. At the conclusion of the confrontation, thirteen women and children were dead. Afterward, three strike leaders were summarily executed. Resistance continued until the end of the month when troops cleared out the strikers. Over the full duration of the strike, from September 1913 to April 1914, over sixty-six individuals on both sides died.

The Advent of Company Unions

The longer-term significance of these events lay not in the massacre itself, but rather in the way CFI responded. Under pressure from President Wilson, Rockefeller implemented the Colorado Industrial Plan giving CFI workers collective representation without unionization. The plan allowed workers to elect their own representatives in order to air grievances. The plan's sponsor suggested that it combined a "maximum of publicity with a minimum of interference in all that pertains to the conditions of employment."[27] The Industrial Plan established a prototype for company unions. The difference between company unions and independent unions was that in the former worker demands could not be supported by collective action. Because employee representation was accomplished on company time with company assistance, workers lacked freedom to chart their own course of action. Workers who spoke out too vehemently against the company were likely to be summarily dismissed. Although representation increased the flow of information from workers to management, inconvenient news could safely be ignored by management. A grievance without a meaningful threat of retribution was like a barking dog without teeth.

The author of the Colorado Industrial Plan, F.L. MacKenzie King, anticipated the effects of the European war on American industry and labor. In 1914, he recognized that as the war progressed unions would become stronger. Accordingly, King believed corporations could position themselves best as progressive and creative protectors of labor. Without succumbing to unionization themselves, they could even ally themselves with the labor movement. Open-shop corporations must promote fair labor standards among themselves and these, in turn, would be emulated by smaller firms. While it was assumed that large firms could discipline themselves, it would fall to unions to monitor compliance by smaller firms.

When the war came, it not only increased labor demand, but also the demands of labor for industrial democracy. Workers logically included their worksites among the places the Great War was fought to make safe for democracy. Was it not clear that the importance of work required that workers have some say in the way it was conducted? The courts, of course, had long answered that workers might have such a say, but only through the contracts they signed. However, there was widespread skepticism that, in this era of large-scale firms, workers' common problems could readily be resolved through individual contract. Instead, there was growing consensus that it was time to reconceptualize labor relations. Industrial democracy became labor's rallying cry during the war. With the war's conclusion, workers formed their own work councils in large corporations. This, along with the militant explosions of 1919, stiffened corporate attitudes against collective bargaining. Company unions constituted corporations' primary concession to the rising tide.

At International Harvester, employee representation was borrowed straight from Colorado Fuel and Iron. CFI consultant Arthur Young explained the value of the plan to Harvester boss Cyrus McCormick, saying:

> I feel certain that the activities of the labor organizers will be much more radical in character, now that the war is over, than they have been heretofore. Furthermore, there is a greater need for the adoption of clearer statements of fair and democratic principles by leading industries, because such pronouncements will serve as beacons on the very turbulent sea of industrial relations existing just now. If we withhold action and make no move to combat the efforts of the labor agitators and anarchistic workers, it is certain that some of our employes [sic] will be influenced by their propaganda.[28]

Harvester's new council gave workers representation in a forum separate from management. To change policies, both the council and management had to approve. When the opposing sides were at odds, the issue was passed up to the president to make his own decisions. In the early years, the council was energetic, even if it often assumed the role of a surrogate management, dismissing strikers and validating wage cuts. By the late 1920s, chronicler Robert Ozanne notes the council had "atrophied," its work reduced to such "trivia" as the purchase of Russet potatoes for Christmas celebrations. Indifference and absenteeism set in.[29] Wages were not even discussed between 1925 and 1931, and after that only because the Great Depression portended huge cuts.

Even though the works council had atrophied, it had nonetheless served management's purpose. After strikes in 1919, Harvester faced few significant labor problems. Like many of the larger firms, the company had arrested labor turbulence with a combination of aggressive open-shop campaigns, dismissals of agitators, the promotion of welfare works, and a semblance of industrial democracy.

The significance of industrial relations in the 1920s is still debated. For some, the period demonstrates that labor could be bought; that, protestations to the contrary, workers cared little about democracy and rights so long as they had a good paycheck and reasonable security. Others, however, believe that only active repression against union members and radicals succeeded in quelling labor's restiveness. For both, the welfare work of corporations was pivotal. Corporate welfare work provided labor's fence sitters with a reason to stay put and proclaim contentment.

No discussion of paternalism is more troubling than that of historian David Brody. Rejecting the idea of continued and active resistance to employers' "arbitrary control," Brody argues, "It is comforting to think that welfare capitalism never was a success, never persuaded workingmen that they were best off as wards of the employer, and never took deep root in the American industrial order. The facts," says Brody, "suggest otherwise."[30]

Chapter 6

Free Education

[T]he gradual widening of the present merely temporary and social difference between the Capitalist and the Labourer was the key to the whole position . . . the increasing refinement of their education, and the widening gulf between them and the rude violence of the poor . . . which is due to the length and expense of the higher educational process and the increased facilities for and temptations towards refined habits on the part of the rich—will make that exchange between class and class, that promotion by intermarriage which at present retards the splitting of our species along lines of social stratification, less and less frequent. So in the end above ground you must have the Haves, pursuing pleasure and comfort, and beauty, and below ground the Have-nots, the Workers getting continually adapted to the conditions of their labour.

—H.G. Wells, *The Time Machine*

In his 1894 novel *The Time Machine,* British writer H.G. Wells conjured up an imaginary future in which two species of man co-habitated the earth. One was a "graceful" childlike people he called the Eloi. The other was that "nocturnal Thing," the Morlock, who lived below ground and only surfaced to feed the Eloi, and then to slaughter them like cattle for food. The novel's time traveler made the startling discovery that the two species were common descendants of humankind from his own time. The Eloi were the delicate descendants of a gentility whose education and circumstances placed ever greater distance between themselves and the industrial base that sustained them. The Morlock were all that remained of a working class whose disagreeable conditions were hidden by removing economic activity to below ground. Wells was cautioning the members of his class that the social divisions their education sustained would come back to haunt them.

Wells wrote in Britain, where conditions differed from those prevailing in the United States. Not only did a larger proportion of the labor force work in mines, but the recent construction of an underground railroad in London also suggested that labor could be consigned to work below the earth's surface. More fundamentally, however, Britain made far fewer efforts than did the United States to use education to elevate the prospects of its lowest socioeconomic strata. Perhaps because America counted on immigrants to do much of the dirty work, or perhaps because of the lingering legacy of republicanism, U.S. citizens expected more. As traditional forms of work decayed, Americans demanded new platforms for independence. The old symbols of opportunity and equality, the yeoman farmer and the master craftsman, were, by the early twentieth century, pale shadows of their former selves. The professions became their idealized replacements and, with them, education became the central element conditioning labor's freedom.

The Educational Crusade

Education was increasingly viewed as the last countervailing force to the tendencies within the law, within management, and within technology that undercut key aspects of labor freedom in the United States. Without opportunity, the growing sense of deprivation in America would have been hard to contain and courts, for example, would have had a far more difficult task in checking organized labor's advance if they could not realistically argue, as they did, that "the road to advancement is open to all." But as the West was increasingly settled, opportunities for independence appeared scarcer.[1] In eastern cities, grown swollen with an uneducated laboring class that survived on day work, the case for state-supported education gained favor. As early as the 1840s Horace Mann promoted universal education arguing that it was an investment that would yield returns as high as fifty cents on each dollar spent.[2] An educational crusade set sail that would not retreat until the ports to every trade and occupation had been seized. The crusade was a radical argument in that schooling was made the vessel that would more fairly remap economic opportunity. Nonetheless, the crusade was conservative in that it did not threaten a major immediate redistribution of wealth. Even though education's appeal was great, few agreed on either its form or its content.

Business efficiency demanded that resources not be excessively squandered on educational equality. If there was a best way of producing goods, so, too, there was a best way of producing education. That best way might not equalize everyone's opportunities, but it would prepare children for their careers as workers and adjust them to society as it existed. In the late nineteenth century, efficiency and bigotry combined with the result that schools, in the minds of many, became a means to tame immigrant youths made wild by slums, poor discipline, crime, sloth, and drink. Education was charged with the task of nativizing foreigners.[3]

To the extent that labor took a position on education, most often it allied itself with progressives for whom education was central in the efforts to promote merit and expertise.[4] Many progressives saw in schools an agency to foster democracy and the fulfillment of human potential. While most agreed that education should develop the whole child, how it was to do so proved more controversial. Neither labor nor the larger society was highly consistent on issues regarding education. Some working citizens actually rejected the expansion of schooling, seeing in it the profusion of "diploma mills." Others were so poor that they needed their children's labor and consequently resisted state attempts to impose schooling upon them.[5] Most, however, desired the opportunities opened by education. Although some, like Irish Catholic New Yorkers in the 1840s, resisted Protestant domination, they did not reject education per se, but sought instead local control over their schools.[6] Accordingly, those concerned by the great educational project under way held markedly different views, particularly as regards the schools systems' responsibility to promote equality.

Despite democratic rhetoric boosting education as the best means to equalize opportunities, education nursed new class distinctions as well as being conditioned by old ones. The advantaged saw in education a way to pass their privileges on to their progeny. Many disadvantaged regarded education as one more barricade separating them from the more promising world enjoyed by others. Critical to the shape education would take were the middle classes. This educated assemblage of clerks, nurses, accountants, teachers, lawyers, architects, chemists, and social reformers constituted the visible proof that education expanded the path toward upward mobility. To the extent that their skills were both scarce and widely useful, they maintained their own independence and eluded the heavy hand of personal patronage. To preserve that independence they cultivated objective measures of their value, including degrees, certifications, licenses, and civil service examinations.[7] This middle class identified with both the civility of the gentry and the work ethic of the laboring classes. As professionals, they were creatures of the scientific revolution that produced so many jobs where systematic application of knowledge was used to solve wide varieties of industrial, social, personal, medical, environmental, and organizational problems.[8] It was the previous dearth of scientific understanding that had enabled craft, faith, and custom to dominate society for so long. Knowledge over those produced by tradition-bound workers and the demonstrable superiority of its products yielded power to its practitioners. That power was manifest in the creation of educational institutions that challenged virtually all outside authority.

Education was so central to society and to the labor question that the most enduring novels of the period invariably expressed themselves as a vision of a society education could or did create. We have already seen how H.G. Wells sought to awaken society to the terrors awaiting it should the agency of education fail to stop the degeneration of the masses. The tense polarization of late-nineteenth-century American society buttressed demands for educational reforms that would reduce the threat of class warfare. Edward Bellamy fictionalized the turmoil of 1886 to drive home a point identical to that of H.G. Wells. The gentlemanly, but idle, American protagonist of Bellamy's *Looking Backward,* Julian West, fell asleep in 1887, waking 113 years later to the realization that:

> To educate some to the highest degree, and leave the mass wholly unculti-
> vated, as you [Bellamy's nineteenth-century generation] did, made the gap
> between them almost like that between different natural species, which have
> no means of communication. What could be more inhuman than this conse-
> quence of partial enjoyment of education![9]

West's adventures in the year 2000 provided the forum for Bellamy to outline an educational program that would transform late-nineteenth-century society.

The initial setting of the novel was 1887, a time when, as Julian West notes, "Strikes had become so common at that period that people had ceased to inquire into their particular grounds."[10] Indeed it was a time when workers struck for wages, for eight-hour days, for job conditions, to protest scab labor, and even to control apprenticeship. This last issue, nearly unnoticed amid the general havoc, was at the vortex of major realignments in labor. Several craft unions had bolted from the Knights of Labor in order to better organize themselves as the American Federation of Labor (AFL). These and other craft unions took firmer steerage over apprenticeship in order to better control their trades.[11] Employers and educators responded by reconceiving schooling as the alternative to apprenticeship.

Nothing separated craft workers from their less-skilled compatriots so much as their training, and to this, access was restricted. In 1880, only 2 percent of high school–aged boys gained access to skilled trades through apprenticeship. Alternatively, secondary education provided a strong alternative guarantee to good employment, but it enrolled virtually an equivalent number of boys. A few more girls than boys enrolled in high schools, but many fewer entered trade apprenticeships. In short, direct routes to prosperous jobs, particularly for the children of the poor and unskilled, were few.[12] This was the context of Julian West's commentary and of Edward Bellamy's ideas for educational reform.

The Industrial Labor Relations Context

As unionists became more militant in defense of their trades during the 1880s, employers launched their own counteroffensives. Unions, they contended, were selfish monopolies that restricted entry into the trades. Employers called for "a new era . . . when the workman was to work with both hands and brains; when he was to be the peer of any man; when he was no longer to stand as suppliant before some self-constituted ruler to ask permission to work; when the test of admission to a trade organization will be the skill of the applicant."[13] In seeking to convince a larger audience that the rising power of unionism was bad, employers and their spokesmen also played on American nativism. They argued that apprenticeship had come to be dominated by the German and Irish immigrants and excluded "American boys," by which they meant third-generation white Protestants. "Foreign" unions were additionally tarred by charges of anarchism, especially after the violent 1886 bombing in Chicago's Haymarket Square. If employers hoped their attacks would win sympathy from those unskilled workers who lacked the connections to get a foothold in the trades, their aim was off the mark. Compared with the African Americans, Southern and Eastern European immigrants, Catholics, Jews, Native Americans, and women who formed the backbone of the drudge labor force, few third- and fourth-generation Americans were anxious to enter the trades. By 1886, these youth were generally much better favored by circumstance. Instead the employers principally won sympathy from the middle classes, who did not need entrance into the trades. Nonetheless their support was crucial to public policy makers.

Skilled workers were inclined to think differently about the issues. Craftsmen knew that American apprenticeship had undergone a progressive degradation over the century. Few employers were willing to train workers thoroughly, and instead preferred to rely upon skilled immigrants, or upon machines involving such a fine division of labor as to enable untrained workers to operate them. Apprenticeship was frequently a burden to employers who, under terms of an indenture, were obligated to provide training and continuous employment, even when there was little work.[14] To unionists, the battle was between good and evil: Employers willingly debased trades solely to profit themselves. In the process they destroyed the basis of worker independence.

Between 1886 and 1887, a New York City strike demonstrated all these issues. Journeymen plumbers struck their masters to enforce new union apprenticeship rules that stipulated employers must not hire more than one apprentice for every four journeymen. The masters cried foul, asserting that "it is the inalienable right for the employer to say who shall or who shall not be in his employ."[15] In an attempt to undo the union, the masters sought the help of Colonel Richard T. Auchmuty and his newly formed New York Trade School. In existence for five years, the fledgling school operated under the premise that the fundamentals of most trades could be learned through systematic instruction lasting no more than three to six months. While such schooling would not bring a boy up to full journeyman speed, practice on the job would finish his education. Thus when the Master Plumbers Association approached Auchmuty, they found not only a willing partner in the reconstruction of apprenticeship, but also a forceful proponent of trade education. Auchmuty rebuked unions for obstructing "the right of a man to follow any honest calling he may see fit." "It is not," said Auchmuty, "the province of any body of men, certainly not of any self-constituted organization, to decide who or how many shall be allowed to work. . . . Mechanics did not invent their trades, they have no proprietary rights in them."[16] The Master Plumbers Association supported the trade school both with money and by enrolling nearly one hundred of its apprentices during the strike, an action that branded the school as an institution designed to produce strikebreakers and scabs.

The journeyman's strike failed and the union nominally lost control over apprenticeship. In part, this was the result of internal tensions. The strike appears to have been an attempt by the Knights of Labor to demonstrate their ability to defend craft organization and thereby stem the flood of deserters going over to the more trade union–oriented American Federation of Labor.

The plumbers' action was one of many hastily conceived and underfinanced strikes in 1886 that followed a major victory by the Knights against the railroad baron Jay Gould. Impatient workers, sensing power, flocked to join the Knights of Labor where assembly after assembly applied for permission to strike. The Knights' grandmaster workman Terrence Powderly attempted to dissuade the strikers, but the fever was contagious. The lack of discipline in these strikes, the shortage of funds for strike relief, and the backlash they inspired among employers across the nation proved fatal to the strikers. Employer associations joined forces, traded blacklists, and sought both state troops and injunctions for support as they locked their workers out. As with New York's plumbers, most of the other strikes were lost and the membership of the Knights sank almost as quickly as it had risen.[17]

The failure of these strikes helped the American Federation of Labor become the leading labor organization, and with it craft and craft control—as epitomized by apprenticeship regulation—became the most important basis for labor organization. Although New York's journeymen plumbers lost the first round in the battle over apprenticeship, other rounds followed. Unsuccessful in their attempts to put trade schools out of business, labor unions shifted their strategy and instead advocated that trade education be located in public, rather than private, schools. There labor could more reasonably expect to influence the form and content of trade education. As democratic institutions, public schools did indeed prove responsive to articulate and well-organized groups including labor.

Strikes in the building trades during 1886 and 1887 are especially significant to our account because they kept the fictitious Julian West from building his wedding home. West's problem gave author Edward Bellamy a convenient excuse to write about labor issues. In Julian West, we have a caricature of upper-middle-class values. The strikes that delayed his marriage led the inconvenienced West to rail that "the unprincipled conduct of the labor agitators . . . [was] going from bad to worse very fast, and that there was no telling what we should come to soon." Along with much of the middle class, West shared a propensity to see the world according to abstract principles that, if adhered to, would prevent the disturbances he had to endure. Although his class had sympathy for workers' attempts to improve their condition, they believed labor too frequently pursued these interests by tearing down the property rights of others, rather than by seeking advancement through moral elevation. To the successful, education suggested a more viable path to economic success than did agitation.

A Path to Success?

Until the mid-eighteenth century few citizens pursued education past eighth grade, and less than 1 percent went on to college. As educational historian Laurence Veysey has put it, much of secondary and post-secondary education was devoted to classical subjects and "mental discipline," which had limited application to everyday life. Private academies and colleges satisfied the elite's demand for credentials, but they did little to prepare students for work.[18] By the 1850s, this was beginning to change. Increasingly, citizens began to demand a more practical education, one that justified the long and costly investments students undertook. The federal government responded to concerns of farmers and mechanics by passing the Morrill Act of 1862 setting aside land grants to endow state universities. As science revolutionized trade, wealthy businessmen, too, began to appreciate the value of education to their organizations. In the late 1850s, inventor and industrialist Peter Cooper was among the leaders in starting institutes of technology. Cooper's Union provided full scholarships for working-class men to pursue science and engineering; it also provided opportunities for young women to learn trades.[19] A parade of businessmen, including Johns Hopkins, Ezra Cornell, John D. Rockefeller, Anthony Drexel, Leland Stanford, and Andrew Carnegie, soon endowed new institutions of higher learning. These institutions were both more practical and more scientific than older institutions like Yale and Harvard, which emphasized the classics.

Concern with the practical clearly made education more attractive to almost everyone. However, that attractiveness was not accompanied by equal access to all. As noted, few children went on to high school and fewer still to college. Because duration in school was highly dependent upon the income of a student's family, Edward Bellamy and H.G. Wells had grist for their complaints. Novelists and educators alike were free to imagine other worlds in which money played a less crucial role. In St. Louis during the 1870s, Calvin Woodward designed a program of manual training to provide all children, rich and poor alike, with an education in the rudiments of tools and mechanics. Woodward's manual training was designed to supplement a liberal education, not to displace it.[20] It was argued that even those destined for brain work would benefit from an education that included handicrafts as well. Implementation of his ideas increased the popularity of secondary education in America. Even Edward Bellamy made manual training a central element in the profoundly changed schools of the utopia in which Julian West awoke in the year 2000.

In this future, schools eliminated "one of the great wastes, as well as one of the most common causes of unhappiness" of West's and Bellamy's earlier day. West explained, "The vast majority of my contemporaries, though nominally free to do so, never really chose their occupations at all, but were forced by circumstances into work for which they were relatively inefficient, because [they were] not naturally fitted for it."[21] The Cooperative Commonwealth in year 2000 instead sorted individuals into work that maximized their talents and preferences:

> As an individual's satisfaction during his term of service depends on his having an occupation to his taste, parents and teachers watch from early years for indications of special aptitudes in children. A thorough study of the national industrial system, with the history and rudiments of all the great trades, is an essential part of our educational system. While manual training is not allowed to encroach on the general intellectual culture to which our schools are devoted, it is carried far enough to give our youth, in addition to their theoretical knowledge of the national industries, mechanical and agricultural, a certain familiarity with their tools and methods. Our schools are constantly visiting our workshops, and often are taken on long excursions to inspect particular industrial enterprises.[22]

Education integrated children into the larger society by making clear the importance of labor to their lives. Bellamy's Cooperative Commonwealth required workers from age twenty-one to forty-five to serve in an industrial army. The first years of industrial service were spent in common labor and constituted a "strict" school in "obedience, subordination, and devotion to duty." Upon completion "without serious disgrace," youth were given "an equal opportunity to choose the life employment they have most liking for."[23] They could freely enter apprenticeships entitling membership in the trades and guilds of their preference. Bellamy's was an ingenious attempt to restructure social opportunity by requiring national service as a quid pro quo for the freedom to choose a vocation.

His utopia seems almost to have been constructed to solve the apprentice situation in New York. The plumbers' strike had gained notoriety. Even the city's 1886 mayoral candidates, radical economist Henry George and reform-minded iron magnate Abram Hewitt, spoke and wrote on related issues. George, famous for his single tax proposal designed to level out inequalities created by chance, argued that schooling had its limits.

> So long as competition for employment on the part of men who are powerless to employ themselves tends steadily to force wages to the minimum that gives the laborer but a bare living, this is all the ordinary laborer can get. So long as this tendency exists—and it must continue to exist so long as private property in land exists—improvement (even if possible) in the personal qualities of the laboring masses, such as improvement in skill, in intelligence, in temperance or in thrift, cannot improve their material condition.[24]

Where plumbers argued that employers ruined their craft through the unregulated hiring of helpers and apprentices, George argued in a similar vein that the present conditions of society tended to "destroy independence, to dispense with skill and convert the artisan into a 'hand.' " He chastised the trade schools that "vomited" out graduates to the detriment of skilled workers.[25]

George's mayoral opponent, Abram Hewitt, professed opposite concerns regarding trade education. Sitting on the board of the famous workingman's institute, Cooper's Union, founded by his business partner and father-in-law, Hewitt argued that education opened closed doors. On schooling, his business and social concerns ran together:

> The masses of the people have never demanded equality of fortune, and indeed understand it to be impossible; but they have always insisted and always insist, upon equality of opportunity. With free schools and universal education, with opportunities for the youth of exceptional ability in the ranks of the rich or the poor to secure the highest instruction, the approaches of communism need never be feared. Equality of opportunity insures the ultimate distribution of wealth upon just conditions and within reasonable periods of time.[26]

Where Hewitt and George were bound by the constraints of their time, fiction enabled Bellamy to imagine a different future ahead. Looking backward from the year 2000, Bellamy rejected Hewitt's insistence that equality was an "impossibility." In his Cooperative Commonwealth, workers competed for jobs, not on the basis of wages—which were all to be equal—but on the basis of hours. More agreeable jobs were rationed by requiring more hours than disagreeable ones. Because wages were to be equal, Bellamy was also able to overcome George's concerns that schools would graduate too many workers. Bellamy's vision was to make schools the cornerstone of a true equality in opportunity, fostering skills and talents that enhanced peoples' lives. At the same time, by insisting upon absolute equality, he denied industry the ability to use an abundance of skill to the detriment of workers.

Even Auchmuty's concern that unions unnecessarily lengthened apprenticeship were allayed under Bellamy's scheme. In the Cooperative Commonwealth, the length of apprenticeships varied as necessary for the specific profession. Graduates were graded into different ranks according to their skill and were allowed, as Auchmuty proposed, to progress at their own pace over their careers.

Bellamy's ideas on governance, however, seemed to respond to different concerns. He divided the nation into guilds. Those guilds oversaw the different trades and the education necessary to stock them. These guilds, however, were not democratic. Only retired members could vote. Bellamy thought it obvious that the self-interest of workers must not be permitted to control guild agendas. The industrial army was, after all, an army. This, more than anything else, defined Bellamy's plan as a middle-class socialism rather than a worker's state. Although labor leaders including the American Federation of Labor's Samuel Gompers read, discussed, debated, and were often even inspired by *Looking Backward,* they could not follow Bellamy unreservedly until he admitted the necessity of greater worker participation. His ideas titillated, but did not satisfy, an increasingly militant labor movement. Among the middle classes, however, his ideas had immediate appeal.[27]

The Transformation of Education

The middle classes were so positioned as to believe themselves free to criticize the destructive and destabilizing tendencies emerging within capitalism. Economist and gadfly Thorstein Veblen envisioned the middle class as the brains of the industrial system, the engineers of a giant economic machine, who—unlike the absentee owners that employed them—could improve its workings without fear that doing so would lead to their own displacement.[28] Readership among these free-thinking middle-class men and women made Bellamy's novel the most popular of the period. Across the country "National" clubs sprouted to promote the Cooperative Commonwealth. Although, like Bellamy's book, this Nationalist program remained largely a fantasy, it nonetheless helped transform education.

Looking Backward framed a coherent theory of freedom in which education was made responsible for enabling individuals to reach their potential. "[T]here are three main grounds on which our educational system rests: first, the right of every man to the completest education the nation can give him on his own account, as necessary to his enjoyment of himself; second, the right of his fellow citizens to have him educated, as necessary to their enjoyment of his society; third, the right of the unborn to be guaranteed an intelligent and refined parentage."[29] Quietly, but surely, America came to believe that education had a deep responsibility for social well-being in an industrial democracy.

Many in the middle class took the position that children should go to school for as long as possible. From the 1880s on, school curricula were increasingly vocationalized, not simply to prepare children for work, but in order to induce them to attend. Manual arts programs swept the country. Once in place, however, many began to distinguish between manual and industrial arts. The latter program was associated with Colonel Auchmuty's New York Trade School and involved full preparation for the trades. Not a novelist, Auchmuty catered to simple reality: Most children could not afford a long apprenticeship or liberal education and instead preferred short trade courses. Indeed, such programs were often huge successes, particularly with lower-income students and parents. Yet their implementation began a debate that has still not ended. Was it education's duty to probe students for their natural proclivities and talents, or was it education's responsibility to fit children to their "probable destinies?" The first scenario constituted a child-centered approach. Advocates of the alternative argued that the limited number of positions at the helm of society's productive machinery made it essential not to educate students for positions and status they could not achieve. To do so would produce educational misfits. Progressives divided; some adopted the managerial efficiency inherent in the second approach while others idealistically hoped education could change economic reality.

Schools could only do so much without a fundamental transformation of society. In Bellamy's novel, the industrial system was based on equality and meaningful opportunity. In reality, however, the industrial system depended upon a hierarchical stratification of the labor force. Where Bellamy would have required everyone to share in society's unpleasant labor in the first years of their careers, few Americans showed a real proclivity to respond to social inequality in this way. Consequently, even if the schools had aimed unambiguously at equal opportunity, without an industrial transformation, Henry George was probably right that expanded training would result in increased competition for a limited number of good jobs. When it came down to hard decisions, business efficiency took precedence over social equality.

In the early 1900s academic studies repeatedly chastised the social waste of a system that destined most poor children for dead-end jobs. Reformers searched for the causes of school-leaving while noting its devastating consequences on wages and employment. Their work increased emphasis upon vocational guidance and pre-vocational education. Although secondary school enrollments increased, Sylvester Counts's studies of high schools in the early 1920s demonstrated that the occupational status of parents continued to matter greatly in determining the extent of their children's educational attainment levels.[30] Although high schools did prepare students for better jobs, only a small number of poor children persisted to graduate from high school. The would-be eighth-grade dropout who now persisted to tenth grade discovered that he or she had to compete against a larger number of high school graduates. Increasingly, the inability to invest time in school tended to sort children from different economic classes into separate educations that reproduced social inequalities.

Managerial efficiency dictated limits on how much could be spent overcoming the disadvantages nature and society imposed. If some children came from privileged homes with greater opportunities, efficiency required society to take advantage of the resources they brought and not to offset them with compensatory subsidies to the poor. By establishing educational and vocational tracks, the advantaged few could make fast progress while bypassing the common or ordinary work of society. The few could go to Harvard, Yale, or Cornell and by age twenty or twenty-one enter managerial positions that were designed to launch them straight to the top of large organizations. Managerial efficiency implied a form of education in which students were fitted to the needs of society. A new and larger conception of efficiency was required if society was to ferret out the waste of unfulfilled lives.

The renowned and influential philosopher John Dewey advocated education as the means to achieve this enlarged notion of social efficiency. Openly acknowledging his debt to Bellamy, Dewey castigated separate educations for managers and workers. Such schooling left "unchanged the existing industrial order of society, instead of operating as means of its transformation." Dewey's desired transformation required

> a society in which every person shall be occupied in something which makes the lives of others better worth living, and which accordingly makes the ties which bind persons together more perceptible—which breaks down the barriers of distance between them ... [and in which] the interest of each in his work is uncoerced and intelligent: based upon its congeniality to his own aptitudes.[31]

However, until the educational system succeeded in changing the industrial order, its chief danger lay in the production of educational misfits like Sinclair Lewis's female protagonist in his 1920 novel *Main Street.* Lewis's character Carol simply wanted more than was available. College educated, Carol was the perpetually frustrated reformer at odds with the dull and smug small-town life in Gopher Prairie. Women, particularly college women, were frequently educated for positions beyond those society would pay them to occupy. Carol's estrangement from the reality of life in Gopher Prairie made her miserable while also rendering her unfit for her self-defined role as change agent. Town folk resented Carol's cultural pretensions and superiority. By implication, they also resented higher education as the wellspring of pointy-headed intellectuals. Such associations made it difficult to see how education could ever gain sufficient steam to achieve Dewey's or Bellamy's transformation.

Separate But Equal?

Schooling suffered yet another problem hindering it from achieving its transformation of society. Educational technology soon proved too crude to fulfill the promise of a truly child-centered pedagogy. Instead, it produced classifications of students not as individuals, but rather as members of groups. Curricula were tailored to fit homogeneous classes comprised of the gifted, the vocationally bound, the discipline problems, the mentally retarded, the handicapped, and assorted others. Intelligence, aptitude, and vocational tests probed students to determine what group treatment each child should receive. The results usually recycled children into the economic classes from which they came, exactly opposite stated intentions.

The problem was most acute among identifiable minorities like African Americans, women, and Native Americans. Demonstrably faulty IQ tests usually confirmed social biases and resulted in separate educations for these groups.[32] Even when testing did not require these results, school officials were not above creating their own classifications catering to society's prejudices. In the South, states actually created schools separated by race, a discriminatory act which, through its infamous 1896 *Plessy v. Ferguson* decision, the Supreme Court upheld as "separate, but equal." Even when separate educations were not specially designed, school personnel generally submitted to existing social inequities rather than challenging them head on. Educational historian David Tyack, for example, points out that northern educators faced a stark choice in designing vocational education for African Americans when rigid racial job segregation was the norm. Tyack asks,

> Were schoolmen simply to accept the low job ceiling as a given and to prepare Negroes to be good janitors and housekeepers? If so, how much and what kind of schooling did a janitor really need? Or was it the duty of schoolmen to open up new career opportunities for black graduates, to perforate the job ceiling to let talented individuals slip through? Or did such piecemeal progress simply postpone the major reconstruction of society that would create genuine equality for blacks and other dispossessed groups? During the years from 1890 to 1940 ... most appear to have accepted the racism of unions and employers as a fact they could do little about.[33]

When schools attempted to train blacks for trades, "Again and again, principals told ... of their failure to place highly qualified black graduates in positions as clerks, machinists' apprentices, dressmakers and in other trades."

Women, too, received separate educations that restricted their freedom of occupational choice. As the curriculum of schools grew more vocational, women were generally encouraged to take home economics or to pursue the few careers open to them, particularly nursing, clerical work, or teaching. Although such choices were not altogether disagreeable (even typing and clerical work were improvements over the factory and domestic employment to which less-educated women had previously been consigned), the chief problem was the systematic elimination of opportunity based on gender alone.

The Limits of Education

In such ways, despite the work of Bellamy, Dewey, and a raft of other reformers, education failed to fulfill its liberating promise. It did not succeed in transforming society, at least not in the period of its most fantastic expansion. What it did do was to enable a limited number of youth from lower socioeconomic status to compete in arenas to which their admittance had previously been barred. It also created a large number of misfits who, in keeping the rest of society apprised of their dissatisfaction, challenged that society to adapt its work to their needs.

While failing to transform society, education did succeed in modifying employment conditions. As schools became more vocational, parents more willingly accepted the income loss required by long periods of classroom attendance in exchange for higher wages afterward. By the end of the 1940s, roughly half of America's youth graduated from high school. Just as these high schools prepared typists, bricklayers, and bookkeepers, now colleges, too, carved out their own niches defining new professions in management, health, engineering, chemistry, statistics, social work, and economics. Persistence in school more dramatically increased wages than did union participation. Just before the World War II, for example, when union workers were estimated to be earning roughly 22 percent more than non-union workers, male college graduates earned 57 percent more than high school graduates, and 89 percent more than dropouts.[34] No fact was so striking as this steady increase in wages that accompanied higher levels of educational attainment. Not only that, higher degrees generally yielded more fulfilling and less arduous or dangerous work as well. Even if skilled unions did limit the number of apprentices, increasingly fewer boys aspired to apprenticeships in the trades when a like investment of three to five years in education yielded far greater monetary and psychic returns.

That is why the tendency to segregate and track different students into different vocational outcomes was so pernicious. If higher education was largely reserved for white males, the plebeian class of menial workers had to be drawn primarily from children of color, new immigrants, or women. Even when not the result of intentional discrimination, income inequality made it more difficult for the poor to send their children to school for extended periods. Although women and minorities averaged lower earnings than white males at every stage of their careers, they too found their earnings also rose with education.[35] In this way, education tugged at class loyalty, informing individuals that advancement was not based on group solidarity, but instead on one's own efforts.

The irony was that collective interests were still served by restricting entry. When Colonel Auchmuty of the New York Trade Schools argued to have schools open opportunities to American boys, he simultaneously argued for a higher grade of workmen that would be measured and licensed by academic credentials. As Auchmuty put it, "The higher the standard of workmanship is made by which the admission to a trade could be procured, the better for the trade and the public. Such a system would be better than 'cards of protection' obtained by favor or by purchase." This was a lesson even the most elite professions noticed as they closed down "diploma mills" with loose standards and tightened admission requirements. Professions like medicine, law, and music, no less than the trades, understood the value of scarcity. Society's failure to do everything possible to promote talent from the least privileged social classes served the privileged by limiting the competition they faced.

Perhaps the greatest danger in all this was the silent reversal of Bellamy's dream. Attempts to unleash each person's talents and proclivities could be subverted into a mechanism that conditioned individuals to accept their "predestined" lot in life. Aldous Huxley's *Brave New World* spelled out the most horrific possibilities by conjuring up a society just close enough to existing conditions as to be believable. His new world prevented the dangerous class cleavage H.G. Wells's *Time Machine* predicted. In Huxley's world, education conditioned, rather than liberated, workers. Batches of alpha, beta, and gamma children were genetically engineered to perform, and to like, their separate tasks. Social conditioning, free sex, rampant drug use, and virtually ubiquitous, yet compulsory, pleasure distracted workers from any sense of themselves or any desire to chart their own destinies. In 1932, when Huxley wrote, serious social commentators advocated a policy of eugenics designed to purge society of its mental defectives and physical deviants. In Huxley's world, it was the malprogrammed misfits who provided the only threat to its smooth functioning. Perhaps, as intimated by Sinclair Lewis's novel *Main Street,* our greatest hope for freedom lies in mistraining individuals for the world in which they live.

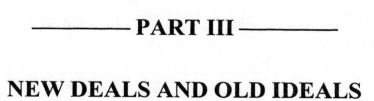

PART III

NEW DEALS AND OLD IDEALS

———————— **Chapter 7** ————————

Union Compromise

True individual freedom cannot exist without economic security and independence. "Necessitous men are not free men." People who are hungry—people who are out of a job—are the stuff of which dictatorships are made. In our day these economic truths have become accepted as self-evident.
—Franklin D. Roosevelt, January 11, 1944

For the generation that came of age in the early twentieth century, the freedom to shape their own lives became hopelessly entwined with consuming public events. In the span of a single lifetime, national heroes and villains—Lenin, Wilson, Mussolini, Hitler, Stalin, Roosevelt, and Mao—confounded everyone's personal ambitions. International revolutions, world wars, depression, genocide, cults of personality, and cultural revolutions ensnared individual citizens like tiny ships in the ocean playground of reckless state leviathans.

It is not surprising, then, that these times created a sea-tide of change that reconfigured the dimensions of American freedom. Political economist Robert Higgs has argued that demands for governmental activity ratchet upward when crisis emerges and reliance upon markets begins to appear cumbersome and inefficient. Crisis leads more people to appreciate how the state can be used to forcefully redirect the activities of men, women, and their economy. Although post-crisis backlash usually ensues, Higgs argues that, once enlarged, the state never reverts completely to its pre-crisis level of activity. Those who, like Higgs, resent active government, saw the succession of crises in the first half of the nineteenth century as a threat to the liberty of individuals to choose their own destinies. Indeed, the noted Austrian philosopher Friedrich Hayek spoke of the West's march down *The Road to Serfdom.*[1]

Corporatism and the Centralization of Government Power

By mid-century the United States had, like other major industrialized countries, experienced a profound centralization of power. The change was particularly noticeable under Franklin Roosevelt's New Deal, but it had been brewing at least since World War I and was firmly in place by World War II. The main lines of change involved increasing governmental responsibility for economic welfare, greater federal supervision over state affairs, and the overthrow of absolute liberty of contract as the guiding legal doctrine of the economy.[2] The visible effect of these changes was to institute a corporatist sharing of power that saw government broker the deals made between labor and capital.[3] This was indeed a jolt to business as usual. However, it would have been extremely surprising if the generation that lived through such abnormal times had not broken with established precedents.

Unlike Higgs and Hayek, many more believed that changes came none too soon. For them the depression ushered in a long overdue recognition that economic realities had changed since the revolutionary days of the eighteenth century. In place of older and harsher assumptions about the nature of individual responsibility, Roosevelt's New Deal officially served notice that the days of rugged individuals had passed and that those of large-scale organizations had taken their place. These entities—businesses, unions, trade and professional associations—were leviathans in their own right. Where theory held that liberty of contract restrained private power through competition, corporatism instead balanced one bastion of private power by offsetting it against another.

Balancing corporate interests can never be a totally satisfying experience.[4] Not only are the interests of the group as a whole left unfulfilled by the compromises bargaining imposes, but the members comprising the group have already surrendered many of their individual aspirations to achieve solidarity. Thus, individuals are twice removed from the pursuit of their own preferences. For many, the new test of freedom lay in the voluntariness of one's affiliation with a corporate interest. The dissatisfying circularity of the system stopped only if the individual opted out of the corporatist system of balancing. However, the effect then was to eliminate the individual's volition as unaffiliated persons were unrepresented and therefore had no voice. It is not surprising, then, that many people violently rejected the corporatist balancing act in its entirety. Unfortunately, the alternative was individual freedom of expression or choice, but without effective power or resources to consummate either.

The New Deal thus saluted the success of organization. Conditions had changed such that few individuals could pretend to be masters of their own fate. Instead, individuals were now harnessed to large organizations that, for better or worse, altered the nature of their options. Navigation of the new economic waters required organizational charts, whether that of Ford or that of the United Auto Workers Union (UAW). All too often those who wished to maintain their independence by going it alone exploited themselves with long hours and low wages. Harrowing insecurity plagued small business proprietors. Lacking capital to buffer themselves in hard times, these small owners had little choice but to chip away at workers or creditors when times were rough. Consequently, employees often preferred large to small employers. According to Steven Fraser smaller firms in the clothing industry found it difficult to provide reliable wages, conditions, and prospects for advancement. As one woman acknowledged, compared to small employers she preferred the huge Chicago clothier, Hart, Schaffner, and Marx, saying there was "nothing like a big place to work" to "better" oneself.[5] Voluntary affiliation with large collectivities occurred because the cost of independence rose, especially in comparison with the benefits of incorporation. Nonetheless, the ideology of individualism left its mark in frequent expressions of remorse over such affiliations.

Efficiency Through Standardization

The industrial efficiency of large-scale enterprise generally undercut the prices of individual craftsmen and small proprietors alike. Big business generated economies of scale at the same time that it coordinated the many disparate elements of production processes. Management's "visible hand," as Alfred Chandler calls it, wrung out savings by orchestrating otherwise separate and discreet market transactions. In other words, organization eliminated transaction costs associated with negotiating, monitoring, and enforcing each and every separate purchase and sale. Ronald Coase received a Nobel prize for explaining that firms grow large because they are easily able to redirect the work of their industrial servants. Smaller firms had to engage in more costly contracting with outside suppliers and then had to renegotiate every unanticipated event. In essence, Coase argues that workers give up their liberty to contract over each managerial decision and instead, for a price, sell to management the rights to govern their day-to-day labor.[6] This situation challenges the conceptual basis of contract, which is to give up something in exchange for something else of equal or greater value: How could such conditions be met when from day to day managers could change what workers were expected to deliver?

While Coase argued that firms grew large because they could redesign work relationships instantaneously, it was also true that large-scale organization achieved efficiency by standardizing elements of production. When it came to their labor relations, this meant that big businesses had to learn to control the dominion that local bosses exercised over the works under their charge. Such bosses could and often did act like petty tyrants, extracting favors and payoffs in exchange for continued employment. The power of local bosses was the chief impediment to standardization. In just one of countless examples that could be cited, we learn that at Hart, Schaffner, and Marx, one local boss asked an employee not to reveal her pay rate to the workers she trained so that they would not know that theirs were lower.[7] Yet, the logic driving the success of corporate control was to standardize. Increasingly central personnel offices dictated policies that reined in arbitrary discretion.[8] Nepotism, favoritism, and simple meanness exercised in violation of company standards became causes for discipline. Scientific managers advanced a movement to train foremen and to give them less authority. In these ways, the arbitrary control that bosses had over their employees was subdued by the implementation of personnel policies. Even if those policies could not dictate all the specific requirements employees might have to fulfill under their contracts, the policies provided some semblance of justice by limiting the extent of managerial discretion and by providing some mechanism to seek redress when employees believed those limits had been breached.

For the firm, standardized inputs and outputs increased productivity. For the worker, standards also defined ideals of justice and freedom: equals should be treated alike, and rules for one were rules for all. Known rules gave workers the freedom to obey or find situations more to their liking. However progressive this solution was, the appeal of liberty of contract had to have been greatly deflated by the conditions to which large-scale enterprise forced it to succumb. Conformity to company standards imposed major limits upon individual bargaining.

Separate from any legislative changes, the impetus toward corporate standardization robbed liberty of contract of its lifeblood. Surprisingly, the organization of labor into unions also abetted this process. Sidney Hillman's relationship with Hart, Schaffner, and Marx illustrates how one labor union helped stabilize business and standardize industrial relations. Between 1912 and 1913 the Chicago clothier cooperated with Sidney Hillman in his drive to organize the firm. After a successful strike, owner Joseph Schaffner explained, "Careful study of the situation has led me to the belief that the fundamental cause of the strike was that the workers had no satisfactory channel through which minor grievances, exactions, and petty tyrannies of underbosses could be taken up and amicably be adjusted."[9] The firm's labor manager acknowledged that Hillman's work was valuable: "Mr. Schaffner even grew to have as much and even more confidence in him than in some of his own superintendents. . . . The influence which he quickly and legitimately came to have with the board and the company conferred a natural authority among the workers."[10] Although Hart, Schaffner, and Marx's distinction lay in its willingness to accept labor's participation in making and controlling labor policy, many other firms also found union organization helpful in regularizing labor relations.

Union leaders like Hillman frequently used bureaucratic grievance procedures to try to dampen shop floor rebellions. When labor leaders chose this path, they were often accused of having been co-opted to management's side.[11] There were always workers who regarded as unfair any grievance whose resolution was not finally decided among the workers themselves. Best represented in the United States by the ill-fated Industrial Workers of the World (IWW), the anarchist and syndicalist workers were determined to keep power in their own hands rather than to surrender it to a system they knew to be hostile to their very existence. They used work stoppages, sabotage, or other exertions of power to force employers to address their needs.[12] Their actions ran counter to the more legalistic formulations that labor leaders like Sidney Hillman advocated. Hillman's contracts generally involved a no-strike clause for the duration of the negotiated contract. This put the onus on unions to enforce labor peace, even when many members were against it; obviously, this was a delicate position for a labor leader to hold. Militant workers regarded no strike clauses as a violation of their liberty to leave work when they saw fit.[13]

What has been described thus far is the process by which large-scale organization, both of industrial enterprise and of labor, forced a change in the regime of liberty of contract. When we come to the effects of crisis, we will need to recognize that advocates of change were divided between those like Hillman, who urged formal mechanisms to resolve labor disputes, and those to the left of him, who urged that labor seize control of the workplace for itself. In the interim, it is helpful to outline the difficulties confronting the rule of contract as it stood in the 1920s and early 1930s.

The Rule of Contract

Contract implies real bargaining over the terms of an agreement. However, corporate standardization and business conditions generally made it impossible for one individual to bargain separately from co-workers. How could one individual bargain separately from coworkers to demand a slower work pace or a separate ventilation system? It was difficult, too, for individuals to secure written agreements that could be made available as evidence in the event of a dispute over their terms. Workers were simply hired at the will of their employer. Courts did not find this problematic and maintained that workers' freedom to quit *at will* had to be balanced by employers' freedom to likewise dismiss or fire them *at will.*[14]

Many economists then, and still today, argue that firms acted as if they had held direct talks with their workers. When disgruntled employees walked away from their employment new workers had to be recruited and trained. Indeed, the high cost of an annual labor turnover rate in excess of 300 percent was a primary reason for Henry Ford's unsolicited and unprecedented announcement in 1913 that he would pay five dollars a day, more than twice the rate unskilled workers received elsewhere. Money, according to this perspective, becomes the medium through which labor resentments are freely surrendered. Economists argue that high wages are used to compensate for poor amenities like unsafe, stultifying, or simply unsavory work. They explain that labor mobility mimics contract and forces management to come to terms with worker demands. This abstraction breathes a new life into liberty of contract debates and infuses great significance into workers' rights to accept or reject a contract: this is a significance few workers willingly acknowledge.

Albert O. Hirschman has argued that the indirect negotiations described above are flawed because such a process forces a choice between blind loyalty or exit.[15] The alternative, he suggests, is *voice,* by which he means that workers must be allowed a meaningful say in their conditions. This, according to Hirschman, improves managerial efficiency by providing information on the conditions workers desire *before* they quit. Bargaining prevents the costly all-or-nothing choices of loyalty or exit. In large organizations, it was collective bargaining that gave workers their voice. Collective bargaining altered the entire power structure of labor relations. If it was easy to replace one worker in an unorganized work force of 10,000, it ceased to be so when workers as a group stood their ground. Management quickly found it important to listen.

The Promotion of Labor Peace

This is the underlying premise of the famous Wagner or National Labor Relations Act of 1935. The law declared national policy required the promotion of labor peace. This was accomplished by balancing management's power with that of labor. It was a policy whose adoption was cinched by the crisis of the Great Depression. Once in place, a second crisis, World War II, gave it specific shape by fostering contractualism over confrontation.

The Wagner Act evolved out of Franklin Roosevelt's earlier National Industrial Recovery Act (NIRA). The NIRA was the direct result of the economic crisis whose peak brought Roosevelt to power. In this act and in his other attempts to provide relief, Roosevelt broke sharply from tradition. In his first 100 days, Roosevelt advanced several bills to reverse the destructive collapse in business confidence and prices. The NIRA encouraged firms to combine to set fair trade standards for themselves, promoting, in effect, cartels and collusion that previously would have been illegal. Whole industries enacted codes of fair practice. The NIRA was designed to restore confidence, limit deadly competition, and increase prices. In exchange for NIRA relief, employers were supposed to give their workers a new deal as well.

When the NIRA passed in 1933, 25 percent of the labor force was unemployed, and many of those who had kept their jobs were working part time. Section 7 of the NIRA suggested new rights for workers and called upon firms to implement fair labor codes. The law encouraged firms to permit workers to organize without interference or coercion. As with the broader industry codes, NIRA labor policy was designed to play a major role in economic recovery. Its purpose was to restore confidence, stabilize sinking wages, and encourage consumption that would help put more people back to work.

In 1935 the Supreme Court held that the NIRA was unconstitutional. Even before this, Robert Wagner had been drawing up replacement legislation for the unworkable and hotly contended law. As opposed to the NIRA's broader industry codes, Wagner's National Labor Relations Act (NLRA) was concerned solely with employees. The NLRA guaranteed workers the right to organize without management interference. Among other things, this meant that workers could not be discriminated against—fired or passed over for promotions or other benefits—because of union activity. It also meant that workers were entitled to petition the government to supervise elections in order to certify a union as their bargaining agent. Once certified, the law required management and labor representatives to negotiate in good faith—though it stopped short of requiring that they submit unresolved differences to arbitration. The Wagner Act also outlawed company-dominated unions. Most importantly, the NLRA set up a National Labor Relations Board (NLRB) to hear complaints regarding abuses of the law. Altogether, the Wagner Act gave labor a bill of rights with which to organize itself. Even though the law was subsequently modified, there can be no doubt that it changed American labor relations dramatically.

A Shift in Labor Strategy

New Deal legislation spawned an upsurge in labor activity. In the coalfields, mine union president John L. Lewis proclaimed, "The President

Wants You to Join the Union," omitting mention whether this was Roosevelt's desire or that of Union President Lewis. Lewis, more than anyone else, was responsible for seizing the opportunities making possible organized labor's resurgence. He began by restoring membership among the dispirited miners, where 300,000 workers had lost their jobs in the four years following 1929. From this base he targeted other key industries, most notably steel and automobiles.[16]

Steel companies owned "captive" mines that they jealously maintained as non-union operations. Consequently, it was logical that once these mines were organized Lewis then launched an assault upon the steel mills themselves. In 1937, U.S. Steel agreed to surrender its company-dominated union to the Steel Workers' Organizing Committee. After years of successfully running non-union steel plants, many were surprised how peacefully U.S. Steel recognized the rights of the new independent union to represent its 200,000 workers. Following U.S. Steel's lead, resistance also crumpled at the adamantly anti-union Jones & Laughlin Company .

Smaller firms, known as "Little Steel," feared unionization would undermine their ability to compete with the giants and accordingly put up fiercer resistance. Republic Steel's president, Tom Girdler, spent $50,000 arming his own 370–man police force with firearms, gas guns, grenades, and night sticks. In May of 1937 Girdler provoked the steelworkers into a premature battle by locking them out of work. Eleven days later at a Chicago rally, in what subsequent investigators called a police riot upon the strikers and their supporters, ten workers were killed, another thirty were shot, and almost two score were reported beaten. The tenacious firms in Little Steel resisted the standards set by Big Labor and Big Steel, fearing they would place them at a competitive disadvantage.[17]

Individual company battles are less important than was the shift in labor strategy that John L. Lewis engineered. Lewis, like Sidney Hillman and Eugene Debs before him, realized that the old AFL policy of organizing workers by crafts was obsolete. The AFL's strategy of skimming off carpenters and placing them in one organization, segmenting machinists in another, and separating welders in yet a third union left workers within modern industrial enterprises weak and divided. Although many members personally favored industrywide organization, the interests of the skilled men prevailed in setting AFL policy.

It remained to John L. Lewis to demonstrate that only by organizing industrial unions could labor successfully redesign the workplace. Organized in this way, workers forced management to choose between replacing entire work forces—sometimes numbering in the hundreds of thousands—or recognizing their collective bargaining rights. In 1935 Lewis organized the

Committee for Industrial Organization (CIO) without AFL sanction. For their sins, CIO leaders were excommunicated from the AFL. Liberated from the AFL, Lewis and his colleagues were free to design their own organizational strategies.

Auto workers simply sat down on the job refusing to relinquish their factories to their nominal owners. To capital, this militant tactic constituted a revolutionary seizure of private property. Indeed, the courts generally agreed. Nonetheless it was an effective organizing technique that literally yielded control over the shop floor. In battles at GM, Ford, and Chrysler, the United Auto Workers eventually prevailed in their fights to gain recognition.

The successes in coal, steel, and autos were instrumental in realigning power within the United States. In fields as divergent as clothing and rubber, new industrial unions kept the momentum going. Aided by federal law, labor was clearly on the rise.

Even as labor rolled up these successes, problems internal to the movement began to shape the face of the freedoms it extolled. Labor was not immune to the tensions that all democratic movements experience; rifts between individual and common interests, and between the desire for solidarity and the necessity of dissent. During the war years a fork in the road came between those who advocated direct shop floor control and those who thought it necessary to establish labor's reputation as a reliable bargaining partner.

Two crises, first World War II and then the Cold War, advanced the perspective held by the latter group. James Atleson and others argue that World War II brought labor pluralists like Sidney Hillman to the forefront of labor policy. These men argued that organized labor must act responsibly and prevent disruptions, which, particularly in times of war, could prove disastrous. Just as wars made it imperative for the state to deal squarely with labor, so too did wars make it necessary for labor to recognize its new position in the councils of power was dependent upon its cooperation in maintaining production. Says James Atleson, "World War II . . . provided a rational basis for stressing bureaucratic dispute resolution, the restriction of midterm strikes and union control over rank-and-file action."[18]

The Role of the Communist Party

Within this environment, the Communist Party played an interesting and important role in the American Labor movement. The party sought a country in which vast inequalities did not overpower the rights of individual citizens. Not only did Communists press for a substantive change in industrial conditions, they also championed the aspirations of African Americans and other minorities. Although Communists rejected the capitalist system, their numbers were small in America and realistically they did not expect to take over the government any time soon, if at all. Instead they believed their best hope for changing power relations lay within the labor movement. Many chose to challenge the system and build their base by organizing workers to confront their bosses. In pursuing this goal, Communists succeeded in broadening organized labor's appeal precisely among those groups that the AFL had long abandoned. Many within labor's old guard found their activities problematic.

Communists occupied important positions in several key unions, particularly the United Auto Workers and the United Electrical, Radio and Machine Workers' Union. Numerically, Communists were never a large percentage of the labor movement, but their dedication and discipline gave them an influence that far exceeded their numbers. Within labor, as elsewhere, they kept their party affiliation to themselves. Even in the 1930s, to be a Communist was problematic. Many outside the party were aghast at the credulous reception American Communists gave to Stalin's claims to have alleviated inequality. Communists regarded themselves as loyal Americans who looked to Russia as the exemplar of what this nation could and should be. When Stalin made peace with Hitler just prior to the outbreak of European war, many American Communists were stunned. They could not understand his alliance with a force that represented everything they loathed. Still, true believers among them argued that the Soviet Union's success was vital to the prospect of a humane economic system. Although they viewed themselves as loyal Americans, Communists followed their party when its leaders urged policies designed to promote Soviet interests. Despite America's increasing effort to mobilize for war, the Communist Party pressed for militant labor strikes when the 1939 Stalin–Hitler non-aggression accord was in place and only altered course after Hitler attacked the Soviet Union in 1941. Such actions earned Communists a poor reputation within the labor movement. Post-war battles culminated in CIO acquiescence to the 1947 Taft–Hartley Act provision that effectively expelled Communists from positions of labor leadership. The situation of rank-and-file Communists grew more difficult with the McCarthy hearings of the 1950s.[19]

Although Communists in the labor movement were disciplined, they were nonetheless associated with the militants who promoted shop-floor democracy. The desire on the part of many unionists to contain Communist influence was symptomatic of labor's transition from dissenter to co-partner within the power structure of America. Labor leaders sought to distance themselves from their fringe elements in order to appear more responsible. Labor's revolutionary victory was to win state protection for workers' rights to independent representation. To achieve those rights it abandoned radical calls for the abolition of private property and privilege. In this, the new industrial unionism of the 1940s and 1950s was in accord with the trade unionism of the past when, desperate for acceptance, the AFL rejected militant resistance and calls for state ownership. Union recognition was ultimately a form of property that, like all property, gave its owners a vested interest in the status quo.

Conservative tendencies within labor were reinforced by the horror stories told about Europe's authoritarian regimes. Their wholesale usurpation of individual property rights and disrespect for individuals were regarded as deadly to western freedoms. George Orwell's *1984,* published in 1949, reflected the widespread distrust of any paternalistic Big Brother. This disdain was shared by many. Enough of America's immigrants had escaped oppressive governments or had relatives who experienced firsthand encounters with powerful states to vividly remind workers here of the potential dangers. Thus, the benign image of Edward Bellamy's Cooperative Commonwealth that briefly flourished in the populist 1880s and 1890s was cast aside for more disparaging views of state power.

Labor's Trade-off

Americans attempted to finesse the dangerous cross currents of laissez-faire and authoritarianism by constructing a corporatist world in which big business was offset by big labor and in which big government did their bidding. Although individual rights could and did get trampled, this was an inescapable trade-off conditioned by the pursuit of freedom in a world composed of large organizations. The nation now not only tolerated, but purposefully grew, its own giants as part of a new system of checks and balances designed to replace the failed promises of republicanism. To take its rightful place within this system, labor disassociated itself from the elements of its militant syndicalist past. The class warfare responsible for achieving power became a liability once labor was accepted as a responsible partner. Syndicalism was a guerrilla war on legal authority waged to obtain justice on the shop floor. Once recognized, organized labor itself became part of that legal authority and, consequently, could no longer condone syndicalist tactics. The unauthorized boycott, the wildcat strike (a strike call by local unionists without approval of their leadership), the seizing of plants, and the sabotage of production—all these could no longer be openly tolerated by unions unless their leaders could call off these actions as easily as workers initiated them. This was hard medicine for rank and file unionists who continued to believe that law and contract were always dominated by moneyed interests. In surrendering what they regarded as inalienable rights to resist management, many workers came to believe they had simply traded one set of masters for another.

Although costly, the trade-off enabled unions to achieve real gains.[20] Labor contracts protected worker freedoms by limiting managerial discretion. By definition, however, contracts also defined the limit of worker discretion. One-hundred-page contracts requiring interpretation by shop stewards and union lawyers stripped away workers' rights to manage themselves and instead put control into the hands of labor experts. When gains in wages and working conditions faded in memory, the rules and constraints remained visible. It often looked as if unions did the corporations' dirty work by disciplining their members. Unions worked best when their moral claim was so strong that workers recognized their interests were best served by adhering to their leaders' advice—but a moral claim that strong required ever greater advances.

The crises in the period under discussion were so compelling and organized labor's successes so great that the sacrifices associated with the new rules seemed justified. Along with federal standards, labor helped raise wages and lower hours. Their right to speak collectively about their own situation and to demand that individual grievances be heard gave workers a new sense of dignity. Labor's larger vision, however, remained to be defined. Would it seek to transform the industrial system or would it merely seek to extract larger wage and benefit concessions for its members? Would it embrace the most disinherited workers in America, or would it content itself with representing its own membership? The purge of its most radical members coupled with the drive to impose discipline upon the remaining members limited the directions labor could take.

David Brody provides the most telling example of how organized labor came to temper its own visions.[21] Following World War II, Walter Reuther of the United Auto Workers (UAW) decided to use contract negotiations with GM to resolve fundamental social problems, particularly the issue of unemployment. Reuther urged GM to raise auto workers' wages without increasing prices on the autos it produced. Reuther reasoned that doing so would force GM to operate at higher levels of production—to make up through volume what it could not achieve through markups—and thereby reduce the impact of post-war unemployment that was widely anticipated. The UAW struck GM hoping to force the company to open its books to disprove the merits of Reuther's scheme. GM argued that the UAW strike assaulted fundamental management rights. The union, GM negotiators reasoned, had the right to negotiate on pay and working conditions, but pricing was outside their prerogative. On this issue, GM was not willing to negotiate.

Despite a presidential commission's authorization allowing arbitrators to open GM's books to determine their ability to pay, GM stood its ground refusing to have price or wage decisions dictated. The commission recommended a raise of 19.5 cents, but GM would not go over 18.5 cents, extending the three-month-old strike for yet another month.

Faced with a choice between a hard struggle to transform industry or settling for advances in worker pay, Reuther prudently chose the latter. Over the next few years, GM and the UAW agreed to pay raises tied to the cost of living and productivity indices while not mentioning price policy. GM was able to claim that it had "conceded no ground whatsoever on fundamental principle matters which would have the tendency of watering down management's responsibility to manage the business." The pattern was established whereby auto workers—both union and non-union—secured higher pay funded through the higher prices that workers, as consumers, across the country had to pay. Over the next twenty-five years, while domestic car prices steadily climbed upward, auto workers were among the best paid labor in the country. By the late 1960s and early 1970s, however, the auto workers' formula was coming undone due to the recovery of the war-ravaged producers in Germany and Japan.

Reuther's UAW, one of the nation's most progressive unions, gained power at the expense of its dreams. Although those dreams involved greater worker participation in every facet of management, the fact was that Reuther believed his moral claim to auto workers' allegiance would not permit him to press the battle so far. Organized labor, in general, had to settle for better pay and working conditions. In so doing it proved itself a responsible partner, bargaining in good faith, and controlling the unruly or disruptive influences within its own ranks.

Chapter 8

"Rights" of Passage

*The first [issue] was whether it [the 1946 Full Employment
Bill] made sense to declare the existence of a right to a job or
to employment, as the proponents of the original bill wished.
On this question there was a good deal of logic chopping, with
philosophic analyses of the rights of man, the Declaration of Independence, and the Bill of Rights. But it was clear as soon as
the issue was raised that, although some people had an affection for the "rights" language, no one seriously meant to
endow individuals with a legally enforceable right to jobs.*
—Herbert Stein, *The Fiscal Revolution*

In the aftermath of World War II, sports, entertainment, and politics combined in an unlikely conspiracy to remind America that the conditions of
freedom facing labor had not been perfected. Events in each arena signaled
tensions that would dominate American life for the next thirty years. In
baseball, the death of Josh Gibson and the hiring of Jackie Robinson called
attention to the fictions in liberty of contract. In film, the contempt citations
of the Hollywood Ten demonstrated that what liberty of contract we had
was very clearly dependent upon government patronage. And finally, in
Congress, politicians hemmed in their patronage toward labor, first by rejecting a national commitment to full employment as a right, and second by
trimming back organized labor's collective bargaining rights. First these
issues are explored and then their interconnections and implications are
analyzed in this chapter.

Baseball and Discrimination

It is a terrible irony that Josh Gibson should die in 1947 as that was the year
when Jackie Robinson was hired by the Dodgers. Both men were African
Americans, yet one of them would achieve national fame and fortune where the
other was to remain virtually unrecognized. Gibson hit seventy-five home runs
in the single season of 1931, more home runs than the records set by Roger

Maris and Babe Ruth. His lifetime batting average of .347 and his career total of nearly 800 home runs would normally have been expected to earn him a place in the gallery of baseball's greats. Yet Gibson was never allowed to play in baseball's all-white major leagues and consequently was never accorded the recognition such accomplishments were due. In a sense, however, his death hailed the demise of a discredited system.

Jackie Robinson was, by all accounts, a gifted and hardworking athlete. In college he participated in several sports, baseball being his least favorite. Robinson was recruited to the majors by Brooklyn Dodger's general manager Branch Rickey. Although there were many outstanding players in the Negro League, Rickey chose Robinson because of the young player's self-assurance. Rickey knew the first player to break the color barrier would need this attribute. He accurately forewarned Robinson of the abuse he would receive from players and fans. Although Rickey understood that he was asking a great deal from Robinson, he made the rookie agree not to react to provocations for three years, not until he had proven to the doubters both his character and his ability. In fact it took only two years before Robinson earned the National League's Most Valuable Player award signaling that he had also won the profession's respect. His self-control and brilliant performance on the field helped reshape public consensus on integrating baseball.

For our story, however, it is more significant that the Dodgers' decision to hire an African American was quickly replicated by other teams hiring great players like Satchel Page, Roy Campanella, and Elston Howard. The episode reads like a picture-perfect lesson in competitive economics. Indeed, as Milton Friedman, the doyen of free markets, has put it, "an impersonal market separates economic activities from political views and protects men from being discriminated against in their economic activities for reasons that are irrelevant to their productivity—whether these reasons are associated with their views or their color."[1] The market operates on profit, not politics. Any team that bypassed talent was in jeopardy of losing to any other team willing to buck the taboos of race. Once the Dodgers had hired Robinson, it was open season to recruit players of any color, and that is how teams behaved.

Yet, how did it come to pass that the pressures of competition did not cause this sport, whose history dates back to the nineteenth century, to integrate earlier? The main secret lies in the fact that baseball, like most markets, is not conducted in abstract or "impersonal" settings. Players are known to fans, to team mates, and to owners. Each may have a reason to discriminate and, if allowed freedom of contract and association, may choose not to buy services from people of color. An employer who disregards the preferences of his or her patrons quickly learns not to do so. The Washington Senators were reputed to have moved to the predominately white city of Minneapolis, in part to insulate themselves from eastern fans who might prefer black players. That an African American player would have to withstand much harassment, an agony to which many a player might succumb, was attested to by Branch Rickey's concern over Jackie Robinson's character. In general, then, employers had reason not to rock the boat by hiring employees whose personal attributes would disrupt workplace productivity. Moreover, although they might pay an economic price for it, employers who used ownership to discriminate often saw themselves as merely exercising the personal liberty and independence that was the reward, indeed was the very point, of property.

Worse, however, was the fact that economic penalties could not always be counted upon to counter discriminatory tendencies. Employers who based their hiring on group attributes did lower costs when their assessments were even partially correct. Like insurance companies that give discounts to young female drivers because, on average, they have fewer accidents, employers who noticed that one type of employee lowers costs over another—however slightly—actually had economic reason to discriminate. In employment, for example, the fact that women of child-bearing age had and have a somewhat higher propensity to need or want maternity leave gave economic reinforcement to society's long-standing differential treatment of men and women. Even where the preponderance of women were committed to their jobs, such a statistical difference between men and women alters employment costs and makes discriminating employers better, rather than worse, off.[2] The assumption that capitalism mitigates social tendencies toward discrimination must be tempered by the realization that (a) most markets are not completely impersonal—even when customers do not know the sellers, employees and bosses do; and (b) some involuntary characteristics, like sex and race, may affect workplace productivity—even if the difference arises for socially unacceptable reasons.

That said, capitalism and private property do provide some incentive to employers to look beyond race and sex. In doing so, however, capitalism has been known to foster even more violent prejudice. Employers were frequently less than shy in hiring foreign or minority labor, whether black, Welsh, Irish, Filipino, or Slovenian.[3] When they did, however, they often segregated their multi-ethnic labor forces in separate workplaces: Greeks, Italians, or Chinese would work in their own gangs on the railroads; Poles and blacks in separate areas within steel mills; Jews and Italians under different proprietors within the garment industry. Physical segregation was frequently accompanied by an occupational segregation that afforded better work for well-organized groups. Such differences in treatment gave sub-stance to inter-group hostilities that weakened labor solidarity. In just one example of how employers used inter-group hostility to their own advantage, historian Ronald Takaki notes that in 1903 Hawaiian sugar plantations "began importing Korean laborers in order to pit them against the Japanese. Aware of the antagonism between these two groups, planters believed that the Koreans were 'not likely to combine with the Japanese at any attempt at strikes.' "[4] Such practices successfully exacerbated labor's divisions. None-theless, as David Roediger points out, even if workers were manipulated by employers, it is incorrect to omit the realization that "racism comes from both above and below."[5]

For African Americans, open or free markets often offered greater re-wards than alliance with their white counterparts. After reconstruction, southern labor markets were not free. Although competition for labor some-times enabled black workers to walk away from peculiarly harsh employers, their freedom to quit work was curtailed by public law and by private force. Employment contracts were enforced through criminal sanctions in a way that would elsewhere have been considered involuntary servitude.[6] As dis-criminatory as such laws were, the Klu Klux Klan and other groups went beyond them by intimidating blacks and whites who deviated from the practices they prescribed for southern society. As if this was not enough, Southern statutes compounded the divisions between blacks and whites by legally mandating separate restrooms, water fountains, public transport, and other accommodations.

African Americans turned to the North for signs of hope. Blacks migrated north in great numbers. There the rising industrial corporations sometimes overlooked the southern color bar to hire African American workers. Be-tween 1910 and 1920 employers like Henry Ford helped increase Detroit's black population from 5,000 to over 40,000. In addition to their willingness to work hard under adverse conditions, black workers were also attractive because their presence made unionization more unlikely.[7]

A Chicago race riot in 1919 soon alerted people to the fact that the North had no magic solution to ethnic strife. Racial division intensified during the depression of the 1930s as skin color became an important factor in the allocation of scarce jobs. Although organizations like the CIO or the Com-munist Party attempted to unite dispossessed white and black workers, well-organized trade unions often countered their efforts by fighting to retain the few privileges their white members possessed. World War II, a terror in almost all other respects, forced changes that might otherwise have come more slowly or, perhaps, not at all.[8] Labor shortages created wartime em-ployment for blacks, and the nation's reliance upon African Americans, both at work and in war, made their unequal treatment more conspicuous and more indefensible. It was this that contributed to Branch Rickey's outrage and set the stage for baseball's integration.

This brief discussion should make it clear that liberty of contract was not sufficient to ameliorate the problems of discrimination and segregation. Although Jackie Robinson's success put the race issue before the public eye, it also enabled the country to congratulate itself, somewhat prematurely, on having solved the race problem. Baseball was in many ways a unique employment situation. It involved a highly public sport in which a player's productivity was established through observable statistics. For jobs where no such track records existed, it was all too easy to rely upon stereotypes and prejudices to predict how an individual would fare. In markets where educational credentials were less revealing than batting averages and where openings to training institutions were restricted, the separation of races continued. After examining other currents in American life we will return to this issue.

The Hollywood Ten and Political Discrimination

Whereas baseball backed away from racial discrimination in 1947, in that same year Hollywood undertook a boycott with a different objective. Eric Johnston, president of the Motion Picture Association of America, issued a proclamation announcing that Hollywood "would not knowingly employ a Communist or a member of any party or group which advocates the overthrow of the government."[9] This change in policy followed on the heels of Congress's contempt citations against writers and directors who refused to name Communists before the House Un-American Activities Committee (HUAC). These individuals, collectively known as the Hollywood Ten, became the core of Hollywood's soon-to-burgeon blacklist. The story of Herbert Biberman's attempt to make an independent film after serving six months in jail for contempt of Congress demonstrates how the absence of government patronship undermined liberty of contract.

Without the backing of major studios, Biberman could continue making films only by working independently. However, even his independent venture was foiled by Johnston's invitation to the "Hollywood talent guilds to . . . eliminate any subversives."[10] Roy M. Brewer, president of the International Alliance of Theatrical Stage Employees Union proved particularly instrumental in securing sanctions against Biberman's independent film efforts. Brewer made sure that no union labor was available to work on *Salt of the Earth*. Later, he would also ruin Biberman's opportunities to get the film seen by securing the refusal of unionized film projectionists to show the movie. Finally, Biberman was effectively prevented from distributing his work. The greatest paradox in this was that Biberman fell victim to union pressure when he himself was an ardent unionist. Failing to enlist official union assistance in securing technicians to make the film, Biberman nonetheless insisted that his crew organize itself.

Biberman's film, no less than the story surrounding it, epitomized key issues of the time. He chose to make a film based on a real miners' strike in New Mexico. The union involved—the International Union of Mine, Mill and Smelters Workers (MMSW)—was ejected from the, until then, progressive Congress for Industrial Organization (CIO) because its leadership was Communist. Chicano workers used the MMSW to reject to the conditions eastern mine owners imposed upon them. The film testifies to the MMSW's ability to recruit minority workers and to give them voice and dignity. Unfortunately, the employers secured an injunction prohibiting the miners from picketing. When this happened, the women formed their own auxiliary to take up the union fight. This shift in strategy resulted in a surprising twist as the Chicana women used their new power and status to put forward their own issues regarding water and sanitation, and also to secure greater authority within the household. Thus, Biberman's film not only told how one disenfranchised group, the Chicanos, used the labor movement to achieve solidarity, but it also foreshadowed the increasing militancy of women, who felt themselves even more marginalized and powerless.

In Congress, calls went up to stop the film as subversive to American interests. The film was decried as propaganda designed to portray America in a bad light, and also as a piece of work intended to incite domestic discontent. Congressional hearings on communism strengthened the Hollywood boycott. Not only the studios and the Hollywood guilds, but the American Legion also sabotaged on Biberman's work.

It was in direct reference to the Hollywood boycott that Milton Friedman argued individual liberty was ensured by "impersonal" capitalist markets. These markets "made it costly for people to preserve the blacklist."[11] Indeed, it is true that by 1958, when Friedman wrote, that the boycott against the Hollywood Ten writers had largely been disbanded. Numerous writers, such as Dalton Trumbo, worked under pseudonyms. The employment of "ghost" writers was widely winked at. But it was not true that everyone was equally protected. Friedman incorrectly argues that under capitalism, "people who are running enterprises have an incentive to make as much money as they can, [and therefore that they] protected the freedom of the individuals who were blacklisted by providing them with an alternative form of employment." The impersonal market worked best for writers, not for actors like Zero Mostel, who remained visible to audiences, advertisers, and censors. Perhaps this is also why directors were more likely to name names at congressional hearings than were writers. Directors, even those as powerful and influential as Elia Kazan, could not become ghosts. More correctly, Friedman argues that whatever power the boycott had was achieved, not through the market, but through the use of "collusive arrangements that used coercive power to prevent voluntary exchanges."[12] Presumably, by this he meant the unholy alliance between the Hollywood guilds that enforced the boycott and the Congress, which publicly censured individuals. Together they wrecked the lives of scores of individuals who refused either to recant their affiliations or to name names. Liberty cannot be ensured by relying on the market alone. The government always weighs in on one side of a conflict or another. In this case, if the government had not created and tolerated a climate in which liberty of contract was freely curtailed in the private sector, Hollywood's scandalous behavior would never have occurred.

The 1947 Taft–Hartley Law

One irony in the plight of the Hollywood Ten was that the boycotts they endured were not penalized under Congress's new prohibitions in its 1947 Taft–Hartley Law. We turn now to an examination of the broad thrust of that law, which trimmed the rights organized labor had recently won under the New Deal's Wagner Act by forcing unions to accommodate themselves to an older, more conservative understanding of freedom. The law resurrected individual liberties to the detriment of collective rights. It did this by eliminating specific types of group boycotts, by allowing states to enact so-called right-to-work laws, and by enabling the federal government to secure injunctions to halt strikes in a national emergency. Separately it hindered militant unionism by denying legal recognition for unions headed by Communists, precisely those unionists who had been leading labor down more progressive pathways. Ultimately, what the law did was to increase the internal divisions within labor by ensuring that industrial democracy did not prevail in American workplaces.

Taft–Hartley limited workers' rights to collective action by outlawing sympathy and secondary boycotts. Boycotts have an important history in the United States.[13] From the Boston Tea Party to the Hollywood Ten, boycotts have been used to impose financial hardship in order to make a point. At one time or another, nations, employers, consumers, civil rights activists, and labor organizations alike have chosen boycotts as a key weapon in their attempts to achieve their objectives. Successful boycotts are often difficult to conduct because they impose hardships on those who boycott as well as those who are boycotted. Nonetheless, organized labor has often used boycotts to pressure firms that refuse to recognize its unions. Boycotts by powerful unions like the Teamsters or the Longshoremen have been important in helping organize weaker labor unions. Thus, when Congress banned secondary labor boycotts, it mounted one more serious obstacle to the spread of unionization. Nevertheless, an evenhanded application of the law might have prevented union projectionists from boycotting theater owners who wanted to show Biberman's *Salt of the Earth.*

Taft–Hartley did not concern itself with the motive behind a boycott, but rather relied upon the concern that independent, neutral, or innocent bystanders could be unwillingly coerced. And indeed, the history of boycotts suggests many instances in which the power of the boycott is used to achieve unsavory results. Baseball's boycott of African American players is one powerful example. The boycott against the Hollywood Ten is, for many, another. Still, the lines between freedom and coercion, on the one hand, and between innocence and participation, on the other, is often fine. Market demand is thought to be an expression of voluntary, or free, behavior. When consumers change their minds about a product, for any reason, they may legally boycott it. The greater the shift in their demand (i.e., the extent of their boycott), the greater the harm or coercion inflicted upon a seller. The boycott question boils down to whether employees have the right to change their minds about working for an employer whose associates or whose activities they dislike. Do workers have the right to boycott bosses who violate their moral standards? Taft–Hartley said no.

Under old law, boycotts enforced through the use of force or threat of force were criminal activities. Similarly, boycotts enforced by contract were often illegal under anti-trust law. Before the Wagner Act union boycotts were frequently subject to court challenges on both these grounds. Although many thought the Wagner Act changed all this, the Taft–Hartley Law halted that impression just twelve years later. But unlike earlier criminal conspiracy and anti-trust laws, the boycott's illegality under Taft–Hartley was determined simply by whether the boycotters were employed by the party with whom they were in dispute. This inhibited unionists' freedom in a way that would not be tolerated elsewhere. For example, no one would suggest that consumers should be barred from boycotting the products of companies that do business with dictators merely because they do not live in the country in which the abuses take place.

Broadly speaking, any systematic discrimination is a boycott, and up to the war years labor was as guilty of discrimination as were the other constituents of the market. Yet the Taft–Hartley Law hit hardest at the faction of labor that had been most aggressive in seeking to change this. This faction involved the industrial unionists in the emerging CIO. Among this group, no element was so united against discrimination as the CIO's small Communist core, a core whose hard work, dedication, and discipline yielded it a disproportionate number of leadership positions. The most immediate effect of Taft–Hartley was to strip from leadership those courageous individuals who most aggressively sought ties between labor and the emerging civil rights movement. The law required union leaders to sign an affidavit stating that they were not Communists before it would certify a union and protect it under the provisions of the Wagner Act.[14] Thus the very leaders that most wholeheartedly embraced disenfranchised minority workers were forced to leave the field. Their abdication signaled labor's retreat from aggressive inter-ethnic solidarity, a retreat that was to have profound consequences for at least the next thirty years.

Historian Michael Honey explains that "Communist party members in the CIO promoted genuine concern and commitment on racial questions and built alliances between blacks and whites." According to Honey, "White party members could be relied upon to join picket lines and organizing drives with blacks, in sharp contrast to many other white unionists, who were willing to join bi-racial unions but did little else to demonstrate solidarity with black workers."[15] When CIO unions started purging left-wing members, prospects for achieving a powerful multi-racial coalition of workers dimmed. Communist-led unions, like the Mexican American Mine, Mill and Smelters Workers portrayed in Biberman's *Salt of the Earth,* became vulnerable. Indeed, the MMSW's leaders had to defend themselves against charges that they had falsely submitted non-Communist affidavits in order to keep their union's NLRB certification. Clifton Jencks, the MMSW organizer who played himself in the film, defended himself against such accusations all the way to the Supreme Court, where the charges were dropped.[16]

Taft–Hartley did not occur in a vacuum. Labor's post-war ascendancy had aroused genuine concerns and these ultimately aided the business community that sought to contain it. Many minorities, anti-Communists, anti-racketeers, and dissenters within labor focused their worries on the rising power of labor rather than the old villain called "capital." One example helps illustrate the situation. Roy M. Brewer, the cold warrior from IATSE (International Alliance of Theatrical and Stage Employees) who supervised the Hollywood blacklist, came to the presidency of his union as the result of a campaign to clean up corruption. When radical opposition within the union surfaced he found the charge of Communist a convenient device to consolidate power. At a time of intense national concern over Stalin's intentions, red-baiting and similar acts became effective techniques for polarizing debate and neutralizing opposition.

Labor turned on itself in these ways, clearing the field for its opponents. The battles were reflected in popular culture.[17] For instance, Elia Kazan's 1954 award winning film *On the Waterfront* took legitimate concerns about the organized crime to heroize the act of a labor racketeer who turned against his mobster buddies. Although the film is nominally sympathetic toward labor, its most vivid scene portrays labor as cowed workers making payoffs to secure their jobs on the waterfront. Although East Coast ILA (International Longshoremen's Association) officials were linked to the mob, some critics have nonetheless suggested that the film is a thin ploy to justify Kazan's role as an informer during congressional hearings.[18] Politics and art combined to create an environment hostile to labor's power.

With rising membership and power, labor's shortcomings received more scrutiny, helping to build an anti-union lobby. Business wanted to revamp, if not rescind, the moderate labor experiment that had been ushered in with the 1935 Wagner Act. Under that law, government had become organized labor's patron, establishing and protecting workers' rights to collective action. Using that patronage, the years surrounding World War II became labor's heyday. By the early 1950s, organized labor represented 35 percent of the labor force, a level unparalleled before and since. Nonetheless, the Wagner Act proved itself to be merely a reform in that it failed to institutionalize labor in all workplaces. The law sidestepped the necessity of making a national commitment to workplace democracy. That is, unlike several European countries which required workers' councils in most places of work, U.S. law only protected workers who sought collective action without insisting upon it.

This omission was to harm the union movement in two pivotal ways. First, organized firms were pitted against non-unionized firms, considerably raising the costs of contract concessions to labor. At the same time, workers were allowed to opt out of union governance schemes, giving dissidents greater incentive to avoid or oppose unionization rather than improve it, while also yielding firms greater reason to convince employees that exit from the union was the wisest course. In these ways, the Wagner law was an incomplete revolution that prevented labor from consolidating its tentative victory. The deficiencies within the law promoted adversarial rather than accommodative strategies. Taft–Hartley limitations followed naturally.

In the post-war period, employers who had long resisted collective bargaining renewed old complaints and sought relief from closed and union shop contracts. Such provisions required union membership as a condition of employment. According to employers, this violated employees' rights to work. It was an interesting argument made in blissful forgetfulness of employers' own past defense of the yellow dog or iron clad contract, which required, as a condition of employment, that workers agree never to join a union. Employers sought and obtained "right-to-work" provisions in the Taft–Hartley Law that abolished shops closed to all but union members and gave states the discretion to also ban the union shop—in which workers were required to join the union after being hired. Right-to-work laws were adopted more frequently in southern and western states.

Organized labor argued that industrial democracy could not survive unless participation was a duty rather than an option. If workers were free to join and leave unions at will, free riders would partake in the benefits of collective bargaining without paying for it, and organizational survival would become nearly impossible. Economist Mancur Olson pointed out that in the first four months after Taft–Hartley became law, more than 90 percent of all unionists voted for compulsory union membership despite the fact that only a small minority of workers regularly attended union meetings.[19] Individual unionists apparently agreed that without compulsion inertia would set in. Labor citizenship, it seems, had its duties as well as its rights.

By denying unions the ability to impose duties (and dues) upon workers in exchange for the rights and benefits they provided, Taft–Hartley aggravated prior weaknesses within the Wagner Act. Where the Wagner Act had at least encouraged unionization, Taft–Hartley threw a damp towel over it. Whereas in 1946 it was possible to imagine that worker participation and governance were inalienable rights that would in time be extended to all workplaces, Taft–Hartley destroyed any such illusion by dictating perpetual competition between union and non-union labor.

Workers who wanted a collective voice would have to fight for it, making it unlikely that low-skilled, migrant, transitory, or otherwise vulnerable workers would ever successfully gain workplace representation. Such workers too often found labor unions irrelevant at best, and threatening at worst. Despite organized labor's advocacy of minimum labor standards covering all workers, a big divide existed between union labor and the rest of working America. Many workers actually agreed with their employers that using the state to raise wages, increase safety standard, cut hours, regulate pensions, and dictate training could jeopardize their jobs. Their fears were not groundless as, in fact, without federal guarantees for full employment, government-imposed standards often did hit the weakest elements of the labor force first. Labor's inability in 1946 to secure congressional guarantees of full employment was, therefore, a major defeat in its attempt to represent all of the working classes and it instead fell victim to claims that labor merely protected unionists from non-union labor.[20]

It is unfair to suggest that white male workers were the backbone of organized labor while minorities, whether they were African American, Chicano, Asian, or women, constituted their unprotected adversaries. There are too many exceptions to this categorization to allow it to stand. Nonetheless, it is clearly true that the most vulnerable factions of the working class did come from these groups. The disproportionate incidence of poverty among minorities alone suggests that their experiences were, and continue to be, distinctly outside of the mainstream of American life. And while organized labor alone did not create that difference, its record vis-à-vis minorities had to be better. Whether because it promoted discriminatory immigration policies, eliminated apprenticeship to outsiders, created differential barriers to entry, or simply created artificial distinctions, organized labor delivered by giving its membership—more often than not, drawn from the white native or European male stock—something that non-members did not have. Until those distinctions between in and out groups were broken, organized labor could not claim to represent all workers.

Ultimately, two broad strategies existed for organized labor, just as two broad strategies existed for minorities. Each could separately seek its own accommodations with the prevailing capitalist order, or each could join forces against capitalism by working toward a socialist alternative. This alternative would be socialist in the sense that it represented all of productive society in opposition to what might be considered the unwarranted privileges and prerogatives of capital. If it had been unlikely before, Taft–Hartley and the expulsion of Communists in the AFL and CIO made this second alternative even more remote. Instead, the separate drives to achieve freedom within the capitalist order by minorities and by labor pit the two groups against one another at pivotal junctures.

Minorities and Labor

This description is not meant to imply that socialism was necessarily the better alternative to capitalist accommodation. Indeed, there is value in Milton Friedman's outdated argument that,

> the groups in our society that have the most at stake in the preservation and strengthening of competitive capitalism are those minority groups—the Negroes, the Jews, the foreign-born, to mention only the most obvious. Yet, paradoxically enough, the enemies of the free market—the Socialists and Communists—have been recruited in disproportionate measure from these groups. Instead of recognizing that the existence of the market has protected them from the attitudes of their fellow countrymen, they mistakenly attribute the residual discrimination to the market.[21]

Friedman's argument correctly accents the ability of competition to provide market choices when discrimination prevails. Yet, it fails to recognize both the personal nature of the market that limits the extent of discrimination-busting competition and the extent to which competition itself exacerbates inter-group rivalry. Still, it is not yet clear that the alternative path—class-based opposition—should be regarded as a more compelling strategy, particularly when modern history is rife with examples of the corruption of socialist enterprises that ultimately justified the elimination of economic opportunities for one minority or another because they were enemies of the state or of the collective good. The point here is not to choose between these two alternatives, but rather to emphasize that viable options that could bolster freedom became more difficult to implement once labor and minority groups began to articulate opposing strategies. While both strategies relied upon a conception of rights based on group experience, the similarity ends there. One advocated individual rights for excluded groups whereas the other sought rights to collective action for individuals who organized themselves. The collision of these two strategies brought existing contradictions within the law to a head.

American law has always had its contradictions, but the nature of these contradictions changed radically in the 1930s. Prior to this decade the law made individual liberty practically consonant with property ownership. Any economic regulation that limited the liberties associated with property was suspect as a class-based attempt to redistribute wealth. This mindset turned contract into a nearly sacred expression of the individual's liberty. It was the individual's right to dispose of his or her property or labor as he or she saw fit and it was the state's duty to enforce and protect that freedom. This arrangement turned discrimination into a personal, but quite legal, choice. After all, liberty of contract gave individuals the authority to decide when and with whom they conducted business.

Until the 1930s the Supreme Court continuously reiterated these conditions as the terms upon which American liberty was founded. Not until the famous 1938 case known as *Carolene Products,* did the Supreme Court recognize the legitimacy of an alternative conception of liberty in which individuals' rights apart from property and contract became important. In *Carolene* the Court reversed its prior direction by allowing states to regulate business whenever a "rational basis" for it could be found. Whether the Court agreed with that rationale was no longer the determining factor. Instead the Court came to terms with democracy and sanctioned the liberty of legislative majorities to make the law.[22] In this it acted contrary to the earlier Madisonian conceptions of rights, which were based upon fears that a tyranny of propertyless majorities might be imposed upon the wealthy few. The Court now restricted its review of the laws majorities enacted to those cases where they impaired the freedoms of "insular and discreet minorities," that is, precisely those who were denied such protection by the pre-existing liberty of contract regime.

This shift in judicial rulings marked the Court's realization that large-scale organizations had undermined the prevailing conceptions of individual liberty. Prejudice, as well as capital, had become incorporated into the key American institutions upon which individuals depended for economic success and independence. The most crucial of those institutions—corporations, unions, and schools—actively discriminated against minorities and women. By tolerating this private discrimination, the law winked at, and sometimes actively encouraged, the closure of the main roads to economic success. Although in *Carolene* the Court restricted its warnings to state-imposed discrimination, soon virtually all intra-group cooperation would be scrutinized for evidence of its collusive and coercive effects upon minorities.

Schooling was the most important arena in which states condoned active discrimination. Largely working outside the existing labor movement, the National Association for the Advancement of Colored People (NAACP) initiated legal actions designed to equalize opportunity. Poor education, they believed, was responsible for the large differences between white and black incomes. Notably, in 1940 the annual incomes of black males working full time were equivalent to just 40 percent of corresponding white incomes. The NAACP took the next logical step and sought to overturn the "separate but equal" doctrine protecting segregated public schools. In 1954, the Supreme Court in *Brown v. Board of Education* agreed with the NAACP and held that the Fourteenth Amendment's guarantee of "equal protection under the law" entitled blacks to admission to all public schools. Opening educational doors was one of two important factors, along with migration from the South to the North, that reduced the overall income gap between black and white males to 80 percent by 1980. The difference grew even smaller between individuals with equivalent experience and education.[23]

The Civil Rights Movement

The civil rights movement successfully altered the quantity and quality of human capital minorities brought to the market. Once active state discrimination in schooling was proscribed, rights activists turned their focus toward the residential housing patterns that contributed to segregated schools and school districts. Unlike *de jure* discrimination—unequal treatment enforced through the law—the pattern of *de facto* segregation created thornier problems. As late as 1964, southern housing patterns kept all but 2 percent of blacks from attending integrated schools. When blacks sought access to white schools through bussing, a renewed furor ensued. The relief of discrimination now required more than the mere repeal of laws, and instead necessitated proactive policy regulating a variety of otherwise private transactions, such as rental and real estate contracts. To enforce non-discriminatory standards, the Supreme Court, over which Chief Justice Earl Warren presided, had to eliminate the inviolability of contract.

As the civil rights agenda expanded, it became ever clearer that the northern states had also failed to assimilate African Americans. There, urban areas had their own segregated black neighborhoods characterized by decrepit housing stock, poor schools, and all-white police forces. Additionally, when focus shifted to the rampant trespass of constitutional rights of citizens of color—particularly violations involving search, seizure, arrest, and lack of due process—open expressions of bitterness increased within black communities. Radicals spoke out against an oppressive "system," no longer limiting themselves to attacks on specific laws. The failure of the mainstream labor movement to effectively champion civil rights left no viable coalition to prevent the deterioration in race relations that followed. Instead, as we will see, organized labor quickly became a major source of contention.

By the mid-1960s, militant blacks demanded greater access to public resources. Events and situations that in different times might have caused only protests now occasioned full-scale disruptions. In 1964 rioting broke out in many cities, the worst of which involved a four-day breakdown of order in Los Angeles's Watts district. Shooting, looting, and arson resulted in thirty-four deaths, hundreds of injuries, and damage to nearly one thousand buildings. Between the 1964 riots and the chaos occasioned by Martin Luther King's 1968 assassination, there were at least 329 separate incidents of violence in over 250 cities. Black Americans were increasingly alienated from white Americans, even from their former liberal friends. Militant demands succeeded in bringing change, but not accord.[24]

The structure of change was strongly influenced by the conservative Republican presidency of Richard Nixon. Seeking to shrink the Great Society initiatives of Lyndon Johnson, his Democratic predecessor, Nixon issued executive orders to institute a policy of affirmative action. Where Johnson, under the pressure of welfare reformists and other advocacy groups, had expanded economic entitlements, Nixon instead attempted to foster change without incurring significant federal expenditures. By requiring large government contractors to submit goals and timetables for hiring minority workers, in 1969 Nixon made the first dramatic move toward a policy of affirmative action. Nixon also endorsed a moderate civil rights agenda by offering to set aside government contracts and subsidies for minority-owned businesses. These targeted policies converted poverty into a minority affair—one whose solutions were implemented at the expense of the white majority.

Labor's failure to convincingly place black civil rights within the greater ambit of worker solidarity allowed Nixon to push through divisive half-measures. The president's actions, as well as those of the Warren Court before him, often promoted minority rights rather than universal standards for the poor and the disenfranchised. As the polarizing aspects of government's visible defense of these rights increased, Nixon retreated. He withdrew much of the patronage he had extended and attacked court enforcement of his own programs. Appealing to his natural political constituency, the "silent majority," Nixon devised a "Southern strategy" disavowing most state intervention on behalf of minorities.

While many individuals within organized labor actively supported civil rights legislation, labor unions became one of that movement's key targets. Construction unions, for example, were accused and convicted of restricting minority access to apprenticeships. Because many unions did use ethnicity to promote internal solidarity—"taking care of their own"—it became increasingly hard to argue that organized labor spoke for all working people. The New Deal alliance between minorities, the poor, and organized labor that had been the bulwark of the Democratic Party stood frayed and torn.

With the Democrats in disarray, employment law took a new direction. Prior attempts to balance the representatives of big business with representatives of big labor—a policy called corporatism—now proved dissatisfying. With progress toward universal workplace representation stalled, organized labor's only claim to represent the unorganized consisted of its promotion of minimum labor standards. A strategy that we have seen was truncated, on one side by its inability to ensure full employment and, on the other, by organizational imperatives that unions put their own members first. When minorities sought protection, the state and even corporate benefactors could appear more attractive as partners.

This form of pluralism, for that is what it became, did not completely avoid the pitfalls associated with state protection. Long before the civil rights movement, organized labor had learned that government protection would compromise its independence and turn labor into a ward of the state. Yet neither organized labor nor the civil rights movement had a real choice not to appeal to the state for their rights and entitlements. And, indeed, as the doubters had predicted, the state proved an unreliable guarantor of rights. Just as the Taft–Hartley Law withdrew state support from organized labor, so too would the pendulum swing against civil rights.

In the public eye affirmative action became a system of minority quotas designed to overturn objective standards of merit in allocating jobs and schooling. Its most hard-to-justify practices quickly became the most public ones. Race-norming, for example, infuriated many because it involved upward adjustments to qualification scores on tests taken by minority applicants. Although such practices were only used in order to counter past discrimination, they were widely believed to penalize white male applicants rather than the perpetrators of that prior discrimination. Not surprisingly, courts and politicians backed away from racial set-asides in colleges, in professional training, and in jobs. In part, this was the predictable backlash of a majority that had the power to overturn legislation that benefited the minority.

However, more than simple numbers were responsible for this retreat. After all, when the count was finished a majority of the population had become potential beneficiaries of some form of affirmative action. In addition to African American, the "insular" groups afforded protections expanded to include Hispanics, Native American males, and women, who alone constituted roughly 50 percent of the electorate. The backlash was instead a symptom of the weakness of the core alliances within the Democratic Party. The Democrats' close association with the nation's civil rights agenda contributed to two important party defections. The first was from southern voters. Lincoln's Republican victory over 100 years earlier had created the historical artifact that the South aligned itself with the Democrats. It did so despite the fact that its Dixiecrat block had little in common with their northern and western brethren. The second defection was that of the rank-and-file blue collar workers who had been the mainstays of the Democratic Party. The 1974 *Kaiser Aluminum v. Weber* case signaled latent tensions within the Democratic coalition. Brian Weber, a white steelworker, charged that an agreement by his employer, Kaiser, to set aside 50 percent of its training slots for minorities constituted "reverse discrimination."[25] White union men who identified with this issue increasingly looked to the Republican Party to reverse the tide. As they left the Democratic Party, so did many of their unions.

Equal opportunity and affirmative action programs were never predominantly about quotas, set-asides, or race-norming. Instead, civil rights leaders generally sought state solutions to foil past discrimination. They asked for broader recruitment and better employment practices. Civil rights leaders were concerned that irrelevant criteria and educational credentials were required for jobs. These requirements often left African Americans and other minorities at a disadvantage when their educational attainment levels suffered from long-standing inequalities. Few employers believed they could prudently disregard the "objective" credentials of their workers. The Court, however, required them to demonstrate that the hiring, promotion, and discipline criteria they used did not impose a disproportionate and unfair impact upon protected minorities. Thus the Court wanted to see proof that employment questionnaires, qualification lists, interview techniques, and promotion policies were demonstrably related to job performance.[26] As they complied, employment managers learned much that they had not known before. New procedures developed from this knowledge were often extended to a firm's entire work force. If good cause had to be shown before minorities were dismissed or denied promotions, other employees would demand no less. Rights to expect procedural fairness in employment became the basis of labor justice.

Organized labor was seriously undercut by the growth of minority rights and associated changes in employment law. Legislatively created labor watchdogs like the Equal Employment Opportunity Commission, the Occupational Safety Commission, and the Pension Guarantee Board freed workers from dependence upon the union hall. Redress for their grievances now came from government agents, not union officials. Workers found fewer reasons to undertake the time, risk, and expense of organizing themselves. Yet, without organization, workers had little political clout. Their legislative power was gradually chipped away and, with it, so too were the very laws and agencies upon which their success depended. Organized labor choked on the dust stirred up by the successes of the civil rights movement from the 1950s to the 1970s.

Freedom Under Increasingly Complex Conditions

In summary, the freedom of workers in the third quarter of the twentieth century was increasingly conditioned by a complex balance of active markets, state entitlements, judicial protections from the rights of property, and the collective powers of organized labor and capital. The situation was anything but tidy and had little aesthetic appeal as compared to the competing rhetorics of either free markets or class conflict. Instead, here was a pluralism that involved a messy overlay of competing interests and of forums in which to resolve discrepancies among those interests. The system was hard to explain and harder to justify. It could not claim to have eliminated injustice, but rather only to have moderated systematic abuses that offended major power groups. The only thing facile about the system involved the dissatisfactions it generated.

Labor and the civil rights movements created alternative understandings of freedom that were largely incompatible with one another. Unions and minorities both relied upon collective identities, but here the similarity stopped. Labor required freedom for groups to combine toward a common good. Such freedom necessarily involved the ability of groups to define themselves, act together, and exclude or boycott those who did not. Minorities, on the other hand, required the freedom not to be excluded on the basis of their minority identity. The dilemma of their situation was that recognition of collective identity was required in order to be rid of the constraints that identity imposed. Unlike the union agenda, the goal of the civil rights movement was to be defined not as a group, but as individuals.

Both abandoned naked individualism for its failure to recognize the actual power relations of groups. Both sought not to undo capitalism but to adjust it to their separate and conflicting needs. In embryo, the contradictory outcomes in the baseball and Hollywood boycotts demonstrate the difficulty of finding a general principle upon which to hinge the foundations of labor freedom.

Had labor been more secure, it might have been able to design a common good for majority and minority workers. Taft–Hartley, however, made sure that this was not the case. As it was, labor constantly had to satisfy its existing membership in order to maintain any power. Too often the result was shortsighted with respect to minority relations. Where it continued to hold power, labor continued to make the workplace its primary arena. Minorities succeeded more often on the school and training fronts. Without coordination, the new-found rights of these two groups failed to forge a coherent vision of freedom.

———— Chapter 9 ————

Playing the Global Piano

Anybody that competes with slaves becomes a slave.
—Kurt Vonnegut, *Player Piano*

Headlines from the 1990s make one scratch one's head in disbelief that this is actually the end of the twentieth century. On one day in 1993 we were told that 282 illegal Chinese immigrants were shipwrecked along the coast of New York where they were supposed to take work. It was reported that they would be paid approximately one dollar per hour. Worse, to pay off their passage the immigrants were to assume a status equivalent to that of indentured servants. On another day in August of 1995 it was reported that seventy-two Thai workers living in El Monte, California, were being held behind barbed wire in virtual slavery. They produced garments for a small sweatshop that received orders from brand-name clothiers. This type of subcontracting was used here and in other cases to provide large firms with cheap garments that can be manufactured without regard to compliance with state labor standards. On still another day, the documentary news program *60 Minutes* reported that migrant workers in some of Florida's orange groves were held against their will in debt peonage. These extreme cases illustrate some of the worst labor abuses afoot in the country. Such situations are most common among illegal immigrants who are afraid to protest for fear they will be deported. Although unusual, these and numerous other instances clearly indicate that unbridled capitalism has no great respect for human rights. Moreover, these examples underscore the threat that global competition poses for Americans at large.

In a world where it is alleged that children are increasingly being sold into slavery, where many poor Asian women are physically forced to prostitute themselves, and where Chinese prisoners produce toys for American toddlers, it is clear why the wholesale integration of global commerce rekindles protectionist sympathies. The fear is that trade will erode American labor standards. While some analysts, like Jeremy Rifkin and Paul Krugman, insist that America's diminished expectations owe less to international trade and more to the emergence of new technologies, the two phenomena are interconnected in a world where the nearly costless use of the internet can instantaneously search the globe for the cheapest resources and products available.[1]

Together the twin threats of technology and trade have made it possible to believe that the looming new millennium will challenge many rights that now form the basis of our freedom. Since the 1970s we have experienced a decline in real wages, a relative stagnation in our productivity, and a rapid dismantling of numerous large corporations upon which many workers had counted for their economic security.[2] These trends have given rise to a fear of uncontrolled immigration and trade, a dismay over government and taxes, and a general disillusionment toward involvement in public life. The result is a malaise that makes cynicism the currency of the land. Dilbert, the famed comic strip, is practically a symbol of our time as we become a nation that disbelieves in the prior premises of progress.

However, cynicism will not prevent decline; that can only be prevented with a clear understanding of the conditions under which our strivings for freedom have been sustained in the past and may yet be sustained in the future. In this regard it is important to realize that our challenges are not entirely new, but rather that what we experience today is an intensification of challenges we have previously met and partly mastered.

Technology

In 1801 the French perfected the Jacquard loom, a device that propelled scientific thinking about information processing. The loom automatically responded to wooden cards with holes in them indicating how the threads were to be woven. Like the player piano of today, automatic looms reduced complex patterns to raw storable data. Where the replication of these patterns had required the sure and steady hands of a skilled weaver, the Jacquard loom rendered the knowledge of that worker unnecessary. This invention, along with numerous others, contributed to the first industrial revolution. While it created untold new wealth, that revolution also produced massive dislocations upon traditionally ordered societies.[3] Just as the unleashing of new technologies has not abated since then, nor have the disruptions they cause.

The current information-processing revolution that extends this long tradition began after World War II. The vacuum tube Univac machine produced at the time was crude compared to today's personal computers. The size of these early machines, their computational limitations, the cumbersome nature of their binary coded computer languages, as well as the propensity of their tubes to overheat, limited their primary use to the calculation of ballistic trajectories for the military.

By the 1960s, however, IBM had developed a large main-frame computer that enabled automation of many processes. Reminiscent of the earlier Jacquard loom, key-punch operators filled computer cards with holes. Those holes contained the instructions that automated systematic components of work. In time, punch hole cards were replaced by computer terminals into which operators typed commands. Esoteric computer languages were used less and less frequently and commands began to resemble spoken English. By the early 1980s, computing was no longer restricted to big firms and academic think tanks. Businesses discovered countless new applications for the machines and an information revolution bloomed.

Had the computer simply remained a giant calculator, its usefulness would have been limited. However, programmers recast old problems so that machines could be used to govern production processes. Engineers provided computers with a host of crude sensory devices mocking those of their human creators. Scanners "recognized" bar codes that stood in the place of names. Heat sensors mimicked touch. Microphones translated sound waves into computer language. In short, computers systematically gained the capacity to perform tasks that had previously required human senses. In some instances their capabilities even exceeded those of human senses. For instance, unlike humans, computers can act as though they recognize infrared waves directly.[4]

The computer was not simply a tool, but an imitation person whose uneven capabilities sometimes outstripped those of its human counterparts. The impact of this was important. As a tool, computers would have to be guided by human agents who consciously controlled each calculation and task. As a sensory device, new capacities were grafted onto computers enabling them to operate autonomously from human operators. The roles separating person and machine were reversing. More and more computers came to direct the behavior of human agents. Although it ultimately remains true that computers only do what humans (correctly or incorrectly) program them to do, machines increasingly became management's eyes, ears, and mouth. To workers who receive their directions from computers, this change constitutes a huge shift in the relationship between labor and capital.

While this is not the first time that workers have felt themselves slaves to the tools or machines they wield, sensory-loaded machines intensify that feeling because they can explicitly direct the work process. Sensors recognize problems that are diagnosed by computer programs known as "expert systems." These programs feed information into management-constructed decision trees dictating the course of action workers should take. In the past, speed-ups on assembly lines pressured line workers to step up their pace, but the new wrinkle now is that machines actively instruct workers *how* to do their jobs.

The first stage in this cybernetic transformation of work involved the use of machines to monitor worker behavior. Machines that did this increased productivity by reducing the need for direct supervision. For instance, computers monitor the number of scans per minute by supermarket cashiers. Likewise, on-line inventory programs detect loss or theft of merchandise in retail establishments as soon as it happens. It is not the big brother of government, but the paternal eye of management that now provides constant surveillance of worker behavior.

Computer operators were some of the first workers to endure computerized supervisors. Human operators were used to submit jobs to the large mainframe computers of the 1960s and 1970s. These operators tended terminals that showed the queues of jobs in process, ready for input, or awaiting output. Glued to the screen of his or her control panel, the operator received signals from the computer when it was time to release the next batch of jobs for work. The operator retained control only in the sense that he or she could override computer instructions when he or she chose to. A second operator, however, had even less discretion. This operator was informed by the computer that it needed a new tape, another disk, or more paper. The "operator" became a lackey whose job it was to respond when the computer was unable to take care of its own physical needs. What earlier was the exception has become the rule today. Information age clerks are guided, prodded, or coerced into responding to computer messages telling them how and when to act.

When it is first applied to a new situation, the ability of computers to recognize problems and suggest solutions is generally inconsistent. As a consequence workers must augment the sensory capacity of computers, particularly when information is presented in irregular formats. Attempts to have scanners read and process handwritten checks, for example, have been only about 90 percent successful. The diagnosis of problems often requires that human intelligence be combined with sensory information. To take one example, hospitals have increasingly come to rely upon telephone nursing interventions that are guided by computerized medical diagnosis, but these programs cannot be counted on to gather all the clues available to trained human observers. The *Wall Street Journal* reported that one nurse "gauge[d] pain by watching how fast a drop of sweat formed on faces."[5] That same story exposed problems that can occur when computers exercise set routines while patients in agony become agitated by their irrelevant questions. Computers work best when work is routinized. Robots that perform a single identically repeated weld make good laborers. However, when complete routinization is absent, the human advantage consists in its flexibility, dexterity, and its ability to discern context. On the other hand, with a large enough scale of operations many irregular tasks can be broken down into batches of smaller tasks involving regular responses that can be performed by specialized robots.

With ingenuity, automated work keeps growing. There are mail order pharmacies where machines are given orders to fill prescriptions. Robots travel down aisles, find bar-coded shelves, and dispense the desired pills. This trend of events begs the question whether any human input at all will soon be necessary. As early as 1952, Kurt Vonnegut's novel *Player Piano,* ruminated about an automated society that deprived its workers of self-esteem and purpose.

Although workers have good reason to be ambivalent about the changes our computer-driven revolution is wreaking, that ambivalence should not necessarily progress to outright rejection. Even as it threatens worker autonomy, creativity, and security, new technology simultaneously opens possibilities for vast improvements in workplace conditions. Hopefully, for example, the most mind-deadening, physically grueling, and spirit-killing elements of work can soon be replaced by new technology.

Much mind-numbing labor that can be performed by rote is amenable to mechanization. The introduction of spinning machines, for example, eliminated the human effort that consisted primarily of adding a twist to a constant flow of wool or cotton. Automatic looms replaced the necessity of throwing a shuttle back and forth to weave fabrics. Steam and electric engines replaced human beings as a power source—one in which hands or feet were employed to push, prod, or rotate moving parts. Unfortunately, these mechanical innovations also created a new class of dead-end jobs consisting of tending or monitoring the machines that replaced human labor. Rotting away their youths as runners who fed machines or spotters who watched for breakdowns, in the nineteenth century untutored children were frequently so employed. These jobs were required because not all elements of the manufacturing process were susceptible to automation. There remained an almost impassable divide between the creative solution of problems and the drone work of monitoring or governing machines.

Even before computerization, inventors and engineers undertook the task of finding clever ways to substitute mechanical devices for repetitive mental work governing machine processes. For example, the cam shaft of a car controls the regular rotation of the four-cycle engine so as to open and close valves, allowing automatic intake, compression, combustion, and exhaust within the combustion chamber. In other instances, automatic governors and thermostats were deployed to monitor and control productive operations. Until the invention of computer chips, however, automatic regulators were the exception. More often, mechanical devices such as timers rang out signals to their human agents telling them to come and turn off a machine or change the flow of work. With computer chips, however, engineers were able to program sensors to signal problems that initiated appropriate responses without direct human interface. As long as the contingencies that interrupted the smooth flow of work could be fully anticipated, computational programs might be designed to operate without direct human labor. The quest to improve productivity aims not only at repetitive labor but now even seeks to reduce capital's dependence upon its own scientific and managerial agents, placing their jobs in jeopardy as well.

Although observers go too far when they suggest that all work is being debased, they are correct in noting that technology produces specialization and a minute division of labor. A finely honed division of labor, however, may be one in which much human capital is necessary. In medicine, for example, burgeoning technology and scientific advances mean health professionals are increasingly specialized. While their work is restricted to a smaller specialty, their training nonetheless requires protracted study of many related subjects. Similarly, aeronautical engineers specialize in very small portions of plane design, but they must still be able to call on very broad principles from numerous scientific fields.

What is happening in the broad picture is that manufacturing and extractive occupations are shrinking and service work is expanding. If we include government workers, it is roughly 80 percent of non-agricultural employees.[6] Much service work is menial, relatively unskilled, and poorly paid: such jobs include those of shelf stockers, hamburger flippers, and warehouse guards. The growth in low-paid service employments mops up those workers who have been displaced by higher-productivity manufacturing processes but whose training and background do not lend themselves to better alternatives. Boon or misfortune, it is not clear how such workers would fare if these jobs, which retain just enough variability to make the human touch necessary, were not available.

Much of the new service work resembles older factory work. Many typists, for example, are herded into large production facilities to translate handwriting and dictation into keystrokes. Although programmers have successfully employed computers in character recognition that automatically renders text into computer data, the vagaries of voice and handwriting cause enough irregularity that the demand for typists persists. However, the new typing pool can be a thoroughly oppressive environment in which outside contractors pump assignments into workers via computer. Output can be tallied electronically so as to compare typists' keystrokes to official quotas. More conventional technology enables management to scrutinize personal behavior on closed circuit cameras. To minimize worker distractions, one employer required employees to strip their desks bare. He even forbade his workers the pleasures of windows, turning around, or any other social inter-actions. Ron Edens, whose Electronic Banking Systems, Inc., employed these practices, explained, "I'm not paying people to chat. I'm paying them to open envelopes ... I don't want them looking out—it's distracting. They'll make mistakes."[7]

As an outlet for employment, low-skilled jobs are under constant attack. In many restaurants, the skill of reading has been replaced as cashiers peck away at registers that replace numbers by product icons. However, the need to observe the appearance of food going out, to take orders, and to collect money is just varied enough to require that workers continue to be em-ployed. But even these jobs clearly face assault as debit machines and change dispensers reduce the need for human money-changers. With ma-chines that enable waiters and waitresses to punch in their patrons' orders to the chefs, it is only a matter of time before cost-conscious diners skip their human intermediaries and talk directly to the kitchen. It is likely that waiter and waitress jobs persist only because our longing for personal service prevents their wholesale elimination. But that may change: from gas sta-tions to banks, customers are continually learning to service themselves with an intriguing array of odd mechanical devices.

For those workers whose education and background have prepared them to think abstractly, rewarding or mentally stimulating work is still available. For these individuals, new technology creates real possibilities for empow-erment. It is an empowerment that, in the pre-industrial era, farmers and artisans attained through the ownership of their land and businesses. As the information age reduces the cost of the capital necessary for independence, freelancers have at their disposal a world of new resources to help them operate businesses on their own. Rock bands, for example, can virtually produce their own records, tapes, and compact disks, freeing them from the need to subordinate themselves to recording companies. Likewise, crafts-men buy precision tools and bookkeeping software that enable them to compete with larger companies. Ready access to information deprives the large corporation of many of its advantages vis-à-vis their smaller competi-tors. By making it less expensive to contract out rather than hiring within a firm, inexpensive information attacks the conditions that favor large-scale enterprise.

Still, not everyone benefits equally from economic opportunities. Despite the open tracts of land that lay fallow waiting for settlers in the early nineteenth century, slaves, women, and unskilled factory operatives had few options providing genuine independence. Similarly, today's abundant infor-mation will only be deployed by those few who have the capability to access and use it. Today's bypassed slaves will be those whose training or resources render them unable to exploit the information age.

Whether in service or manufacturing, the uneven spread of computer power leaves behind many unskilled, repetitive, and low-paying jobs. This is the dubious legacy that our disadvantaged citizens stand ready to inherit. In 1994 the *Wall Street Journal* reported that the job of poultry worker was among the six fastest growing occupations. This repetitive, dirty, and hazardous job involves specialized tasks along a chicken disassembly line. These include live hanging, scalding, eviscerating, de-boning, and setting out the chickens on the drip-line. Live hanging is one of the most unpleasant of these tasks as it requires workers to "hitch incoming birds to shackles at a rate of 25 or more a minute. So strenuous that only a few can do it, live-hanging exposes workers to struggling birds that scratch, peck and defecate all over them."[8] Over 200,000 workers, mostly in the southeast portion of the country, labor nearly at the minimum wage in conditions that result in one occupational injury for every four workers each year. The odd sizes and combativeness of the birds pose just enough irregularity to permit low-wage humans to compete with high-priced computers.

Weak as the poultry workers' position may be, their jobs are more secure than those of many unskilled and semi-skilled workers. The poultry processing industry is relatively immobile because it is tied to the location of its resource. The popularity of chicken meat depends upon its relatively low cost, and consequently the product would not likely bear the high costs associated with overseas transportation. However, the same cannot generally be said for higher value items, particularly those with low weight or bulk relative to price. In the impersonal segment of the service market, low tariffs and easy telecommunications make imports more and more seductive. For example, the *Wall Street Journal* reported that the work of inexpensive Russian, Chinese, and even Bulgarian programmers is increasingly being transmitted to U.S. firms to substitute for well-paid domestic programmers who earn between $50,000 and 80,000 annually.[9] The expanding global market even permeates those services that hitherto had been regarded as immobile. While it is extremely costly to transport health services from one region to another, this has not stopped the globalization of health care. It is now reported that India's hospitals have improved so dramatically that they expect to compete with the West for the lucrative business of caring for the wealthy patients from Third World nations that lack good hospitals. Rather than ship the product to the buyer, the buyer is brought to the lowest cost seller. High wages and working standards in such human capital–intensive employments as medicine may be subject to increasing erosion due to global competition.

Global Trade and Competition

Governments are increasingly submitting their economies to the forces of transnational competition. It is a competition that threatens many existing American jobs. Free traders respond, that overall, the stimulus of trade will create more wealth than it destroys.

The acquiescence of national governments to the logic of the market is particularly evident in trade negotiations, which, over several decades, have continuously reduced tariffs. International agreements such as GATT (General Agreement on Tariffs and Trade) have reduced average tariff levels to a low 5 percent of the value of goods and services.[10] When the so-called Uruguay Round of trade talks was completed in 1994, it went even further by aiming to eliminate many non-tariff trade barriers such as import quotas, export subsidies, and bogus quality restrictions.

Even if the free traders are correct that the gains from trade will increase American wealth and jobs, we are not sure what kind of jobs these will be and who will get them. What is clear is that trade reductions have gradually brought about an ever greater economic interdependence among nations. Until recently, the United States, compared to other countries, had been relatively self-reliant with exports and imports. In 1970, for example, imports and exports together added up to 11 percent of the gross domestic product. By 1995 that figure had risen to 23 percent.[11] A good case may be made that governments must yield to the inevitable: they must either support international competition or find their exports undermined by countries that do. Either way, there is little security for workers in trade-based jobs. Even more significant is that trade-based jobs increase as the fundamental barriers of transportation, information, and communication become less formidable.

New telecommunications technologies have radically altered our notions of time and space. Now that the electronic factory can cheaply convey information from the workstation to the manager, distance is no longer the major natural obstacle to trade. Instantaneous communication with suppliers in Malaysia, India, or Mexico give the visible hand of management a far longer grasp than ever before. Where it once took weeks to visit foreign plants, now it takes a day and often it is not even necessary to be there in person as video-teleconferencing, electronic mail, and computer-generated reports provide instantaneous information. As multi-national firms gain hands-on control over far-off outposts, U.S. workers can be more easily disciplined. When they are expensive or unruly, it is not as difficult as it once was to import manufactured components.

Since the post–World War II era, decreased trade barriers and improved communications have been accompanied by a dramatic change in the distribution of U.S. income and jobs. Economic historians have dubbed the decade of the 1940s as the "great compression,"[12] a time when income inequality shrank dramatically. But this was also a time when Americans had a unique advantage. As the only major industrial nation not to fight that war on its own soil, this country's physical plant was preserved while those of Europe and Japan was destroyed. Large industrial concerns were able to pass that advantage along to workers by providing pay increases linked to general productivity indices. Unions created additional security for workers by establishing industrywide patterns that set wage standards ensuring no single U.S. firm enjoyed a significant cost advantage over any other. Consumers paid the higher bills without noticeable grumbling because there were no apparent alternatives. In areas such as transportation, government regulatory agencies fostered agreements to achieve price stability, high wages, and the elimination of cutthroat competition. Even international air transport was cartelized for these same purposes.

However, by the 1960s and 1970s all this was beginning to unravel. In what was a forerunner of things to come, British entrepreneur Freddie Laker avoided international agreements by flying chartered aircraft at rates below those offered by commercial airlines. Other carriers, like Icelandic Air, did the same. By the 1970s, economists of the left and the right joined the chorus of market-oriented analysts who derided government regulations that forced consumers to pay higher prices. The deregulation that followed was the harbinger of coming problems for well-paid pilots, machinists, and flight attendants.

Although formal cartels did not exist among auto, steel, and tire firms, the very small number of domestic producers in these industries made it possible to avoid intense price competition. This helped ensure high American wages for relatively unskilled assembly workers. However, by the 1960s, our European and Japanese competitors were getting back on their own feet. The outcome in the automobile industry was similar to that in many other industries. Germany began to penetrate the American market with large quantities of low-priced Volkswagen Beetles. Soon thereafter foreign cars from Italy, Sweden, France, Britain, and finally Japan penetrated the U.S. market. While the success of foreign car makers was instrumental in completing these foreign nations' rebound from the war, America's basic industries began to look sicker and sicker, making domestic labor standards increasingly vulnerable.

As trade began to threaten American industries and standards, labor found it could no longer depend upon the protection it counted on from Keynesian policy. Keynesian policymakers argued that unemployment could be avoided through appropriate government taxation and spending. Although the deliberate use of Keynesian stimulus to ensure full employment did not take hold until Kennedy used tax reductions to spur on a faltering economy in the early 1960s, by the Vietnam era, fiscal prescriptions were endemic in policy circles.[13] Shortly thereafter, for reasons independent of trade, reliance upon Keynesian policy began to unravel.[14]

Keynesian nostrums lost their allure when the budgetary strains of the Vietnam War were combined with President Lyndon Johnson's War on Poverty. Federal spending soared, and little pressure could be exerted to prevent inflation without causing a sharp rise in unemployment. By the 1970s, the U.S. government operated with seemingly permanent budget deficits. To accommodate these deficits and keep interest rates low, the Federal Reserve printed money. By the mid-1970s so much money was created that the resulting inflation made it harder to keep interest rates low. This, in turn, made it harder to keep unemployment from rising. As the late 1970s rolled in, the nation experienced a problem that Keynesian policy could not effectively control. Unemployment and inflation were rising at the same time.

The increasing disfavor of Keynesianism threw the labor movement into disarray at the exact moment when global competition was destroying its most important enclaves. Even if labor had wanted to turn toward Keynesianism, Keynesians had only short-term pain to offer as an answer to workers' long-term problems. Their solutions, like higher taxes, higher interest rates, or greater competitiveness, all threatened jobs and wages. There was no getting around these poor alternatives. Trade unions were left to advocate an anemic policy of trade restrictions. This was deeply unattractive to the larger public, which believed the labor community was asking it to pay more for goods of lesser quality in order to rescue the unions from a problem of their own making. Dissatisfaction with government made a policy of removing trade fetters more attractive to policy makers.

Problems with global trade only got worse when President Carter selected Paul Volcker to head the Federal Reserve Board. The appointment occurred just as policy talk was consumed by an escalating "misery index"—measured by adding the inflation rate to the unemployment rate. Volcker responded with an abrupt reduction in the growth of the money supply. The immediate result was higher interest rates and an escalation of the misery index to nearly 20 percent. This could only be followed by recession. But more important for the trade story is that the rapid increase in interest rates under Volcker were a sure recipe for an appreciation of the dollar that was bound to hurt American exports and export-related jobs.[15]

The interest rate problem only increased with the election of Ronald

Reagan. Reagan's candidacy was made possible only by the extent of the economic dislocations then underfoot. Before this point he had been regarded as too right-wing to be electable. Reagan succeeded with the voters by calling for a program of reduced government social expenditures, deep tax cuts, and increased military expenditures. Congress accommodated his requests. As it did so, the federal deficit spun out of control, interest rates continued to soar, and the nation moved into its worst depression since the 1930s.

In one respect Reagan's policies were successful. They broke the back of inflationary expectations. Workers no longer expected wage increases and contented themselves when new contracts merely maintained their wages. More often, concessionary bargaining forced workers to accept wage reductions, decreased benefits, and more onerous work rules. When Reagan fired striking air traffic controllers in 1981, workers understood that it would be a long time before old conditions were restored. Bloodletting continued for the first two years of Reagan's administration, and then the economy slowly began to improve. The improvement, however, consisted primarily of additional jobs, not higher wages.

As mentioned, the pressures from global competition intensified as the dramatic rise of interest rates in the early 1980s drove up the value of the dollar. Normally that would have been good news, but coming as it did, in the midst of a recession, the dollar's ascent meant that American exports were ever more expensive on the international market. An intense hollowing out of the industrial Midwest followed. Howls of protest resulted in agreements requiring foreign competitors to "voluntarily" restrict their exports. In place of their exports, companies like Honda and Toyota agreed to set up U.S. manufacturing firms in the United States. That increased the visibility of foreign systems of labor relations.

Trading Labor Relations Systems

Globalization took an unusual turn. Perplexed by our rapid industrial decline, Americans searched for new solutions. Japan and Germany became the focus of increasing attention.[16] Both nations had experienced considerable market expansion. The industrial relations in each nation stood in stark contrast to those found in America. Japan and Germany both put more emphasis upon skill and education than did the United States, albeit each in its own way. To compete globally, the United States not only had to produce better goods at a lower price, but in order to do so it had to consider imitating the labor institutions of its competitors.

Japan emphasizes formal schooling as a prerequisite to future opportunities. Students dread "Hell Week," a time when the nation's sixteen-year-olds take a single exam that will determine their educational future. Japan's emphasis upon testing makes education a great deal more important as compared with the United States. Subjects are studied more intensively and the school year is significantly longer.[17] High school graduates are said to have learned as much as college graduates in the United States. Japanese firms pay attention to educational credentials because broadly educated new recruits are easy to train and therefore raise their firms' productivity. Japanese firms mobilize worker skills in a number of ways, including inexpensive correspondence courses, quality circles, and by eliminating excessive specialization so that workers perform a variety of tasks on the job.

American economist Masanori Hashimoto suggests that Japanese employers provide more training to their workers than do their American counterparts because they couple lifelong employment with large annual bonuses.[18] This makes it possible for employers to secure high returns on their investments in skills. Because bonuses make up a considerable portion of the Japanese worker's compensation, wages can easily be reduced during cyclical downturns. In the United States, wage rigidity results in layoffs when the economy sours. In Japan, workers accept bonuses as a significant element of their compensation because lifelong employment guarantees that bad years are leveled out by good ones. More significantly, Japanese author Kazuo Koike suggests that frontline workers are "white collarized" in that they are trusted to make operating decisions.[19] Overall, despite paternalistic and authoritarian overtones, to Americans the Japanese system appears to generate a high degree of commitment and loyalty from each side of the labor bargain.

Germany differs from Japan by promoting craft mastery, not mere job flexibility. It is noted for its dual system of education and apprenticeship: About 60 percent of its workers learn trades on the job while attending school one day each week. These apprentices are given thorough instruction in their trade and in the context in which it is performed. Workers in clerical and retail trades, as well as those of the traditional crafts, have opportunities to undertake apprenticeships. The journeyman who completes an apprenticeship is well respected in Germany. In turn, workers participate more thoroughly in their firms, taking part in company works councils and sitting on boards of directors as mandated by national co-determination laws. These differences in their labor system are coupled with a strong social policy requiring generous benefits. German workers, for instance, are given six weeks of vacation. They work fewer hours per year than the labor force of any other major industrial country and they do this while maintaining high wages.

Germany and Japan differ from the United States in that they regard labor as their most important resource, one to be nourished and appreciated. As social scientists and business leaders learned more about these cultures, they became more articulate about America's problems. This nation, they complained, looked for easy short-term profits and neglected the long-term investments. This argument gained currency in the late 1980s as financial barons achieved notoriety by buying up long-established firms only to sell them off piece by piece. Junk bond specialists used borrowed money to buy up firms that were underperforming, sell off their non-productive assets, and saddle the remainder of the company with the debt created by the transaction. In the process, communities and workers faced complete upheaval. Meanwhile, large companies like IBM and AT&T made massive cuts in their blue and white collar work forces in an effort to down-size, or in the phrase of the times, to make themselves "lean and mean." Outspoken commentators like Peter Drucker publicly questioned the wisdom of buccaneer capitalism.[20]

First in a report called *A Nation at Risk*, and then in another entitled *Workforce 2000*, a series of alarms were sounded in the 1980s calling attention to the idea that our citizens were undereducated for tasks of effective global competition ahead. As the industrial base continued to shift from manufacturing to services it would require frontline workers capable of thinking critically. But it was not until the 1990s that the fundamental conditions underlying America's swashbuckling behavior had diminished. When inflation and interest rates were high, it did not pay to think about investments that yielded results only in the distant and uncertain future. As the economy stabilized, more firms found it advantageous to imitate foreign human resource policies. Although a few companies, like Motorola, had pioneered new skill investment policies in the 1970s, most had dragged their feet. Even Motorola was slow, not realizing until the mid-1980s the magnitude of the changes it needed to make in order to keep itself competitive.[21] In addition, spurred on by businessmen like David Kearns of Xerox, one state government after another began to look at ways to shore up floundering educational and training systems.

Difficulties in Maintaining International Leadership

As evidence mounts that real wages are at last inching forward, there are those who suggest that American business is once again competitive. For some, understanding the turnaround involved unraveling the great mystery underlying the productivity slowdown of the last twenty years. Many analysts failed to understand why the nation's investments in information-processing technology failed to increase productivity. By the 1990s, two answers were touted. The first was that industry needed to reorganize itself if its workers were to take advantage of the information age. The second was that productivity really was not as bad as we had thought because our measures of prices and output failed to account for vast quality improvements in many products.[22] However, it is now time to realize that U.S. progress was greater than it seemed, in part, because our global competitors soon became equally vulnerable to worldwide competition. Just when their economies appeared to have outstripped America's, Germany, Japan, and other industrialized countries faced their own setbacks.

While the quagmires within which the German and Japanese economies are presently stuck may, to American eyes, seem to represent some sort of exhilarating poetic justice, their longer-term implications are less sanguine. Japan's amazing advance noticeably began to come undone in 1989. In rapid succession, its stock market tumbled, its investments abroad began to drop, the competitiveness of many of its firms was eroded by the advancing value of the yen, and finally its unemployment rate began to rise. Paul Krugman declares that Japan's advance has actually been muted since 1973. Its rapid rates of growth occurred in the decade prior to 1973. Once Japanese wages and living standards began to approach those of the industrialized West, further gains became much more difficult to secure.[23] The distinctive features of Japanese management, like lifetime employment, have increasingly come to be seen as evidence of an inefficiently rigid institution to be overcome rather than praised. The loyalty of workers toward their firms is now challenged by the slower growth of exports, a slowdown that means companies can offer fewer opportunities for advancement. If worker loyalty is eroded, the turbulent labor relations Japan experienced in the two decades after the World War II could return. In the meantime, more Japanese are beginning to look longingly toward the United States, where market-driven companies approach labor much more flexibly and with much less commitment.

The case of Germany, too, is interesting. Although its immediate troubles are located in its idiosyncratic situation, fundamentally its problems stem from the same reality: global competition holds back any industrialized nation that gets too far out in front of the others. German problems can be traced to the country's firm support for the establishment of a single European currency. As an interim step, European Union countries agreed to coordinate their currency values. The arrangement is called "the snake." Nations may bend their respective exchange values, but they may not break off from each other. Thus, if the value of the mark rises relative to the dollar or the yen, so too must those of other European currencies. This created tremendous problems for Germany, and for Europe as a whole, as they headed into the 1990s. When the Berlin Wall fell in 1989, West Germany decided to subsidize the Eastern Republic in order to hasten a union and to prevent massive in-migration. Because German citizens resisted tax increases, the country had to borrow money to execute its rescue mission. Interest rates rose dramatically and, as had happened with the United States in the early 1980s, so too did its currency. As the mark rose in value, German workers had more purchasing power abroad. Another way of saying this, however, is that German wages rose. Germany suddenly faced its own de-industrialization crisis. Surrounded by the low-wage and low-price but high-skilled countries of the ex-Soviet block, German firms found it much more desirable to produce in and buy from those countries than to do so at home. Germany's unemployment rate has risen and its government is having difficulty paying for the extensive social programs it supports. The government has tried, with only partial success, to reduce the size of its social state and the commitments it made to its unions. Resistance has been fierce. Nonetheless, global competition appears to rebuff any nation that gets too far ahead of its neighbors.

The concessionary bargaining to which the United States submitted itself in the 1980s is now afoot internationally. Union battles in France and South Korea, where governments have attempted to withdraw their patronage for labor, provide the most visible examples of the process so far. In the present environment, it is hard to see how any economically advanced nation will be able to make rapid improvements in wages and living conditions. More likely, workers in the economically advanced nations will have to save more and innovate rapidly just to maintain their position vis-à-vis relatively low-wage but high-skill countries like Taiwan or the Czech Republic.

From an international perspective these trends may be desirable. Increasing competition could even out some of the vast inequities in the global distribution of income. From the perspectives of the United States and other industrialized nations there is increasing concern over how the gains from growth, which may be large, will be distributed. In the 1980s and 1990s, incomes have become more unequal in most nations. In part, this represents a scaling back of governmental commitments to equality. However, it also stems from vastly unequal conditions of competition facing individuals within nations.

The International Challenge to American Standards

Former labor secretary Robert Reich argues forcefully that Americans are being divided into three major classes: routine service producers, in-person service providers, and symbolic analysts. The condition of producers is worsening due to global competition. The fate of those providing in-person services, while not euphoric, will depend greatly upon the success of the symbolic analysts. The last class is comprised of individuals who can seize opportunities around the world to identify, broker, and solve problems. They are the engineers, consultants, and market analysts who know how to use information. The size of the routine service producing class will shrink and the rising in-person service sector will cater to the needs of symbolic analysts.

New technology creates information and resources that constitute a global piano upon which symbolic analysts play. Unfortunately, most Americans simply do not know how to program the keyboards to play their own tunes. Reich argues,

> All Americans used to be in roughly the same economic boat. Most rose or fell together, as the corporations in which they were employed, the industries comprising such corporations, and the national economy as a whole became more productive—or languished. But national borders no longer define our economic fates. We are now in different boats, one sinking rapidly, one sinking more slowly, and the third rising steadily.[24]

It is reasonable to fear that those in the sinking boats will only be able to earn their bread by surrendering the vestiges of their independence and becoming servants to the powerful.

The result is that Americans face a new challenge. Just as they earlier confronted the challenge of growing markets, of technology, of unfair and unfree competition, of contract, of paternalism, and of state repression, those same challenges are now writ large on the global level. The challenge lies in devising world labor standards that are compatible with our aspirations for freedom. It looms before us as an arduous process. Not having yet demonstrated mastery over these scores despite long years of practice within their own borders, the question now is whether American workers will have the stomach to confront the same difficult music all over again on a global basis.

Epilogue

Memories and Challenges

*I am not a Labor Leader; I do not want you to follow me or any-
one else, if you are looking for a Moses to lead you out of this
capitalist wilderness, you will stay right where you are. I would
not lead you into the promised land if I could, because if I could
lead you in, some one else would lead you out. YOU MUST
USE YOUR HEADS AS WELL AS YOUR HANDS, and get yourself out of your present condition.*

—Eugene V. Debs, 1910

I have tried to do two things in this text. One is to suggest that the quest for
abstract freedom will always be elusive: that our freedoms are always and
necessarily conditioned by nature, by law, and by society. I have also explored the nature of our freedoms in the hope that we can understand some
of the trade-offs involved when we change the conditions of our liberties.

When constraints weigh on us like shackles, we struggle against them
using the rhetoric of freedom and inalienable rights to rally our troops
around us. That rhetoric is a necessary part of change, but it is not a
substitute for reason. Ultimately, we must engage the material and social
conditions that restrict us if we are to devise institutions that are more free
than those we have today. This is an intellectual endeavor and it requires
that we explain why the usual blandishments regarding liberty of contract
are insufficient to enable us to achieve greater results. In this challenge we
face a long and rich intellectual tradition that has been used to constrain the
forces of change, and sometimes, it must be admitted, correctly so. Nonetheless, the proposition that liberty of contract has been insufficient in improving the position of workers is a proposition requiring an unblushing
defense.

History reminds us that collective action has been essential in our struggle for freedom. It also reminds us that collective action invariably threatens
individual liberties; that to act collectively is to attempt to bind individuals

to their larger group interest. When such attempts involve selective induce-ments they are generally not regarded as worrisome. The use of force, intimidation, or police power, however, raises more than eyebrows. Propo-nents of collective action must deal with both these worries. One defense is that the line between force and incentive is not clear, if it exists at all. As workers who have lost company housing during their strikes know, the denial of accustomed inducements can itself become coercion. A second defense is that overt force is more necessary when an unjust set of rights prevents peaceful resolution of grievances. This is another way of saying that in seeking redress we appeal to our "inalienable rights." Put more directly, whether it was the Civil War or the legislative enactments that northern majorities imposed upon the minority of slaveholders in their states, I have argued that to overthrow slavery required force. Similarly, to eliminate contracts that permit vestiges of slavery also requires legislative or judicial force. It is here, however, that we run into difficulties.

Why should individuals not be allowed to contract away their rights? To this, I would give two answers. The first is that the so-called "race to the bottom," is a real phenomenon. If it is true that free individuals cannot always compete effectively with slaves, we cannot count on competition alone to elevate the position of the working class. A second response is that we can do better. Even Adam Smith, the father of market-oriented thinking, argued that by nature humans are compassionate, empathetic beings. If desperation and want have driven the contracts of indentures, of debtors, of peons, and of many immigrants, then meaningful freedom for them depends upon the availability of alternatives other than destitution or degrading de-pendence. Although the worst conditions are as unlikely to trickle all the way up the socioeconomic ladder as are the best to trickle all the way down, the contracts our poorest citizens sign establish the foundations of freedom upon which our society builds.

This epilogue is not an open invitation to yield to every yearning for freedom or every expression of inalienable rights. In their name, collective action holds the power for ill, as well as for good. But we must learn to intelligently discuss when we can rely on voluntary contract and when we need collective action. The legacy of our race relations suggests the most glaring contradictions. On the one hand, the collective actions of workers have contributed to the most flagrant forms of discrimination. At the same time, voluntary contract will not do away with this, nor, perhaps more importantly, will it eradicate the prejudices that sustain it. Contemporary arguments that the impersonal nature of capitalism promotes individual freedom and diminishes the possibilities for discrimination miss the central point that the labor market is singularly personal in its workings. Such problems require a balance between liberties and restraints.

Labor markets produce an unusual constellation of forces that make it hard to distinguish between interdependence and dependence. That is precisely why the older tradition of equating independence—not voluntary contract—with freedom requires us to reformulate our concerns with greater sophistication. We must learn how to debate whether the specific liberties we yearn for merit the prices they exact. This is a challenge that the memory of history helps us to face.

Notes

Prologue

1. Selig Perlman, *A Theory of the Labor Class*, New York: Kelly, 1928. For more recent considerations, see Kim Voss, *The Making of American Exceptionalism: The Knights of Labor and Class Formation in the Nineteenth Century*, Ithaca: Cornell University Press, 1993; William E. Forbath, *Law and the Shaping of the American Labor Movement*, Cambridge: Harvard University Press, 1991, pp. 10–36.

2. Morton Horwitz, *The Transformation of American Law, 1780–1860–1960*, New York: Oxford University Press, 1992, and "The Historical Foundations of Modern Contract Law," *Harvard Law Review* 87, no. 5 (March 1974): 917–956.

3. Two modern versions of the exploitation thesis appear in Harry Braverman, *Labor and Monopoly Capital: The Degradation of Work in the Twentieth Century*, New York: Monthly Review Press, 1974; and Michael Burawoy, *Manufacturing Consent: Changes in the Labor Process under Monopoly Capital*, Chicago: University of Chicago Press, 1979.

4. See, George S. McGovern and Leonard F. Guttridge, *The Great Coalfield War*, Boulder: University of Colorado Press, 1996, pp. 20–21. For a more general treatment of the issues of control, see also Richard Edwards, *Contested Terrain: The Transformation of the Workplace*, New York: Basic Books, 1979.

5. Milton Friedman is now the classic exponent of this view. See *Capitalism and Freedom*, Chicago: University of Chicago Press, 1982; and, with Rose Friedman, *Free to Choose: A Personal Statement*, New York: Harcourt Brace Jovanovich, 1990.

6. For one of the earliest and best rationalizations of collective bargaining, see J.R. Commons, *The Legal Foundations of Capitalism*, Madison: University of Wisconsin Press, 1957. More recently, see the work of Richard Freeman and James Medoff, *What Do Unions Do?* New York: Basic Books, 1984.

7. For contemporary analyses of the failures of markets, see Robert Kuttner, *Everything for Sale: The Virtues and Limits of Markets*, New York: Knopf, 1997. One important and recent argument that law failed to adjust sufficiently to satisfy the needs of industrialization is found in Forbath's, *Law and the Shaping of the American Labor Movement*.

Chapter 1. Republican Soil

1. J.G.A. Pocock, *Politics, Language, and Time: Essays on Political Thought and History*, New York: Atheneum, 1971, p. 92. See also, generally, Gordon Wood, *The Radicalism of the American Revolution*, New York: Vintage, 1991.

2. Peter Laslett, *The World We Have Lost: England Before the Industrial Age*, 3d ed., New York: Macmillan, 1984, p. 38.

3. See, generally, Douglass North and Robert Thomas, *The Rise of the Western*

World: A New Economic History, Cambridge, England: Cambridge University Press, 1973.

4. Horwitz, "The Historical Foundations of Modern Contract Law," pp. 917–956.

5. Robert Steinfeld, *The Invention of Free Labor: The Employment Relation in English and American Law and Culture, 1350–1870,* Chapel Hill: University of North Carolina Press, 1991, p. 7.

6. David Galenson, *White Servitude in America: An Economic Analysis,* Cambridge: Cambridge University Press, 1981.

7. Stephen A. Epstein, *Wage Labor and Guilds in Medieval Europe,* Chapel Hill: University of North Carolina Press, 1991, p. 259.

8. John U. Nef, *Industry and Government in France and England, 1540–1640,* Philadelphia: American Philosophical Society, 1940.

9. Eugenie Leonard, *The Dear-Bought Heritage,* Philadelphia: University of Pennsylvania Press, 1965, p. 323; and Julia Cherry Spruill, *Women's Life and Work in the Southern Colonies,* New York: Norton, 1972, p. 245.

10. American Social History Project, *Who Built America? Working People and The Nation's Economy, Politics, Culture and Society,* vol. 1, New York: Pantheon Books, 1992, p. 144.

11. Robert J. Steinfeld, "Property and Suffrage in the Early American Republic," *Stanford Law Review* 41, no. 2 (January 1989): 335–376.

12. William Rorabaugh, *The Craft Apprentice, from Franklin to the Machine Age in America,* New York: Oxford University Press, 1986, pp. 16–31.

13. Edmund Morgan, *The Puritan Family: Religion and Domestic Relations in Seventeenth Century New England,* New York: Harper and Row, 1966, p. 123.

14. George Howard, *A History of Matrimonial Institutions,* Chicago: University of Chicago Press, 1904, p. 153.

15. See, generally, Jonathan R.T. Hughes, *The Governmental Habit: Economic Controls from Colonial Times to the Present,* New York: Basic Books, 1977.

16. Philip Greven, "Family Structure in Seventeenth Century Andover, Massachusetts," *William and Mary Quarterly* (April 1966): 244.

17. Daniel Smith, "Parental Control and Marital Patterns: An Analysis of Historical Trends in Higham, Massachusetts," *Journal of Marriage and the Family* (August 1973).

18. Wood, *The Radicalism of the American Revolution,* p. 60.

19. Ibid., p. 57.

20. For fruitful contrasts see, David Galenson, "Rise and Fall of Indentured Servitude in the Americas," *Journal of Economic History* 44 (March 1984): 1–25; *White Servitude in Colonial America;* Steinfeld, *The Invention of Free Labor;* and Horwitz, "Historical Foundations."

21. Galenson, "Rise and Fall of Indentured Servitude in the Americas," *Journal of Economic History* 44 (March 1984): 1–25.

22. Kenneth Stampp, *The Peculiar Institution: Slavery in the Ante-bellum South,* New York: Vintage, 1989, p. 22.

23. David W. Galenson, "Rise and Fall of Indentured Servitude in the Americas," *Journal of Economic History* 44 (March 1984): 1–25.

24. Adam Smith, *The Wealth of Nations,* New York: Modern Library Edition, 1937, p. 250.

25. *Reflections on the Revolution in France by Edmund Burke and The Rights of Man by Thomas Paine,* New York: Anchor, 1973, p. 71.

26. Saul K. Padover, ed., *James Madison, The Forging of American Federalism, Selected Writings,* New York: Harper Torchbooks, 1953, (Federalist Paper No. 10) p. 52.

27. See Samuel Bowles and Herbert Gintis, *Democracy and Capitalism: Property, Community and the Contradictions of Modern Social Thought*, New York: Basic Books, pp. 27–63.

Chapter 2. Contracting Liberties

1. Rorabaugh, *The Craft Apprentice, from Franklin to the Machine Age*, p. 36
2. Ibid., p. 32. Regarding women, see Mary Blewitt, "Conflict among Lynn's Shoemakers," in Eileen Boris and Nelson Lichtenstein, eds., *Major Problems in the History of American Workers*, Lexington: D.C. Heath, 1991, pp. 106–125; more generally, see Horwitz, "Historical Foundations."
3. Lance E. Davis, Richard Easterlin, and William Parker, eds., *American Economic Growth: An Economist's History of the U.S.*, New York: Harper and Row, 1972, pp. 138, 601.
4. Claudia Goldin, *Understanding the Gender Gap: An Economic History of American Women*, Oxford: Oxford University Press, 1990, pp. 60–66. Goldin notes that women were drawn into the labor market when their productivity exceeded their implicit household wage. Women earned under 30 percent of men's agricultural wages in 1820. In manufacturing, women's wages rose from, perhaps, 30 percent of male wages in 1815 to nearly 50 percent of male wages in 1850. Alice Kessler-Harris, *Out to Work, A History of Wage-earning Women in the United States*, Oxford: Oxford University Press, 1982, pp. 10–72, cites opportunities and problems confronting women in the early labor force. She argues that an ideology of domesticity made it difficult for women to work outside the home for wages. This left women more dependent. Regardless, it should be clear that the freedom to barter one's way toward greater freedom could not be prevented without elaborate socio-cultural inhibitions that thwarted the force of market logic.
5. Horwitz, "Historical Foundations."
6. For a statement of the problem and contradictions within it, see James B. Atleson, *Values and Assumptions in American Labor Law*, Amherst: University of Massachusetts Press, 1983, pp. 11–13. Steinfeld, *The Invention of Free Labor*, pp. 154–157. Says Steinfeld, "It is important to understand how thoroughly conservative and profoundly revolutionary this new legal model of employment was.... [B]y making the employer's possessory interest in the labor of his employee determinable at the will of the employee, and by eliminating the employer's coercive authority during the term of the relationship, the old relationship was almost completely transformed. The employer did continue to enjoy the legal right to command the labor he hired, but that right could not legally be enforced through corporal punishment. . . ." Steinfeld notes, however, that by eliminating formal dependence, old doctrines, such as the responsibility of the master to care for workers in time of sickness, came undone. See also, Daniel Jacoby, "The Legal Foundations of Human Capital Markets," *Industrial Relations* 30, no. 2 (Spring 1991): 229–250.
7. Steinfeld, *The Invention of Free Labor*, p. 57, describes the nature of status relationships and incidentally reveals their vulnerability.
8. Alexis de Tocqueville, *Democracy in America*, vol. 2, New York: Vintage, 1990, p. 181.
9. Jean-Jacques Rousseau, *The Social Contract* and *Discourses*, G.D.H. Cole (trans), New York: E.P. Dutton, 1950; John Locke, *Two Treatises of Government*, London: J.M. Dent; Rutland, VT: C.E. Tuttle, 1990.
10. See, generally, Stampp, *The Peculiar Institution*.

11. Alexis de Tocqueville, *Democracy in America,* vol. 1, New York: Vintage, 1990, p. 361.

12. Daniel Rodgers, *Work Ethic in Industrial America, 1850–1920,* Chicago: University of Chicago Press, pp. 1, 31. Jonathan A. Glickman, *Concepts of Free Labor in Antebellum American,* New Haven: Yale University Press, 1991, pp. 12–14, points out some of the anomalies with regard to the North's free labor ideology.

13. Robert Fogel, *Without Consent or Contract: The Rise and Fall of American Slavery,* New York: Norton, 1989, p. 248.

14. See, generally, Eric Foner, *Free Soil, Free Labor, Free Men: The Ideology of the Republican Party,* Oxford: Oxford University Press, 1970; and Harold M. Hyman and William M. Wiecek, *Equal under Law: Constitutional Development 1835–1875,* New York: Harper, 1982. The first tells the story in terms of conflicting ideology and the second in terms of conflicting sectional laws.

15. Hyman and Wiecek, *Equal under Law,* pp. 173–174.

16. Gerald Gunderson, "The Origin of the America Civil War," *Journal of Economic History* (December 1974); Claudia Goldin, "The Economics of Emancipation," *Journal of Economic History* (March 1973).

17. Tocqueville, *Democracy in America,* vol. 1, p. 360.

18. Ibid., p. 366.

19. Robert Fogel and Stanley Engerman, *Time on the Cross: The Economics of American Negro Slavery,* Boston: Little, Brown, 1974, pp. 58–102.

20. Ibid., pp. 196–199.

21. Fogel and Engerman's *Time on the Cross* is responsible for publicizing most of the revisionist view of slavery. Their analysis is not, however, without its critics. A unified critique can be found in Paul David, Herbert Gutman, Richard Such, and Gavin Wright, *Reckoning with Slavery,* Oxford: Oxford University Press, 1976. Much of the debate centers on data interpretations and upon the generalizability of Fogel and Engerman's sources, which overrepresent large slaveholders. But twenty years later, in *Without Consent or Contract,* Robert Fogel garnered enough support to justify a largely unapologetic stance.

22. Fogel, *Without Consent or Contract,* and Fogel and Engerman, *Time on the Cross.* Ultimately, their main point is that slavery is, by itself, morally wrong. They have had some difficulty convincing their critics of this because of their insistence on revising the draconian picture of master–slave relationships that existed. What needs more emphasis in their account is not that every slave was brutally treated, but that slaves were always vulnerable to such treatment and had no recourse when it occurred. This absence of legal standing is what makes slavery morally repugnant.

23. Claudia Goldin, *Urban Slavery in the American South,* Chicago: University of Chicago Press, 1976.

24. Tocqueville, *Democracy in America,* vol. 1, p. 363.

25. Frederick Douglass, *Life and Time of Frederick Douglass,* New York: Collier Books, 1962, pp. 76–87

26. For an opposing view, see Elizabeth Fox-Genovese and Eugene Genovese, *Fruits of Merchant Capital: Slavery and Bourgeois Property in the Rise and Expansion of Capitalism,* Oxford: Oxford University Press, 1983, pp. 59–60. Earlier, Eugene Genovese, *The Political Economy of Slavery: Studies in the Economy and Society of the Slave South,* New York: Vintage, 1967, p. 17, had made the point that capitalism depended upon qualitative change brought about through investment and expansion of capital, whereas slavery could persist through the quantitative expansion of labor and land as inputs.

27. Milton and Rose Friedman, *Free to Choose.*

28. Stampp, *The Peculiar Institution,* p. 89.

29. Steinfeld, "Property and Suffrage in the Early American Republic."

30. Stephen Mayer, "People v. Fisher: The Shoemakers' Strike of 1833," *New York Historical Quarterly* 62, no. 1 (1978): 6.

31. For a classic treatment, see, generally, Norman Ware, *The Industrial Worker, 1840–1860: The Reaction of American Industrial Society to the Advance of the Industrial Revolution,* Boston: Houghton Mifflin, 1924. For a more contemporary treatment, see Sean Wilentz, *Chants Democratic: New York City and the Rise of the American Working Class, 1788–1855,* New York: Oxford University Press, 1984.

32. Mayer, "People v. Fisher," p. 8.

33. Adam Smith, *Theory of Moral Sentiments,* Indianapolis: Liberty Classics, 1976, p. 162.

34. American Social History Project, *Who Built America,* vol. 1, pp. 334–335.

35. Kenneth Stampp, *The Peculiar Institution,* p. 65; Patricia Schechter, "Free and Slave Labor in the Old South: The Tredegar Ironworkers' Strike of 1847," *Labor History* 35, no. 2, (Spring 1994): 165–187.

36. Arthur Schlesinger, *The Colonial Merchants and the American Revolution,* New York: Ungar, 1957, p. 170.

37. *Commonwealth v. Hunt* 45 Mass, 111 (1842).

38. Clarence Danhof, "Farm Making Costs and the Safety Valve: 1855–60," in Vernon Carstenson, ed., *The Public Lands,* Madison: University of Wisconsin Press, 1963.

39. Louis Hartz, *Economic Policy and Democratic Thought: Pennsylvania, 1776–1860,* New York: Quadrangle, 1968, p. 222.

40. Peter Coleman, *Debtors and Creditors in America,* Madison: State Historical Society of Wisconsin, 1974, p. 245

41. *Ogden v. Saunders* 25 U.S. 213 (1827).

42. Hartz, *Economic Policy,* p. 223.

43. Galenson, "Rise and Fall of Indentured Servitude."

44. Farley Grubb, "The End of European Immigrant Servitude in the United States: An Economic Analysis of Market Collapse, 1772–1835," *Journal of Economic History* 54, no. 4 (December 1994): 794–825.

45. *Trask v. Parsons* 7 Gray 473, 478 (1856).

Chapter 3. The Properties of Labor

1. See, generally, David R. Roediger, *The Wages of Whiteness, Race and the Making of American Working Class,* London: Verso, 1991.

2. Jenifer Roback, "Southern Labor Law in the Jim Crow Period: Exploitative or Competitive?" in *Labor Law and the Employment Market, Foundations and Applications,* eds. Richard A. Epstein and Jeffrey Paul, New Brunswick, NJ: Transaction Books, 1985. However, it is important to note that the North imposed draconian vagrancy laws that virtually criminalized poverty. See David Montgomery, *Citizen Worker: The Experience of Workers in the United States with Democracy and the Free Market During the Nineteenth Century,* Cambridge: Cambridge University Press, 1993.

3. Herbert Hovencamp, *Enterprise and American Law 1836–1937,* Cambridge: Harvard University Press, 1991, particularly pp. 116–124. William Forbath, "The Ambiguities of Free Labor: Labor and the Law in the Gilded Age," *Wisconsin Law Review* (1985): 767–817; Robert A. Burt, *The Constitution in Conflict,* Cambridge: Harvard University Press, Belknap Press, 1992, particularly Ch. 7, pp. 233–267; Harold Hyman

and William M. Wiecek, *Equal Justice under Law;* J. R. Commons, *The Legal Foundations of Capitalism.*

4. David Montgomery, *Beyond Equality, Labor and the Radical Republicans 1862–1872,* p. 381, argues that Thomas Cooley is responsible for converting Field's ruling into a "substantive" right. See also Hovencamp, *Enterprise and Law,* pp. 223–224; Commons, *Legal Foundations,* pp. 13–15.

5. Hyman and Wiecek, *Equal Justice under Law,* pp. 435–436, 475–480.

6. Ibid., but note that Morton Horwitz, *Transformation of American Law, 1870–1960, The Crisis of Legal Orthodoxy,* Oxford: Oxford University Press, 1990, p. 158, argues it is a mistake to give the increasing judicial activism a new name. He argues the courts' positions were little changed from before; the change instead lay in the scope of their application.

7. It is usual to cite *Lochner v. New York* 198 U.S. 45 (1905) as the crowning decision invoking Substantive Due Process. Here, a maximum hour law for bakers was rejected despite the state's argument that long labor affected the public health.

8. Sean Wilentz, *Chants Democratic,* pp. 57–59; Stephen Mayer, *"People v. Fisher,"* pp. 6–21; Mary Blewitt, "Conflict among Lynn's Shoemakers," pp. 106–125.

9. Alan Dawley, *Class and Community, The Industrial Revolution in Lynn,* Cambridge: Harvard University Press, 1976, p. 93.

10. William Mulligan, "From Artisan to Proletarian: The Family and Vocational Education of Shoemakers in the Handicraft Era," in *Life and Labor, Dimensions of American Working-Class History,* eds. Charles Stephenson and Robert Asher, Albany: SUNY Press, 1986.

11. Wilentz, *Chants Democratic,* pp. 57–59.

12. Don Lescohier, "The Knights of St. Crispin, 1867–1874: A Study of Industrial Causes of Trade Unionism," *Bulletin of the University of Wisconsin,* no. 355 (1910): 38–48.

13. Ibid., pp. 60–61.

14. Ibid., p. 76.

15. Dawley, *Class and Community,* pp. 144–148.

16. *Walker v. Cronin* 107 Mass 55 (1871).

17. Ibid.

18. *Hitchman Coal and Coke v. Mitchell* 245 U.S. 229 (1917).

19. *Snow v. Wheeler* 113 Mass 185 (1873).

20. See, generally, Roger Ransom and Richard Sutch, *One Kind of Freedom, The Economic Consequences of Emancipation,* Cambridge: Cambridge University Press, 1977; Kenneth Stampp, *The Era of Reconstruction, 1865–1977,* New York: Vintage, 1965; Robert Higgs, *Competition and Coercion, Blacks in the American Economy, 1865–1914,* Cambridge: Cambridge University Press, 1977.

21. Roback, "Southern Labor Law in the Jim Crow Period."

22. *Plessy v. Ferguson* 163 U.S. 537 (1896). See Charles Black, "The Lawfulness of the Segregation Decisions," *Yale Law Journal* 69 (1960).

23. Ransom and Sutch, *One Kind of Freedom,* pp. 44–47.

24. Higgs, pp. 122–123. The methodology is discussed from pp. 95–117. There is controversy over the extent of black gains. Higgs, though he argues he is being conservative, lies on one end of the continuum. Harold Woodman, "Sequel to Slavery: The New History Views the Postbellum South," *Journal of Southern History* 43 (1977): 523–554, argues Higgs uses a faulty competitive model to discuss growth. Woodman finds Ransom and Sutch's discussion more appropriate. However, even they note that black incomes rose. The difference is that they find these incomes to have grown on a one-time basis as a result of emancipation. They argue that inefficient institutions—

often tied to race—kept the South from growing. Woodman argues that Higgs's assertion that the South grew economically largely results from the choice of endpoints from which he measures economic growth.

25. Montgomery, *Beyond Equality*, p. 238. See also David Brody for an account of the earlier hour struggles in the United States, "Time and Work During American Industrialism," in *In Labor's Cause: Main Themes on the History of the American Worker*, Oxford: Oxford University Press, 1993.

26. Ibid., p. 238.

27. *Muller v. Oregon* 208 U.S. 412 (1908).

28. *In re Jacobs* 98 NY 98 (1885).

29. Forbath, *Law and the Shaping of the American Labor Movement*, pp. 39–40.

Chapter 4. A Skillful Control: Managing the Labor Process

1. For a fuller treatment, see David Montgomery, *Beyond Equality: Labor and the Radical Republicans, 1862–1872*, Urbana: University of Illinois Press, 1981, pp. 230–260.

2. See, generally, Daniel Nelson, *Managers and Workers: The Origins of the Twentieth Century Factory System in the United States, 1880–1920*, 2d ed., Madison: University of Wisconsin Press, 1995; Sidney Pollard, *Genesis of Modern Management*, Cambridge: Harvard University Press, 1965; Stuart Brandes, *American Welfare Capitalism, 1880–1940*, Chicago: University of Chicago Press, 1970; Harry Braverman, *Labor and Monopoly Capital*.

3. Nelson, *Managers and Workers*, pp. 35–55.

4. See, for example, *Coppage v. Kansas* 236 U.S. 1, 17 (1915). In upholding the validity of yellow dog contracts, the Court noted, "No doubt, wherever the right of private property exists, there must and will be inequalities of fortune . . . parties negotiating a contract are not equally unhampered by circumstances . . . it is from the nature of things impossible to uphold freedom of contract and the right of private property without at the same time recognizing as legitimate those inequalities of fortune that are the necessary result of the exercise of those rights."

5. Samuel Gompers, *Seventy Years of Life and Labor: An Autobiography*, New York: E.P. Dutton, 1925, pp. 44–45.

6. Ibid., p. 43.

7. David Montgomery, *Workers Control in America*, Cambridge: Cambridge University Press, 1979, p. 13.

8. Gompers, *Seventy Years*, p. 161.

9. Voss, *The Making of American Exceptionalism*, p. 219.

10. James Beek, *30,000 Locked Out*, Chicago: 1887, pp. 170–179.

11. Daniel Jacoby, "Plumbing the Origins of American Vocationalism," *Labor History* 37, no. 2 (Spring 1996): 264.

12. Charlotte Erickson, *American Industry and the European Immigrant*, Cambridge: Harvard University Press, 1957, pp. 47–48, 141; See also, Daniel Creamer, "Recruiting Contract Laborers for Amoskeag," *Journal of Economic History* (May 1941): 54–56.

13. Gompers, *Seventy Years*, pp. 21–22.

14. Erickson, *American Industry*, p. 141. For a similar case, see Yuzo Murayama, "Contractors, Collusion, and Competition: Japanese Immigrant Railroad Laborers in the Pacific Northwest, 1898–1911," *Explorations in Economic History* 21 (1984): 290–305.

15. *Machinists Monthly Journal*, November 1905.

16. Carlos Schwantes, "Unemployment, Disinheritance and the Origins of Labor Militancy in the Pacific Northwest, 1885–86," *Western Historical Quarterly* (1982).

17. New York Bureau of Labor Statistics, *Annual Report,* 1886, p. 399.

18. See Daniel Jacoby, "The Transformation of Industrial Apprenticeship in the United States," *Journal of Economic History* 51, no. 4 (Winter 1991): 887–910.

19. Gompers, *Seventy Years,* p. 108.

20. Nathan Rosenberg, *Technology and American Economic Growth,* New York: Harper, 1972, pp. 98–107.

21. Martin Segal, *The Rise of the United Association: National Unionism in the Pipe Trades, 1884–1924,* Cambridge: Harvard University Press, 1970, pp. 3–5.

22. David Brody, *Steelworkers in America: The Non-Union Era,* New York: Harper & Row, 1960, pp. 50–54.

23. David Brody, "The American Worker in the Progressive Era," in *Workers in Industrial America,* p. 6. Brody points out that in 1910 unskilled workers actually fell as a percentage of the labor force. Skilled workers rose from 28 percent to 30.5 percent and semi-skilled operatives also increased from 36 percent to 39 percent of the labor force. However, in the leading firms, like Ford, the process of "homogenizing" the workplace toward semi-skilled operatives went much further. See David M. Gordon, Richard Edwards, and Michael Reich, *Segmented Work, Divided Workers: The Historical Transformation of Labor in the United States,* Cambridge: Cambridge University Press, 1982, pp. 133; and, Charles Stephenson, "There's Plenty Waitin' at the Gate: Mobility, Opportunity and the American Worker," in Charles Stephenson and Robert Asher, eds., *Life and Labor: Dimensions of Working-Class History,* Albany: SUNY Press, 1986. Stephenson argues that upward mobility, though not pervasive, was real enough to make it believable.

24. Herbert Hovencamp, *Enterprise and American Law,* pp. 221–224.

25. Gordon, Edwards, and Reich, *Segmented Workers,* pp. 136–141. See, generally, Peter Doeringer and Michael Piore, *Internal Labor Markets and Manpower Analysis,* Lexington, MA: D.C. Heath, 1971; Sanford Jacoby, *Employing Bureaucracy: Managers, Unions, and the Transformation of Work in American Industry, 1900–1945,* New York: Columbia University Press, 1985.

26. Wilentz, *Chants Democratic,* p. 123.

27. Montgomery, *Workers Control,* p. 11.

28. Alfred Chandler, *The Visible Hand, The Managerial Revolution in American Business,* Cambridge: Harvard University Press, Belknap Press, 1977, pp. 62–78.

29. Ibid., pp. 81–187.

30. Murayama, "Contractors, Collusion, and Competition."

31. David Wellman, *The Union Makes Us Strong: Radical Unionism on the San Francisco Waterfront,* Cambridge: Cambridge University Press, 1996, p. 60.

32. Edwards, *Contested Terrain,* pp. 52–54.

33. Fredrick W. Taylor, *Shop Management,* New York: Harper, 1911, p. 35.

34. See, generally, Braverman, *Labor and Monopoly Capital.*

35. Nelson, *Managers and Workers,* makes it clear that Taylor's version of scientific management was not broadly applied, in part because of its exacting nature and, in part, because his followers had their own variations. Nonetheless, even if it does not fully accord with its inventor's own ideas, Taylorism has become the label for the broad movement toward the systematization of management. Fordism and Taylorism are often, though incorrectly, considered interchangeable.

36. In this context, it is useful to note that not everyone railed against Fordism or Taylorism. Gary Cross, "Redefining Workers' Control: Rationalization, Labor Time and Union Politics in France, 1900–1928," in James Cronin and Carmen Sirianni, eds., *Work Community and Power: The Experience of Labor and Europe and America, 1900–1925,*

Philadelphia: Temple University Press, 1983, demonstrates that Taylorism was viewed as part of a constructive socialist vision of the state that would increase French productivity. Likewise, Sidney Hillman of the Amalgamated Clothing Workers also adapted Taylorism so long as its imperatives could be controlled by industrial democracy. See Steve Fraser, "The 'New Unionism' and the 'New Economic Policy,' " also in Cronin and Siranni, eds.

Chapter 5. Incorporating Paternalism

1. Davis, Easterlin, and Parker, eds. *American Economic Growth*, p. 199.
2. Chandler, *The Visible Hand*, pp. 321–326. For developments in corporation law more generally, see Horwitz, *The Transformation of American Law, 1870–1960*, pp. 65–107; Hovencamp, *Enterprise and American Law*, pp. 246–251
3. For general information on establishment size by employees see, Gordon, Edwards, and Reich, *Segmented Work*, p. 116–118; also, Edwards, *Contested Terrain*, p. 23.
4. Thomas N. Maloney and Warren C. Whatley, "Making the Effort: The Contours of Racial Discrimination in Detroit's Labor Markets, 1920–1940," *Journal of Economic History* 55, no. 3 (September 1995): 465–494.
5. Stanley Lebergott, *The Americans: An Economic Record*, New York: Norton, 1984, p. 369; and Davis, Easterlin, and Parker, *American Economic Growth*, pp. 61–88.
6. U.S. Census, *Historical Statistics for the United States*, Series D, Tables 735–738.
7. Ibid., Tables 722–727.
8. See David Montgomery, *Fall of the House of Labor: The Workplace, the State, and American Labor Activism, 1865–1925*, Cambridge: Cambridge University Press, 1989, pp. 328, 453, for a cogent analysis that takes the point of view that repression crippled labor's resistance. David Brody, *Workers in Industrial America: Essays on the 20th Century Struggle*, Oxford: Oxford University Press, 1980, provides the best statement of the converse position. Dana Frank, *Purchasing Power: Consumer Organizing, Gender, and the Seattle Labor Movement, 1919–1929*, Cambridge: Cambridge University Press, 1994, provides a carefully balanced discussion, see particularly, pp. 247–251.
9. See, generally, Almont Lindsey, *The Pullman Strike: The Story of a Unique Experiment and a Great Labor Upheaval*, Chicago: University of Chicago Press, 1942.
10. Ibid., pp. 61–86
11. Ibid., p. 50.
12. Brandes, *American Welfare Capitalism;* Brody, *Workers in Industrial America*.
13. Robert Ozanne, *A Century of Labor–Management Relations at McCormick and International Harvester*, Madison: University of Wisconsin Press, 1967.
14. Ibid. p. 39.
15. Forbath, *Law and the Shaping of American Labor*, p. 16.
16. Ibid., pp. 39–42.
17. Walter Licht, "The Dialectics of Bureaucratization: The Case of 19th Century American Railway Workers," in Stephenson and Asher, eds., *Life and Labor*.
18. Davis, Easterlin, and Parker, eds., *American Economic Growth*, p. 220.
19. Steven Fraser, *Labor Will Rule: Sidney Hillman and the Rise of American Labor*, New York: Free Press, 1991, pp. 129–130. Montgomery, *Fall of the House of Labor*, discusses the role of the National Civic Federation with regard to mediation, p. 279.

Dubofsky, *The State and Labor in Modern America,* pp. 37–60, discusses labor's relationship with the state during the Progressive Era.

20. Dubofsky, *The State and Labor in Modern America,* pp. 74–81.

21. James E. Cronin, "Labor Insurgency and Class Formation: Comparative Perspectives on the Crisis of 1917–1920 in Europe," in Cronin and Sirianni, eds., *Work, Community and Power.*

22. Joseph A. McCartin, " 'An American Feeling': Workers, Managers, and the Struggle Over Industrial Democracy in the World War I Era," in Nelson Lichtenstein and Howell John Harris, eds., *Industrial Democracy in America: The Ambiguous Promise,* Cambridge: Cambridge University Press, 1996, pp. 80–81

23. *Adkins v. Children's* 43 Sup. Ct. 394 (1923).

24. On industrial democracy, see generally Lichtenstein and Harris, eds., *Industrial Democracy in America.*

25. This account relies upon George S. McGovern and Leonard F. Guttridge, *The Great Coalfield War;* Irving Bernstein, *The Lean Years, A History of the America Worker, 1920–1933,* Boston: Houghton Mifflin, Sentry Edition, 1972, pp. 157–164; David Montgomery, *The Fall of the House of Labor: The Workplace, the State, and American Labor Activism, 1865–1925,* New York: Cambridge University Press, 1985, pp. 341–356.

26. David Brody, *In Labor's Cause,* New York: Oxford University Press, 1993, pp. 139–144.

27. Montgomery, *The Fall of the House of Labor,* p. 350.

28. Ozanne, *A Century of Labor–Management Relations,* p. 120.

29. Ibid., p. 142.

30. Brody, *Workers in Industrial America,* p. 78.

Chapter 6. Free Education

1. Stephenson, "There's Plenty Waitin' at the Gate."

2. Maris Vinovski, "Horace Mann and Economic Productivity," in *Education, Society, and Economic Opportunity: A Historical Perspective on Persistent Issues,* New Haven: Yale University Press, 1995, pp. 99–102.

3. David Tyack, "Ways of Seeing: An Essay on the History of Compulsory Schooling," *Harvard Educational Review* 46, no. 3 (August 1976): 355–389.

4. Useful background on this subject is contained in Lawrence Cremin, *The Transformation of the School: Progressivism in American Education 1876–1957,* New York: Vintage, 1964; David Tyack, *The One Best System: A History of American Urban Education,* Cambridge: Cambridge University Press, 1974; Sam Bowles and Herbert Gintis, *Capitalism and Schooling,* New York: Basic Books, 1976; Ira Katznelson and Margaret Weir, *Schooling for All, Class, Race and the Decline of the Democratic Ideal,* New York: Basic Books, 1985; Martin Carnoy and Henry Levin, *Schooling and Work in the Democratic State,* Palo Alto: Stanford University Press, 1985.

5. Forest Ensign, *Compulsory School Attendance and Child Labor,* Iowa City: Athens Press, 1921.

6. Diane Ravitch, *The Great School Wars, New York City, 1805–1973: A History of the Public Schools as Battlefield of Social Change,* New York: Basic Books, 1974, pp. 33–76.

7. Lawrence M. Friedman, "Freedom of Contract and Occupational Licensing 1890–1910, A Legal and Social Study," *California Law Review* 53 (1965): 487–534.

8. Stanley Aronowitz and William DiFazio, *The Jobless Future: Sci-Tech and the*

Dogma of Work, Minneapolis: University of Minnesota Press, 1994, pp. 1–56.

9. Edward Bellamy, *Looking Backward,* New York: Signet, 1960, (first published, 1887), p. 151.

10. Ibid., p. 30.

11. Edward Bemis, "The Relation of Trade Unions to Apprentices," *Quarterly Journal of Economics* 6 (October 1891): 76–93; James M. Motley, "Apprenticeship in American Trade Unions," *Johns Hopkins University Studies in Historical and Political Science* 25 (1907), pp. 9–123; Paul Douglas, *American Apprenticeship and Industrial Education,* New York: Columbia University Press, 1921.

12. Jacoby, "Plumbing the Origins of American Vocationalism."

13. Ibid., pp. 252–253

14. Jacoby, "The Transformation of Industrial Apprenticeship," pp. 889–890.

15. Jacoby, "Plumbing the Origins of American Vocationalism," p. 243.

16. Ibid., p. 250.

17. Voss, *American Exceptionalism,* p. 232, suggests, "American industrial relations and labor politics are exceptional because in 1886 and 1887 employers won the class struggle."

18. Laurence Veysey, *The Emergence of the American University,* Chicago: University of Chicago Press, 1965, pp. 21–56.

19. Allan Nevins, *Abram S. Hewitt: With Some Account of Peter Cooper,* New York: Harper & Brothers, 1935.

20. Cremin, *Transformation of the School,* pp. 26–34.

21. Bellamy, *Looking Backward,* p.101

22. Ibid., p. 59.

23. Ibid., p. 93.

24. Henry George, *Protection or Free Trade,* New York: Schalkenbach, 1886, pp. 268–269.

25. Henry George, *The Standard,* Editorials on April 9, 1887, and December 31, 1887.

26. Nevins, *Abram S. Hewitt,* pp. 578–583.

27. Arthur Lipow, *Authoritarian Socialism in America: Edward Bellamy and the Nationalist Movement,* Berkeley: University of California Press, 1982.

28. Thorstein Veblen, *The Engineers and the Price System,* New Brunswick, NJ: Transaction Books, 1983.

29. Bellamy, *Looking Backward,* p. 152.

30. George Sylvester Counts, *Selective Character of American Secondary Education,* Chicago: University of Chicago Press, 1922.

31. John Dewey, *Democracy and Education,* New York: Macmillan, 1963, pp. 316–317.

32. Stephen Jay Gould, *The Mismeasure of Man,* New York: Norton, 1981. See also for recent commentary, Steven Fraser, ed., *The Bell Curve Wars: Race Intelligence and the Future of America,* New York, Basic Books, 1995.

33. Tyack, *One Best System,* p. 221.

34. Freeman and Medoff, *What Do Unions Do?* p. 53. Temporarily, unions did have a high differential (46 percent) in the early 1930s when the Great Depression severely cut the wages of almost everyone else. Education data culled from Herman P. Miller, "Annual and Lifetime Income in Relation to Education, 1937–1959," pp. 155–158 in H.C. Riker, ed., *Investment in Human Capital,* Columbia: University of South Carolina Press, 1971, pp. 155–158.

35. James Smith and Finis Welch, "Black Economic Progress after Myrdal," *Journal of Economic Literature* 27, no. 2 (June 1989): 519–564.

Chapter 7. Union Compromise

1. Robert Higgs, *Crisis and Leviathan: Critical Episodes in the Growth of American Government*, Oxford: Oxford University Press: 1987, pp. 3–20; Friedrich A. Hayek, *The Road to Serfdom*, Chicago: University of Chicago Press, 1944.

2. See, generally, Melvyn Dubofsky, *The State and Labor*.

3. Ronald W. Schatz, "From Commons to Dunlop: Rethinking the Field and Theory of Industrial Relations," in Lichtenstein and Harris, eds., *Industrial Democracy in America*, pp. 87–112.

4. Ibid., p. 96.

5. Fraser, *Labor Will Rule*, p. 50.

6. Ronald Coase, "Theory of the Firm," *Economica* (1937). For a more radical interpretation of management, see Stephen Marglin, "What Do Bosses Do? The Origins and Function of Hierarchy in Capitalist Production," *Journal of Radical Political Economy* 6, no. 2 (Summer 1974).

7. Fraser, *Labor Will Rule*, p. 33.

8. Nelson, *Managers and Workers*, pp. 35–55.

9. Fraser, *Labor Will Rule*, p. 51.

10. Ibid., p. 73.

11. James Atleson, "Wartime Labor Regulation: The Industrial pluralists, and the Law of Collective Bargaining," in Lichtenstein and Harris, eds., *Industrial Democracy in America*.

12. See, generally, Melvyn Dubofsky, *We Shall Be All: A History of the IWW*, New York: Quadrangle, 1969.

13. James Zetka, *Militancy, Market Dynamics and Workplace Authority*, Albany: SUNY Press, 1995, pp. 34–35, gives a good illustration of how workers viewed their rights to use shop-floor militancy.

14. Richard Epstein, "In Defense of Contract at Will," in Richard Epstein and Jeffrey Paul, eds., *Labor Law and the Employment Market*, New Brunswick, NJ: Transaction Books, 1985; Jay M. Feinman, "Development of the Employment at Will Rule, American," *Journal of Legal Studies* 20 (1976).

15. Albert O. Hirschman, *Exit, Voice, and Loyalty*, Cambridge: Harvard University Press, 1971.

16. John Rhea Dulles and Melvyn Dubofsky, *Labor in America: A History*, 4th ed., Arlington Heights, IL: Harlan Davidson, 1984, pp. 278–300.

17. Irving Bernstein, *The Turbulent Years: A History of the American Worker, 1933–1941*, Boston: Houghton Mifflin, Sentry Edition, 1969, pp. 448–498.

18. Atleson, "Wartime Labor Regulation," p. 149.

19. David Oshansky, "Labor's Cold War: The CIO and the Communists," in Eileen Boris and Nelson Lichtenstein, eds., *Major Problems in the History of the American Workers*, pp. 510–524. In the same volume, see also, Robert Korstad and Nelson Lichtenstein, "How Organized Black Workers Brought Civil Rights to the South," pp. 475–485.

20. David Brody, "Workplace Contractualism, Historical/Comparative Analysis," in *In Labor's Cause*, pp. 221–250.

21. Brody, *Workers in Industrial America*, pp. 173–214. For a larger discussion of the labor–management accord that stemmed from the UAW conflicts see Barry Bluestone and Irving Bluestone, *Negotiating the Future: A Labor Perspective on American Business*, New York: Basic Books, 1992; Zetka, *Militancy, Market Dynamics and Workplace Authority*.

Chapter 8. "Rights" of Passage

1. Friedman, *Capitalism and Freedom,* p. 21.
2. For discussions of the economics of discrimination, see Gary Becker, *The Economics of Discrimination,* 2d ed., Chicago: University of Chicago Press, 1971; Thomas Sowell, *Ethnic America, A History,* New York: Basic Books, 1981; and Higgs, *Competition and Coercion.* These economists summarize the market-oriented position on discrimination.
3. Gordon, Edwards, and Reich, *Segmented Work,* p. 141, illustrates the position of left-wing economists. According to them, the segmentation of workers by race and gender was an important part of capital's success. This involved, "corporate policies toward ... involv[ing] the manipulation of racial and ethnic differences among workers." More recently, Ronald Takaki, *A Different Mirror: A History of Multicultural America,* Boston: Little, Brown, 1993, makes similar points with graphic examples.
4. Takaki, *A Different Mirror,* p. 252.
5. David R. Roediger, *The Wages of Whiteness,* p. 10. Roediger calls for an analysis that recognizes that race as well as class has its own dynamics. He argues that race has been central to the mentality of the white working class since this nation started. Michael Kazin, *The Barons of Labor: San Francisco Building Trades and Union Power in the Progressive Era,* Urbana: University of Illinois Press, 1989, pp. 145–176, draws a similar conclusion for the San Francisco building trades workers. Likewise, Daniel Cornford, "California Workingmen's Party in Humboldt County," in Daniel Cornford ed., *Working People of California,* Berkeley: University of California Press, 1995, illustrates how race permeated the thinking of those in the Workingmen's Party of California during the late nineteenth century. See also Jim Gregory, "Okies and the Politics of Plain-Folk Americanism," also in Cornford's volume, pp. 116–158.
6. Roback, "Southern Labor" in *Labor Law,* pp. 217–248.
7. Maloney and Whatley, "Making the Effort," pp. 465–494.
8. James D. Anderson, "The Historical Development of Black Vocational Education," in Harvey Kantor and David Tyack, eds., *Youth, Work and Schooling,* Stanford: Stanford University Press, 1982.
9. Herbert Biberman, *Salt of the Earth: The Story of a Film,* Boston: Beacon Press, 1965, p. 13.
10. Ibid., p. 13.
11. Friedman, *Capitalism and Freedom,* p. 21.
12. Ibid., p. 20.
13. For an insightful example, see Gregory Zieren, "The Boycott and Working Class Solidarity, Toledo, Ohio in 1890s," in Stephenson and Asher, eds., *Life and Labor.*
14. Robert H. Zieger, *The CIO, 1935–1955,* Chapel Hill: University of North Carolina Press, 1995, p. 255. Although Zieger maintains "Rank-and-file Communists exhibited a passionate commitment to their conception of social justice. As a group Communists and their close allies were better educated, more articulate, and more class conscious than their counterparts in the CIO," he nonetheless takes the view that expulsion of Communist-led unions from the CIO was the correct and necessary path to take because of the politics of Stalin's party, toward which American Communists turned a blind eye. Zieger is taken to task for this by Bruce Nelson, "Zieger's CIO: In Defense of Labor Liberalism," *Labor History* 37, no. 2 (Spring 1996): 161–162.
15. Michael Honey, *Southern Labor and Black Civil Rights: Organizing Memphis Workers,* Urbana: University of Illinois Press, 1993, p. 243.
16. Jack Cargill, "The Salt of the Earth Strike," in Robert Kern ed., *Labor in New*

Mexico: Unions Strikes and Social History since 1881, Albuquerque: University of New Mexico Press, 1983, pp. 183–267; see also, *Jencks v. U.S.* 353 U.S. 657 (1957).

17. William Puette, *Through Jaundiced Eyes: How the Media Views Organized Labor,* Ithaca: ILR Press, 1992, makes the case that media sympathy evaporated as soon as labor lost its underdog status.

18. Victor Navasky, *Naming Names,* New York: Viking, 1980, pp. 199–222; and Brian Neve, "On the Waterfront (Film in Context)," *History Today,* 45, no. 6 (June 1995): 19–25.

19. Mancur Olson, *The Logic of Collective Action: Public Goods and the Theory of Groups,* Cambridge: Harvard University Press, 1971, p. 85.

20. Herbert Stein, *The Fiscal Revolution in America,* Chicago: University of Chicago Press, pp. 197–204; see also, Walter Salant, "The Spread of Keynesian Doctrines and Practices in the United States," in Peter Hall, ed., *The Political Power of Ideas,* Princeton: Princeton University Press, 1989, pp. 45–48.

21. Friedman, *Capitalism and Freedom,* p. 21.

22. Robert Burt, *The Constitution in Conflict,* Cambridge: Harvard University Press, Belknap Press, 1992, pp. 265–267; Horwitz, *Transformation of American Law 1870–1960,* pp. 252, 258; both regarding *United States v. Carolene Products* 304 U.S. 144 (1938).

23. Smith and Welch, "Black Economic Progress after Myrdal," pp. 519–564.

24. Thomas Byrne Edsall with Mary D. Edsall, *Chain Reaction: The Impact of Race Rights and Taxes on American Politics,* New York: Norton, 1992, p. 51.

25. Ibid., pp. 199–200.

26. Thaddeus Holt, "Personnel Selection and the Supreme Court," in Kenneth Perlman, Frank L. Schmidt, and W. Clay Hamner, eds., *Contemporary Problems in Personnel,* 3d ed., New York: Wiley, 1983, pp. 38–51.

Chapter 9. Playing the Global Piano

1. Jeremy Rifkin, *The End of Work: The Decline of the Global Labor Force and the Dawn of the Post-Market Era,* New York: Tarcher Putnam, 1995, p. 8. See also Richard Freeman, "Are Your Wages Set in Beijing?" *Journal of Economic Perspectives* 9, no. 3 (Summer 1995): 15–31. For varying perspectives see also, in the same issue, J. David Richardson, "Income Inequality and Trade: How to Think, What to Conclude," pp. 35–55, and Adrian Wood, "How Trade Hurt Unskilled Workers," pp. 57–80.

2. See, generally, Bennett Harrison and Barry Bluestone, *The Great U-Turn: Corporate Restructuring and the Polarizing of America,* New York: Basic Books, 1988.

3. For good discussions of the industrial revolution, see David S. Landes, *The Unbound Prometheus: Technological Change 1750 to the Present,* Cambridge: Cambridge University Press, 1972; and Joel Mokyr, *The Lever of Riches: Technological Creativity and Economic Progress,* Oxford: Oxford University Press, 1990.

4. Aronowitz and DiFazio, *The Jobless Future: Sci-Tech and the Dogma of Work,* particularly Part 1, does a excellent job discussing the impact of technology on professional workers. For solid discussions of the impact of technology on the transformation of work, see, generally, Shoshanna Zuboff, *Work in the Age of the Smart Machine: The Future of Work and Power,* New York: Basic Books, 1984; Braverman, *Labor and Monopoly Capital;* and Rifkin, *The End of Work.*

5. George Anders, "How Nurses Take Calls and Control the Care of Patients from Afar," *Wall Street Journal,* February 4, 1997, p. 1.

6. Office of Economic Advisors, *Economic Report of the President, 1996,* Washing-

ton, DC: U.S. Government Printing Office, 1996, Table B-42, p. 327.

7. "Mr. Edens Profits from Watching His Workers Every Move," *Wall Street Journal,* December, 1994, p. A11.

8. Tony Horwitz, "9 to Nowhere," *Wall Street Journal,* December 1, 1994. p. A1, col. 6.

9. Pascal Zachary, "U.S. Software: Now It May Be Made in Bulgaria," *Wall Street Journal,* February 21, 1995, p. B1, col 3.

10. Paul Bairoch, *Economics and World History: Myths and Paradoxes,* Chicago: University of Chicago Press, 1993, p. 35.

11. Office of Economic Advisors, *Economic Report,* 1996, p. 225.

12. Claudia Goldin and Robert Margo, "The Great Compression: The Wage Structure in the U.S. at Mid-Century," *Quarterly Journal of Economics* 107, no. 1 (February 1992): 1–32.

13. See, generally, Stein, *The Fiscal Revolution in America.*

14. Salant, "The Spread of Keynesian Doctrines," in Peter Hall, ed., *The Political Power of Ideas,* pp. 49–51.

15. See, generally, Benjamin Friedman, *Day of Reckoning,* New York: Vintage, 1989; and David Calleo, *The Bankruptcy of America: How the Federal Budget Is Impoverishing the Nation,* New York: Avon, 1992.

16. As examples, see Lester Thurow, *Head to Head: The Coming Economic Battle among Japan, Europe, and America,* New York: Morrow, 1992; Jeffrey Garten, *A Cold Peace: America, Japan, and Germany and the Struggle for Supremacy,* New York: Times Books, 1992; Ray Marshall and Marc Tucker, *Thinking for a Living: Education and the Wealth of Nations,* New York: Basic Books, 1992; and Stephen Hamilton, *Apprenticeship for Adulthood: Preparing Youth for the Future,* New York: Free Press, 1990.

17. Thomas P. Rohlen, *Japan's High Schools,* Berkeley: University of California Press, 1983.

18. Masanori Hashimoto, "Firm Specific Human Capital as a Shared Investment," *American Economic Review* 71 (June 1981).

19. Kazuo Koike, "Human Resource Development and Labor–Management Relations," in Kozo Yamamura, ed., *Political Economy of Japan,* vol. 1, Stanford: Stanford University Press, 1987.

20. Peter Drucker, "Corporate Takeovers—What Is to Be Done?" *Public Interest* 82 (Winter 1982): 3–24.

21. William Wiggenhorn, "Motorola U: When Training Becomes an Education," *Harvard Business Review* (July–August 1990): 71–83.

22. See James K. Galbraith, "Self-Fulfilling Prophets: Inflated Zeal at the Federal Reserve," *American Prospect* 18 (Summer 1994): 31–40; Peter Gottschalk, "Inequality, Income Growth, and Mobility: The Basic Facts," *Journal of Economic Perspectives* 11, no. 2 (Spring 1997): 21–40.

23. Paul Krugman, *Pop Internationalism,* Cambridge: MIT Press, 1996, pp. 178–180. Regarding other Asian tigers, particularly Singapore and Hong Kong, Krugman asserts most of their growth has been achieved through increased use of inputs rather than greater efficiency.

24. Robert Reich, *The Work of Nations,* New York: Vintage Knopf, 1992, p. 208.

Bibliography

American Social History Project. *Who Built America? Working People and The Nation's Economy, Politics, Culture and Society.* Vol. 1. New York: Pantheon Books, 1992.

Anderson, James D. "The Historical Development of Black Vocational Education," in Harvey Kantor and David Tyack, eds., *Youth Work and Schooling, Historical Perspectives on American Vocationalism.* Stanford: Stanford University Press, 1982.

Aronowitz, Stanley, and William DiFazio. *The Jobless Future, Sci-Tech and the Dogma of Work.* Minneapolis: University of Minnesota Press: 1994.

Atleson, James B. *Values and Assumptions in American Labor Law.* Amherst: University of Massachusetts Press, 1983.

———. "Wartime Labor Regulation, the Industrial Pluralists, and the Law of Collective Bargaining," in Nelson Lichtenstein and John Howell Harris, eds. *Industrial Democracy in America: The Ambiguous Promise.* Cambridge and New York: Cambridge University Press, 1996.

Bairoch, Paul. *Economics and World History: Myths and Paradoxes.* Chicago: University of Chicago Press, 1993.

Becker, Gary. *The Economics of Discrimination.* 2d ed. Chicago: University of Chicago Press, 1971.

Beek, James. *30,000 Locked Out.* Chicago: Press of the Franz Gindele Printing Co., 1887.

Bellamy, Edward. *Looking Backward.* New York: Signet, 1960.

Bemis, Edward. "The Relation of Trade Unions to Apprentices," *Quarterly Journal of Economics* 6 (October 1891): 76–93.

Bernstein, Irving. *The Lean Years: A History of the America Worker, 1920–1933.* Boston: Houghton Mifflin, Sentry Edition, 1972.

———. *The Turbulent Years: A History of the American Worker, 1933–1941.* Boston: Houghton Mifflin, Sentry Edition, 1969.

Biberman, Herbert. *Salt of the Earth: The Story of a Film.* Boston: Beacon Press, 1965.

Blewitt, Mary. "Conflict among Lynn's Shoemakers," in Eileen Boris and Nelson Lichtenstein, eds., *Major Problems in the History of American Workers,* Lexington, MA: D.C. Heath, 1991, pp. 106–125.

Bluestone, Barry, and Irving Bluestone. *Negotiating the Future: A Labor Perspective on American Business.* New York: Basic Books, 1992.

Boris, Eileen, and Nelson Lichtenstein, eds. *Major Problems in the History of American Workers.* Lexington, MA: D.C. Heath, 1991.

Bowles, Samuel, and Herbert Gintis. *Capitalism and Schooling.* New York: Basic Books, 1976.

———. *Democracy and Capitalism: Property, Community and the Contradictions of Modern Social Thought.* New York: Basic Books, 1986.

Brandes, Stuart. *American Welfare Capitalism, 1880–1940*. Chicago: University of Chicago Press, 1970.

Braverman, Harry. *Labor and Monopoly Capital: The Degradation of Work in the Twentieth Century*. New York: Monthly Review Press, 1974.

Brody, David. *In Labor's Cause: Main Themes on the History of the American Worker*. Oxford: Oxford University Press: 1993.

———. *Steelworkers in America: The Non-Union Era*. New York: Harper Torchbacks, 1960.

———. 1980. *Workers in Industrial America, Essays on the 20th Century Struggle*. Oxford: Oxford University Press, 1980.

Burawoy, Michael. *Manufacturing Consent: Changes in the Labor Process under Monopoly Capital*. Chicago: University of Chicago Press: 1979.

Burke, Edmund. *Reflections on the Revolution in France and The Rights of Man by Thomas Paine*. New York: Doubleday Anchor, 1973.

Burt, Robert A. *The Constitution in Conflict*. Cambridge: Harvard University Press, Belknap Press, 1992.

Calleo, David. *The Bankruptcy of America: How the Federal Budget Is Impoverishing the Nation*. New York: Avon, 1992.

Cargill, Jack. "The Salt of the Earth Strike," in Robert Kern, ed., *Labor in New Mexico: Unions Strikes and Social History since 1881*. Albuquerque: University of New Mexico Press, 1983, pp. 183–267.

Carnoy, Martin, and Henry Levin. *Schooling and Work in the Democratic State*. Stanford: Stanford University Press, 1985.

Chandler, Alfred. *The Visible Hand: The Managerial Revolution in American Business*. Cambridge: Harvard University Press, Belknap Press, 1977.

Coase, Ronald. "Theory of the Firm," *Economica* (1937).

Coleman, Peter. *Debtors and Creditors in America*. Madison: State Historical Society of Wisconsin, 1974, p. 245

Commons, J.R. *The Legal Foundations of Capitalism*. Madison: University of Wisconsin Press, 1957.

Cornford, Daniel. "California Workingmen's Party in Humboldt County," in Daniel Cornford ed., *Working People of California*, Berkeley: University of California Press, 1995, pp. 287–310.

———. ed. *Working People of California*, Berkeley: University of California Press, 1995.

Counts, George Sylvester. *Selective Character of American Secondary Education*. Chicago: University of Chicago Press, 1922.

Creamer, Daniel. "Recruiting Contract Laborers for Amoskeag," *Journal of Economic History* (May 1941).

Cremin, Lawrence. *The Transformation of the School: Progressivism in American Education 1876–1957*. New York: Vintage, 1964.

Cronin, James E. "Labor Insurgency and Class Formation: Comparative Perspectives on the Crisis of 1917–1920 in Europe," in James E. Cronin and Carmen Sirianni, eds., *Work, Community and Power: The Experience of Labor in Europe and America, 1920–1925*. Philadelphia: Temple University Press, 1983.

Cronin, James E., and Carmen Sirianni, eds. *Work, Community and Power: The experience of Labor in Europe and America, 1920–1925*, Philadelphia: Temple University Press, 1983.

Cross, Gary. "Redefining Workers' Control: Rationalization, Labor Time and Union Politics in France, 1900–1928," in Cronin and Sirianni, *Work Community and Power: The Experience of Labor and Europe and America, 1900–1925*. Philadelphia: Temple University Press, 1983.

Danhof, Clarence. "Farm Making Costs and the Safety Valve: 1855–60," in Vernon Carstenson, ed., *The Public Lands,* Madison: University of Wisconsin Press, 1963.

David, Paul, Herbert Gutman, Richard Such, and Gavin Wright. *Reckoning with Slavery.* Oxford: Oxford University Press, 1976.

Davis, Lance E., Richard Easterlin, and William Parker, eds. *American Economic Growth: An Economist's History of the U.S.* New York: Harper and Row, 1972.

Dawley, Alan. *Class and Community: The Industrial Revolution in Lynn.* Cambridge: Harvard University Press, 1976.

Dewey, John, 1916. *Democracy and Education.* New York: Macmillan, 1963.

Doeringer, Peter, and Michael Piore. *Internal Labor Markets and Manpower Analysis.* Boston: Lexington, 1971.

Douglas, Paul. *American Apprenticeship and Industrial Education.* New York: Columbia University Press, 1921.

Douglass, Frederick. *Life and Time of Frederick Douglass.* New York: Collier Books, 1962.

Drucker, Peter. "Corporate Takeovers—What Is to Be Done?" *Public Interest* 82 (Winter 1982): 3–24.

Dubofsky, Melvyn. *The State and Labor in Modern America.* Chapel Hill: North Carolina Press, 1994.

———. *We Shall Be All: A History of the IWW.* New York: Quadrangle, 1969.

Dulles, John Rhea, and Melvyn Dubofsky. *Labor in America, A History.* 4th ed. Arlington Heights, IL: Harlan Davidson, 1984.

Edsall, Thomas Byrne E., with Mary D. Edsall. *Chain Reaction: The Impact of Race Rights and Taxes on American Politics.* New York: Norton, 1992.

Edwards, Richard. *Contested Terrain: The Transformation of the Workplace.* New York: Basic Books, 1979.

Ensign, Forest. *Compulsory School Attendance and Child Labor.* Iowa City: Athens Press, 1921.

Epstein, Richard, and Jeffrey Paul, eds. *Labor Law and the Employment Market: Foundations and Applications.* Brunswick, NJ: Transaction Books, 1985.

Epstein, Stephen A. *Wage Labor and Guilds in Medieval Europe.* Chapel Hill: University of North Carolina Press, 1991.

Erickson, Charlotte. *American Industry and the European Immigrant.* Cambridge: Harvard University Press, 1957.

Feinman, Jay M. "Development of the Employment at Will Rule," *American Journal of Legal History* 20 (1976).

Fogel, Robert. *Without Consent or Contract: The Rise and Fall of American Slavery.* New York: Norton, 1989.

Fogel, Robert, and Stanley Engerman. *Time on the Cross: The Economics of American Negro Slavery.* Boston: Little, Brown, 1974.

Foner, Eric. *Free Soil, Free Labor, Free Men: The Ideology of the Republican Party.* Oxford: Oxford University Press, 1970.

Forbath, William. "The Ambiguities of Free Labor: Labor and the Law in the Gilded Age," *Wisconsin Law Review* (1985): 767–817.

———. *Law and the Shaping of the American Labor Movement.* Cambridge: Harvard University Press, 1991.

Fox-Genovese, Elizabeth, and Eugene Genovese. *Fruits of Merchant Capital: Slavery and Bourgeois Property in the Rise and Expansion of Capitalism.* Oxford: Oxford University Press, 1983.

Frank, Dana. *Purchasing Power: Consumer Organizing, Gender, and the Seattle Labor Movement, 1919–1929.* Cambridge: Cambridge University Press, 1994.

Fraser, Steven. *Labor Will Rule: Sidney Hillman and the Rise of American Labor*. New York: Free Press, 1991.

————. "The 'New Unionism' and the 'New Economic Policy,'" in James Cronin and Carmen Sirianni, eds., *Work Community and Power: The Experience of Labor and Europe and America, 1900–1925*. Philadelphia: Temple University Press, 1983.

Freeman, Richard. "Are Your Wages Set in Beijing?" *Journal of Economic Perspectives* 9, no. 3 (Summer 1995): 15–31.

Freeman, Richard, and James Medoff. *What Do Unions Do?* New York: Basic Books, 1984.

Friedman, Benjamin. *Day of Reckoning*. New York: Vintage, 1989.

Friedman, Lawrence M. "Freedom of Contract and Occupational Licensing 1890–1910, A Legal and Social Study," *California Law Review* 53 (1965): 487–534.

Friedman, Milton. *Capitalism and Freedom*. Chicago: University of Chicago Press, 1982.

Friedman, Milton, with Rose Friedman, 1979. *Free to Choose, A Personal Statement*. New York: Harcourt, Brace Jovanovich, 1990.

Galbraith, James K. "Self-Fulfilling Prophets: Inflated Zeal at the Federal Reserve," *American Prospect* 18 (Summer 1994): 31–40.

Galenson, David W. "Rise and Fall of Indentured Servitude in the Americas: An Economic Analysis," *Journal of Economic History* 44 (March 1984): 1–25.

————. *White Servitude in America: An Economic Analysis*. Cambridge: Cambridge University Press, 1981.

Garten, Jeffrey. *A Cold Peace: America, Japan, and Germany and the Struggle for Supremacy*. New York: Times Books, 1992.

Genovese, Eugene. *The Political Economy of Slavery, Studies in the Economy and Society of the Slave South*. New York: Vintage, 1967.

George, Henry. *Protection or Free Trade*. New York: Schalkenbach, 1886.

Glickman, Jonathan A. *Concepts of Free Labor in Antebellum America*. New Haven: Yale University Press, 1991.

Goldin, Claudia. "The Economics of Emancipation," *Journal of Economic History* (March 1973).

————. *Urban Slavery in the American South*. Chicago: University of Chicago Press, 1976.

————. *Understanding the Gender Gap: An Economic History of American Women*. Oxford: Oxford University Press, 1990.

Goldin, Claudia, and Robert Margo. "The Great Compression: The Wage Structure in the U.S. at Mid-Century," *Quarterly Journal of Economics* 107, no. 1 (February 1992): 1–32.

Gompers, Samuel. *Seventy Years of Life and Labor: An Autobiography*. New York: E.P. Dutton, 1925, pp. 44–45.

Gordon, David M., Richard Edwards, and Michael Reich. *Segmented Work, Divided Workers, The Historical Transformation of Labor in the United States*. Cambridge: Cambridge University Press, 1982.

Gottschalk, Peter. "Inequality, Income Growth, and Mobility: The Basic Facts," *Journal of Economic Perspectives* 11, no. 2 (Spring 1997): 21–40.

Gould, Stephen Jay. *The Mismeasure of Man*. New York: Norton, 1981.

Gregory, Jim. "Okies and the Politics of Plain-Folk Americanism," in Daniel Cornford, ed. *Working People of California*. Berkeley: University of California Press, 1995, pp. 116–158.

Greven, Philip. "Family Structure in Seventeenth Century Andover, Massachusetts," *William and Mary Quarterly* (April 1966).

Grubb, Farley. "The End of European Immigrant Servitude in the United States: An Economic Analysis of Market Collapse, 1772–1835," *Journal of Economic History* 54, no. 4 (December 1994): 794–825.

Gunderson, Gerald. "The Origin of the American Civil War," *Journal of Economic History* (December 1974).

Hamilton, Stephen. *Apprenticeship for Adulthood: Preparing Youth for the Future.* New York: Free Press, 1990.

Harrison, Bennett, and Barry Bluestone. *The Great U-Turn: Corporate Restructuring and the Polarizing of America.* New York: Basic Books, 1988.

Hartz, Louis. *Economic Policy and Democratic Thought: Pennsylvania, 1776–1860.* New York: Quadrangle, 1968.

Hashimoto, Masanori. "Firm Specific Human Capital as a Shared Investment," *American Economic Review* 71, no. 3 (June 1981): 425–482.

Higgs, Robert. *Competition and Coercion: Blacks in the American Economy, 1865–1914.* Cambridge: Cambridge University Press, 1977.

–––––––. *Crisis and Leviathan: Critical Episodes in the Growth of American Government.* Oxford: Oxford University Press, 1987.

Honey, Michael. *Southern Labor and Black Civil Rights: Organizing Memphis Workers.* Urbana: University of Illinois Press, 1993.

Holt, Thaddeus. "Personnel Selection and the Supreme Court," in Kenneth Perlman, Frank L. Schmidt, and W. Clay Hamner, eds., *Contemporary Problems in Personnel,* 3d ed. New York: Wiley, 1983, pp. 38–51.

Hovencamp, Herbert. *Enterprise and American Law 1836–1937.* Cambridge: Harvard University Press, 1991.

Howard, George. *A History of Matrimonial Institutions.* Chicago: University of Chicago Press, 1904.

Horwitz, Morton. "The Historical Foundations of Modern Contract Law," *Harvard Law Review* 85, no. 5 (March 1974): 917–956.

–––––––. *Transformation of American Law, 1870–1960: The Crisis of Legal Orthodoxy.* Oxford and New York: Oxford University Press, 1992.

–––––––. *The Transformation of American Law, 1780–1860.* Oxford and New York: Oxford University Press, 1977.

Hughes, Jonathan R.T. *The Governmental Habit: Economic Controls from Colonial Times to the Present.* New York: Basic Books: 1977.

Hyman, Harold M., and William M. Wiecek. *Equal Justice under Law, Constitutional Development 1835–1875.* New York: Harper, 1982.

Jacoby, Daniel. "The Legal Foundations of Human Capital Markets," *Industrial Relations* 30, no. 2 (Spring 1991): 229–250.

–––––––. "Plumbing the Origins of American Vocationalism," *Labor History* 37, no. 2 (Spring 1996): 235–237.

–––––––. "The Transformation of Industrial Apprenticeship in the United States," *Journal of Economic History* 51, no. 4 (Winter 1991): 887–910.

Jacoby, Sanford. *Employing Bureaucracy: Managers, Unions, and the Transformation of Work in American Industry, 1900–1945.* New York: Columbia University Press, 1985.

Katznelson, Ira, and Margaret Weir. *Schooling for All: Class, Race and the Decline of the Democratic Ideal.* New York: Basic Books, 1985.

Kazin, Michael. *The Barons of Labor: San Francisco Building Trades and Union Power in the Progressive Era.* Urbana: University of Illinois Press, 1989.

Kessler-Harris, Alice. *Out to Work: A History of Wage-Earning Women in the United States.* Oxford: Oxford University Press, 1982.

Koike, Kazuo. "Human Resource Development and Labor–Management Relations," in Kozo Yamamura, ed., *Political Economy of Japan*. Vol. 1. Stanford: Stanford University Press, 1987, pp. 289–330.

Korstad, Robert, and Nelson Lichtenstein, "How Organized Black Workers Brought Civil Rights to the South," in Eileen Boris and Nelson Lichtenstein, eds., *Major Problems in the History of American Workers*. Lexington, MA: D.C. Heath, 1991, pp. 475–485.

Krugman, Paul. *Pop Internationalism*. Cambridge: MIT Press, 1996.

Kuttner, Robert. *Everything for Sale: The Virtues and Limits of Markets*. New York: Knopf, 1997.

Landes, David S. *The Unbound Prometheus: Technological Change 1750 to the Present*. Cambridge: Cambridge University Press, 1972.

Laslett, Peter. *The World We Have Lost: England Before the Industrial Age*. 3d ed. New York: Macmillan, 1984.

Lebergott, Stanley. *The Americans: An Economic Record*. New York: Norton, 1984.

Leonard, Eugenie. *The Dear-Bought Heritage*. Philadelphia: University of Pennsylvania Press, 1965.

Lescohier, Don. "The Knights of St. Crispin, 1867–1874: A Study of Industrial Causes of Trade Unionism," *Bulletin of the University of Wisconsin*, no. 355 (1910).

Licht, Walter. "The Dialectics of Bureaucratization: The Case of 19th Century American Railway Workers," in Charles Stephenson and Robert Asher, eds., *Life and Labor: Dimensions of American Working-Class History*. Albany: SUNY Press, 1986.

Lichtenstein, Nelson, and Howell John Harris, eds. *Industrial Democracy in America, The Ambiguous Promise*. Cambridge: Cambridge University Press, 1996.

Lindsey, Almont. *The Pullman Strike: The Story of a Unique Experiment and a Great Labor Upheaval*. Chicago: University of Chicago Press, 1964.

Lipow, Arthur. *Authoritarian Socialism in America: Edward Bellamy and the Nationalist Movement*. Berkeley: University of California Press, 1982.

Locke, John. *Two Treatises of Government*. London: Dent; Rutland, VT: Tuttle, 1990.

McCartin, Joseph A. " 'An American Feeling': Workers, Managers, and the Struggle Over Industrial Democracy in the World War I Era," in Nelson Lichtenstein and Howell John Harris, eds., *Industrial Democracy in America, The Ambigous Promise*. Cambridge: Cambridge University Press, 1996.

McGovern, George S., and Leonard F. Guttridge. *The Great Coalfield War*. Boulder: University of Colorado Press, 1996.

Maloney, Thomas N., and Warren C. Whatley. "Making the Effort: the Contours of Racial Discrimination in Detroit's Labor Markets, 1920–1940," *Journal of Economic History* 55, no. 3 (September 1995): 465–494.

Marglin, Stephen. "What Do Bosses Do? The Origins of and Function of Hierarchy in Capitalist Production," *Journal of Radical Political Economy* 6, no. 2 (Summer 1974): 60–112.

Marshall, Ray, and Marc Tucker. *Thinking for a Living: Education and the Wealth of Nations*. New York: Basic Books, 1992.

Mayer, Stephen. "*People v. Fisher*: The Shoemakers' Strike of 1833," *New York Historical Quarterly* 62, no. 1 (1978): 6–21.

Mokyr, Joel. *The Lever of Riches: Technological Creativity and Economic Progress*. Oxford and New York: Oxford University Press, 1990.

Montgomery, David. *Beyond Equality: Labor and the Radical Republicans, 1862–1872*. Urbana: University of Illinois Press, 1981.

———. *Citizen Worker: The Experience of Workers in the United States with Democracy and the Free Market during the Nineteenth Century*. Cambridge: Cambridge University Press, 1993.

———. *Fall of the House of Labor: The Workplace, the State, and American Labor Activism, 1865–1925.* Cambridge: Cambridge University Press, 1989.

———. *Workers' Control in America.* Cambridge: Cambridge University Press, 1979.

Morgan, Edmund. *The Puritan Family: Religion and Domestic Relations in Seventeenth Century New England.* New York: Harper and Row, 1966.

Motley, James M. "Apprenticeship in American Trade Unions," *Johns Hopkins University Studies in Historical and Political Science* 25 (1907): 9–123.

Mulligan, William. "From Artisan to Proletarian: The Family and Vocational Education of Shoemakers in the Handicraft Era," in Charles Stephenson and Robert Asher, eds., *Life and Labor: Dimensions of American Working-Class History.* Albany: SUNY Press, 1986.

Murayama, Yuzo. "Contractors, Collusion, and Competition: Japanese Immigrant Railroad Laborers in the Pacific Northwest, 1898–1911," *Explorations in Economic History* 21 (1984): 290–305.

Navasky, Victor. *Naming Names.* New York: Viking, 1980.

Nef, John U. *Industry and Government in France and England, 1540–1640.* Philadelphia: American Philosophical Society, 1940.

Nelson, Bruce. "Zieger's CIO: In Defense of Labor Liberalism," *Labor History* 37, no. 2 (Spring 1996): 161–162.

Nelson, Daniel. *Managers and Workers: The Origins of the Twentieth Century Factory System in the United States, 1880–1920.* 2d ed. Madison: University of Wisconsin Press, 1995.

Nevins, Allan. *Abram S. Hewitt: With Some Account of Peter Cooper.* New York: Harper & Brothers, 1935.

New York Bureau of Labor Statistics, *Annual Report,* 1886.

North, Douglass, and Robert Thomas. *The Rise of the Western World: A New Economic History.* Cambridge and New York: Cambridge University Press, 1973.

Olson, Mancur. *The Logic of Collective Action: Public Goods and the Theory of Groups.* Cambridge: Harvard University Press, 1971.

Ozanne, Robert. *A Century of Labor–Management Relations at McCormick and International Harvester.* Madison: University of Wisconsin Press, 1967.

Oshansky, David. "Labor's Cold War: The CIO and the Communists," in Eileen Boris and Nelson Lichtenstein, eds., *Major Problems in the History of American Workers.* Lexington, MA: D.C. Heath, 1991, pp. 510–524.

Padover, Saul K., ed. *James Madison: The Forging of American Federalism, Selected Writings.* New York: Harper Torchbooks, 1953.

Perlman, Selig. *A Theory of the Labor Class.* New York: Kelly, 1928.

Pocock, J.G.A. *Politics, Language, and Time: Essays on Political Thought and History.* New York: Athenaeum, 1971.

Pollard, Sidney. *Genesis of Modern Management.* Cambridge: Harvard University Press, 1965.

Puette, William. *Through Jaundiced Eyes: How the Media Views Organized Labor.* Ithaca, NY: ILR Press, 1992.

Ransom, Roger, and Richard Sutch. *One Kind of Freedom: The Economic Consequences of Emancipation.* Cambridge: Cambridge University Press, 1977.

Ravitch, Diane. *The Great School Wars New York City, 1805–1973: A History of the Public Schools as Battlefield of Social Change.* New York: Basic Books, 1974.

Reich, Robert. *The Work of Nations.* New York: Vintage Knopf, 1992.

Richardson, J. David. "Income Inequality and Trade: How to Think, What to Conclude," *Journal of Economic Perspectives* 9, no. 3 (Summer 1995): 35–55.

Rifkin, Jeremy. *The End of Work: The Decline of the Global Labor Force and the Dawn of the Post-Market Era.* New York: Tarcher Putnam, 1995.

Roback, Jenifer. "Southern Labor Law in the Jim Crow Period: Exploitative or Competitive?" in Richard A. Epstein and Jeffrey Paul, eds., *Labor Law and the Employment Market: Foundations and Applications.* Brunswick, NJ: Transaction Books, 1985.

Rodgers, Daniel. *Work Ethic in Industrial America, 1850–1920.* Chicago: University of Chicago Press, 1979.

Roediger, David R. *The Wages of Whiteness: Race and the Making of American Working Class.* London and New York: Verso, 1991.

Rohlen, Thomas P. 1983. *Japan's High Schools.* Berkeley: University of California Press, 1983.

Rorabaugh, William. *The Craft Apprentice, from Franklin to the Machine Age in America.* Oxford and New York: Oxford University Press, 1986.

Rosenberg, Nathan. *Technology and American Economic Growth.* New York: Harper, 1972.

Rousseau, Jean-Jacques. *The Social Contract; and Discourses.* London: J.M. Dent; Rutland, VT: C.E. Tuttle, 1993.

Salant, Walter. "The Spread of Keynesian Doctrines and Practices in the United States," in Peter Hall, ed., *The Political Power of Economic Ideas, Keynesianism Across Nations.* Princeton: Princeton University Press, 1989.

Schatz, Ronald W. "From Commons to Dunlop: Rethinking the Field and Theory of Industrial Relations," in Nelson Lichtenstein and Howell John Harris, eds., *Industrial Democracy in America: The Ambiguous Promise.* Cambridge: Cambridge University Press: 1996. pp. 87–112.

Schechter, Patricia. "Free and Slave Labor in the Old South: The Tredegar Ironworkers' Strike of 1847," *Labor History* 35, no. 2 (Spring 1994): 165–87.

Schlesinger, Arthur M. *The Colonial Merchants and the American Revolution, 1763–1776.* New York: Ungar, 1957.

Schwantes, Carlos. "Unemployment, Disinheritance and the Origins of Labor Militancy in the Pacific Northwest, 1885–86," *Western Historical Quarterly* (1982).

Segal, Martin. *The Rise of the United Association: National Unionism in the Pipe Trades, 1884–1924.* Boston: Harvard University Press, 1970.

Smith, Adam. *Theory of Moral Sentiments.* Indianapolis: Liberty Classics, 1976.

———. *The Wealth of Nations.* New York: Random House, Modern Library Edition, 1937.

Smith, Daniel. "Parental Control and Marital Patterns: An Analysis of Historical Trends in Hingham, Massachusetts," *Journal of Marriage and the Family* (August 1973).

Smith, James, and Finis Welch. "Black Economic Progress after Myrdal," *Journal of Economic Literature* 27, no. 2 (June 1989): 519–64.

Sowell, Thomas. *Ethnic America, A History.* New York: Basic Books, 1981.

Spruill, Julia Cherry. *Women's Life and Work in the Southern Colonies.* New York: Norton, 1972.

Stampp, Kenneth. *The Peculiar Institution: Slavery in the Ante-bellum South.* New York: Vintage, 1989.

———. *The Era of Reconstruction, 1865–1977.* New York: Vintage, 1965.

Stein, Herbert. *The Fiscal Revolution in America.* Chicago: University of Chicago Press, 1969.

Steinfeld, Robert. *The Invention of Free Labor: The Employment Relation in English and American Law and Culture, 1350–1870.* Chapel Hill: University of North Carolina Press. 1991.

———. "Property and Suffrage in the Early American Republic," *Stanford Law Review* 41, no. 2 (January 1989): 335–376.

Stephenson, Charles. "There's Plenty Waitin' at the Gate: Mobility, Opportunity and the American Worker," in Charles Stephenson and Robert Asher, eds., *Life and Labor: Dimensions of Working-Class History.* Albany: SUNY Press, 1986.

Stephenson, Charles, and Robert Asher, eds. *Life and Labor: Dimensions of Working-Class History.* Albany: SUNY Press, 1986.

Takaki, Ronald. *A Different Mirror: A History of Multicultural America.* Boston: Little, Brown, 1993.

Taylor, Fredrick W. *Shop Management.* New York: Harper, 1911.

Thurow, Lester. *Head to Head: The Coming Economic Battle Among Japan, Europe, and America.* New York: Morrow, 1992.

Tocqueville, Alexis de. *Democracy in America.* Vols. 1 and 2. Vintage, 1990.

Tyack, David. *The One Best System: A History of American Urban Education.* Cambridge: Cambridge University Press, 1974.

———. "Ways of Seeing: An Essay on the History of Compulsory Schooling," *Harvard Educational Review* 46, no. 3 (August 1976): 355–389.

U.S. Census. *Historical Statistics of the United States.* Washington, D.C.: U.S. Government, 1975.

Veblen, Thorstein. *The Engineers and the Price System.* New Brunswick: Transaction Books, 1983.

Veysey, Laurence. *The Emergence of the American University.* Chicago: University of Chicago Press, 1965.

Vinovski, Maris. "Horace Mann and Economic Productivity," in *Education, Society, and Economic Opportunity: A Historical Perspective on Persistent Issues.* New Haven: Yale University Press, 1995.

Voss, Kim. *The Making of American Exceptionalism: The Knights of Labor and Class Formation in the Nineteenth Century.* Ithaca: Cornell University Press, 1993.

Ware, Norman. *The Industrial Worker, 1840–1860: The Reaction of American Industrial Society to the Advance of the Industrial Revolution.* Boston: Houghton Mifflin, 1924.

Wellman, David. *The Union Makes Us Strong: Radical Unionism on the San Francisco Waterfront.* Cambridge: Cambridge University Press, 1996.

Wiggenhorn, William. "Motorola U: When Training Becomes an Education," *Harvard Business Review* (July–August 1990): 71–83.

Wilentz, Sean. *Chants Democratic: New York City and the Rise of the American Working Class, 1788–1855.* New York: Oxford University Press, 1984.

Wood, Adrian. "How Trade Hurt Unskilled Workers," *Journal of Economic Perspectives* 9, no. 3 (Summer 1995): 57–80.

Wood, Gordon. *The Radicalism of the American Revolution.* New York: Vintage, 1991.

Woodman, Harold. "Sequel to Slavery: The New History Views the Postbellum South," *Journal of Southern History* 43 (1977): 523–554.

Zetka, James. *Militancy, Market Dynamics and Workplace Authority.* Albany: SUNY Press, 1995.

Zieger, Robert H. *The CIO, 1935–1955.* Chapel Hill: University of North Carolina Press, 1995.

Zieren, Gregory. "The Boycott and Working Class Solidarity, Toledo, Ohio in the 1890s," in Charles Stephenson and Robert Asher, eds., *Life and Labor: Dimensions of Working-Class History.* Albany: SUNY Press, 1986.

Zuboff, Shoshanna. *Work in the Age of the Smart Machine: The Future of Work and Power.* New York: Basic Books, 1984.

Index

A

Abolition:
  forcible, 43, 168
Absentee owner, 107
Absenteeism, 80
Adams, John, 20
Adkins v. Children's Hospital
  (1923), 93
Affirmative Action, 144–146
AFL. *See* American Federation of
  Labor
African American, 37, 125, 132,
  133, 137, 141, 144, 146
Agricultural labor, 7
  specific performance, 16
  See also farmers
Agricultural Workers, 84
Air Traffic Controllers, 160
Air Travel, 158
Amalgamated Association of Iron
  and Steelworkers, 75
American Emigrant Company, 72
American Federation of Labor,
  (AFL), 67, 77, 87, 88, 90, 91,
  103, 124–127
American Legion, 135
American Plan, 93
American Railway Union (ARU),
  88
American Revolution, 19, 33
American System of Manufacturing,
  75
Andover, Massachusetts, 22
Apprentices, 33

Apprenticeship, 7, 32, 71–72,
  101–104, 92, 106, 107, 112, 161
  guilds, 17
  organized labor, 74
  Knights of St. Crispin, 62
Arendt, Hannah, 84
Artisans, 18–20
Asian, 141
Assembly Line, 82–83
At will Contracts, 121–122
Atleson, James, 125
AT&T, 162
Auchmuty, Colonel Richard T., 103,
  107, 108, 112
Authoritarianism, 127
Authority:
  traditional, 33
Auto workers, 125
Automatic surveillance, 154
Automation, 153
Automobiles, 86, 125
  import competition, 158

B

Bacon's Rebellion, 26
Baltimore, Lord, 16
Bankruptcy, 31, 32
Bankruptcy Laws, 50–51
Beeks, Gertrude, 89
Bellamy, Edward, 101, 105, 107,
  109, 111, 113, 127
Biberman, Herbert, 134–138
Big Steel, 124
Black-codes, 56

Blacklist, 73, 134, 135, 138
Blacks. *See* African American
Bonus, 81, 82
  Japanese system, 161
Bootmakers, 58
Boston, 93
Boston Tea Party, 136
Boycott, 47, 71, 127, 135–137
  See also discrimination
Brave New World, 70
Breach of Contract:
  debt, 49–50
Brewer, Roy M., 134
Brody, David, 76, 97, 128
Brotherhood of Railroad Firemen, 88
Brown v. Board of Education
  (1954), 143
Buccaneer capitalism, 162
Burke, Edmund, 13, 30
Butchers Benevolent Association,
  56, 57

C

California:
  entry as free state, 39
Campanella, Roy, 131
Capitalism, 141, 149
  and discrimination, 132
  impersonality of, 167
  See also free markets; markets
Carnegie, Andrew, 75, 76, 105
Carolene Products (1938), 142, 143
Cartels, 158
Cash economy, 33
Chandler, Alfred, 80, 120
Chicago, 133
Chicanos, 135
  See also Mexican Americans
Child Labor, 92
Children. *See* marriage and
  inheritance
Chinese, 73, 149
  Exclusion Act, 73

Chrysler, 125
Cigar Manufacturers Association, 71
Cigar workers, 66, 67, 70, 73, 74
CIO. *See* Committee for Industrial
  Organization
Civil Rights, 9, 143, 144–146
  Act of 1866, 55
  Movement, 138
Civil War, 7, 32, 40, 55, 58, 72, 167
Clark, John Bates, 78
Class warfare, 101, 127
Classes:
  separation of, 98–99
Closed Shops, 62
Clothing, 125
Co-determination, 161
Coal, 79, 125
  Mines, 123
Coase, Ronald, 120
Coffin Hand-bill, 43
Committee for Industrial
  Organization, (CIO), 125, 133,
  135, 137, 141
Central Competitive Field, 94
Cold War, 125
Collective Action, 9, 45–48, 139,
  167
  and boycotts, 47
  and contract, 121
  and early strikes, 44–48
  as threat to property rights, 61
Collective rights, 136
College, 104, 110
Colonists, 14
Colonization:
  and commercial revolution, 16
Color Barrier, 131
  See also race relations
Color Consciousness, 55
Colorado Fuel and Iron Company,
  94–96
Colorado Industrial Plan, 95
Colt, Judge, 62
Commissions, 78, 79

Commonwealth:
  and household, 15
Communism and communists, 133,
  135, 138, 141
Community, 58
  control, 22
Company Unions, 95, 123
Competition, 91, 131
  and division of labor, 44
  market, 32
Compromise of 1850, 39
Compulsory Labor:
  taxes replace, 22
Computers, 151
  problem solving, 151
  as monitoring devices, 151
Congress of Industrial
  Organizations. See CIO
Conservation. See soil depletion
Constitution, 3, 20, 30–32
  designed to constrain rights
    rhetoric, 48
  and slavery, 38
Consumption, 85–86
Contract, 33, 165
  and economic theory, 51
  apprenticeship, 17
  breaches, 61
  contradictions within, 36
  formal relationship to property, 57
  freedom of, 9, 131
  incomplete, 79
  See also Liberty of Contract
indentured servitude, 16
  informed and voluntary, 8
  long term, 72–73
  logic of, 35, 36
  triumph of, 7, 8, 35, 36
Contract clause, 31–32
Contract Labor, 72, 73
Cooper's Union, 104
Cooper, Peter, 104
Cooperative Commonwealth, 105,
  107, 108

Cooperatives, 67
Cordwainers. See shoemakers
Corporate Responsibility, 89
Corporate Welfarism, 94
  See also paternalism
Corporation:
  general purpose, 84–85
Corporatism, 118, 145
Cotton Gin, 38
Counts, George Sylvester, 109
Courts:
  and labor, 63, 66, 67
Craft Control, 103
Craft Union, 92
Craftsmanship, 59, 78
Credit, 24
Crescent City Slaughterhouse, 56
Criminal Conspiracy, 137
Custom, 27
  and authority, 25
  See also manorialism
Cybernetic transformation, 151
Czech Republic, 164

D

Dawley, Alan, 60
Day labor, 68
De-industrialization, 160
  Germany, 164
De-regulation, 158
Deb, Eugene V., 88, 124, 166
Debt, 31, 32, 36, 37, 48–51
Declaration of Independence, 3, 28,
  29
Democracy, 18, 100
  and minorities, 32
  and property, 30
  company towns, 88
  workplace, 139
Democracy In America, 37
Democratic impulse, 31
Democratic Party, 146
Department stores, 79

Dependence:
  corporate paternalism, 90
Detroit, 133
Dewey, John, 109–110, 111
Dilbert, 150
Discrimination, 73, 112, 141–142,
    146
  as boycott, 137
  de jure versus de facto, 143–144
  economics of, 131–134
  state, 143
Dispute resolution, 93, 121
Division of Labor, 83, 154
  capital and management, 80
  shoemakers, 58
Dixiecrat, 146
Drexel, Anthony, 104
Drucker, Peter, 162

E

Economic theory, 78, 80
Economists, 122
Edens, Ron, 154
Education, 29, 98–113
  end of segregation, 143
Educational:
  attainment and income, 109
  Efficiency, 99
  Equality, 99
Edwards, Judge Odgen, 43, 46
EEOC, 147
Eight-hour Day, 67, 69
Emancipation Proclamation, 7,
    55
Empire, 18
Employer Associations, 71–72
Employers:
  large versus small, 119
Employment rights, 147
Engerman, Stanley, 40
Engineering, 75
Engineers, 107
Enlightenment, the, 14, 28

Enticement, 61, 62
  Laws, 64
Enumerated Goods, 19
Epstein, Stephen, 17
Equal Opportunity, 146
Equal Protection Clause, 55, 64
  and eight-hour day, 67
Erie Canal, 34
Ethnic Tensions, 73
Europe, 14, 158
  custom as compared with United
    States, 27, 28
European Union, 163
Exceptionalism, 6
Exchange Rates, 163–164
Exit, 123
Expert Systems, 151
Exploitation, 8
Exports, 159
Ezra Cornell, 104

F

Factories:
  textile, 35
Factory Girls, 43
Factory labor, 78
  shoemaking, 59
Factory Work, 82
  and slavery, 42, 47
  new service workers, 154
Fair Trade Standards, 123
Farrell, Ed, 72
Farmer, 14
Farmers, 18–20
  as symbol, 13
  and debt, 49
  and frontier, 49
  and markets, 14
  self sufficiency, 48
Federal Law, 55
Federal Spending, 160
Federalism, 31
Fee Simple, 16

Feudalism, 15
Field, Stephen J., 57, 59–60
Fifteenth Amendment, 55
Financiers, 80
Firm Size, 85
Firms:
  small, 71
  large-scale, 79
  large v. small, 95
Fiscal Policy, 159
Fogel, Robert, 40, 43
Forbath, William, 67, 91
Forced Labor:
  and progress, 42, 43
Ford Motor Company, 85, 119, 125
Ford, Henry, 82–83, 122, 133
Fordism, 83
Fourteenth Amendment, 55, 67
  equal protection clause, 57
France, 164
Franchise, 79
Fraser, Steven, 119
Free labor ideology, 58
Free market, 131, 141–142
Free riders, 140
Free Soil, 40
  westward expansion, 49
Freedmen:
  economic advances, 65
  failure to provide property, 56
Freedom:
  America, 37
  and money, 16
  and organizations, 8
  collective governance, 17
  conditions of, 6, 7, 9, 30, 32, 166
  defined, 3, 4, 9
  different understandings, 148
  incoherent vision, 148
  independence, 19
  individual, 18
  of association, 61, 131
  of Speech, 61
  republican, 7

Freedom *(continued)*
  tensions in meaning, 3
  to quit, 133
Freedom Dues, 24, 25
Freedom of Contract:
  equivalent to republic
    independence, 57
Freedom-from, 4
Freedom-to, 4
Friedman, Milton, 131, 135, 141–142
Frontiersman:
  as symbol, 24
Frontline workers:
  and education, 162
Full Employment, 130
Full Employment Law, 140
Fundamental Rights, 57

G

Galenson, David, 25, 50
Gatt, 157
Gender, 20, 21, 111
  See also women
General Motors, 85, 125, 128,
  129
Geneva, New York, 45, 46, 58
George, Henry, 106–107, 109
German Reunification, 164
Germany, 160–162, 163
  apprenticeship, 161
  employee benefits, 161
Gibson, Josh, 130
Girdler, Tom, 123
Global competition, 149
Gompers, Samuel, 67, 70, 72, 74,
  75, 77, 88, 107
Governance:
  self, 19, 20
Government, 88, 117–118
  and property, 20
  colonial, 27
  legal monopoly of force, 5
Great Compression, 158

Great Depression, 8, 57, 86, 96, 123
Greven, Phillip, 22
Group discrimination, 132
Grubb, Farley, 50
Guilds, 29, 107
  system, 17
  and property, 21
  trade protection, 58

H

Hancock, John, 19
Hart, Schaffner & Marx, 119–121
Harvard, 105
Hashimoto, Masanori, 161
Hayek, Friedrich, 117–118
Haymarket Square, 102
Health Care, 90
  and globalization, 156
Health and Safety, 92
Hewitt, Abram, 106–107
Higgs, Robert, 65, 117–118
High School, 101
Hillman, Sidney, 120, 121, 124, 125
History, 167
Hitchman Coal and Coke v. Mitchell
  (1917), 62
Hitler, Adolf, 117, 126
Hollywood, 138, 148
Hollywood Ten, 130, 135, 137
Homestead, Pennsylvania, 76, 93
Homesteading, 49
Honey, Michael, 138
House Un-American Activities
  Committee, 134
Households, 14, 34, 35
  governance, 20
  management, 15
  labor, 7
  men, 22
Household appliances, 86
Howard, Elston, 131
Human potential, 100
Human Rights, 5, 149

Hunt v. Commonwealth (1842), 48,
  60
Husbands, 22
Huxley, Aldous, 70, 83, 113

I

IATSE. *See* International
  Association of Theatre and
  Stage Employees
IBM, 162
International Longshoremen's
  Association (ILA), 139
Immigrants, 92, 99, 102
Immigration, 35
  Chinese, 149
In Re Jacobs (1885), 67
Inalienable rights, 3, 5, 29–31, 128,
  140, 166–167
  and debt, 51
  and revolutionary traditions, 47
  and strikes, 45
  and violence, 47, 48
  inherent opposition to liberty of
    contract, 32
Income. *See also* wages
  education, 109
  Inequality, 164
  annual, 86
Indentured Servant, 7, 24, 25, 32
  and debt, 50–51
  and transportation costs, 26, 27, 50
  as distinguished from
    apprenticeship, 17
  contemporary, 149
  immigrants, 16
  terms of, 26
Indentures:
  supply and demand, 26, 27
Independence, 14
  and organization, 118–119
  in information age, 155
  social hierarchy, 24
  and contract, 167

Independence *(continued)*
Capital-Labor Relations, 78
Individual Rights:
pensions, 9
Industrial army, 106
Industrial democracy, 95–96, 108, 139, 140
See also democracy
Industrial revolution, 150
Industrial transformation, 128
Industrial unionism, 124
Industrial Workers of the World (IWW), 121
Inflation, 159, 162
constitution and money, 31, 32
Inflationary expectations, 160
Information processing, 150
and productivity, 162
Inheritance, 22
Insolvency, 31
Integration:
schooling, 144
Interdependence, 79
Interest rates, 159
Internal Improvements, 34
International Association of Theatre and Stage Employees (IATSE), 138
International Harvester, 89–90, 96
ILA. *See* International Longshoremen's Association
International management:
and information systems, 157
International Trade, 149, 157–160
International Union of Mine, Mill and Smelter Workers (MMSW), 135, 138
Internet, 149
Investment:
and legal protection, 57
Investments:
long term, 162
Involuntary servitude, 55, 63, 69, 133

IQ, 110
Irish Catholics, 100
Iron, 79, 80
IWW. *See* Industrial Workers of the World

J

Jacquard loom, 150, 151
Japan, 158, 160–163
schooling, 161
Japanese, 133
Jefferson, Thomas, 20, 28–32, 47, 48
Jeffersonian Republic, 47
Jencks, Clifton, 138
Jim Crow Laws, 64
Johnson, Lyndon, 144, 159
Johnston, Eric, 134
Jones & Laughlin Company, 124
Judicial Review, 30
Junk-Bonds, 162
Justice, 8

K

Kaiser Aluminum v. Weber, 146
Kazan, Elia, 136, 139
Kearns, David, 162
Kennedy, John, 159
Key punch, 151
Keynesianism, 158–159
King Cotton, 38
King, F.L., Mackenzie, 95
King, Martin Luther, 144
Kinship:
security and status, 23, 24
Knights of Labor, 66, 67, 71, 73, 77, 87, 101, 103
Knights of St. Crispin, 59–62
limits on apprentices, 60
Koike, Kazuo, 161
Koreans, 133
Krugman, Paul, 149, 163
Ku Klux Klan, 65, 133

L

Labor:
distinguished from other forms of
property, 57
farming, 13
not the same as unions, 6
sale of, 14
services or dues, 15–17
standards, 67, 140, 145, 165
theory of value, 30–31
Labor and management:
harmony, 78–82
Labor combinations, 58
Labor costs, 75
Labor Force,
agricultural, 34
Labor Laws, 91
Labor Markets, 25
Labor Organizations:
political reform, 66
See also unions
Labor Problem, 7
Labor unions:
lawful activities, 62, 63
Laissez-Faire, 127
Laker, Freddie, 158
Land:
freehold, 24
See also property
Land Ordinances of 1785 and 1787,
29
Lean and mean, 162
Legislation:
and self interest, 29
Lewis, John L., 123, 124
Lewis, Sinclair, 110, 113
Liberty:
collective bargaining, 46
order and security, 83
personal, 17
sale of, 32
two traditions, 48
Liberal Education, 107

Liberty of Contract, 32, 68, 69, 93,
119, 134, 130
in large scale organizations, 121
regime ends, 143
Liberty:
sale of, 83
Licensure, 21
Lincoln, Abraham, 146
Lock-outs, 71, 73
Locke, John, 21, 28, 31
Longshoremen, 137
Louisiana Territory, 29
Lowell, Massachusetts, 35, 43
Loyalty, 163
Ludlow Massacre, 94
Lum, Daniel, 45, 46
Lynn, Massachusetts, 59

M

Machine tools, 75
Machines:
drudge labor, 153–154
mental labor, 152, 154
Madisonian democracy, 142
Madison, James, 30, 31, 32
Mail-order pharmacy, 153
Malicious interference, 61
Management, 68, 71, 75–76, 78, 79,
81–83, 120, 151
Japanese, 163
Managerial Discretion, 128
Managerial Hierarchy, 80
Managers, 80
Mann, Horace, 99
Manorialism, 15
customs of, 15
Manual and industrial arts, 108
Manual Training, 105
Manufacturing, 154
Maris, Roger, 131
Market expansion, 33
Markets, 25
and social change, 35

Markets *(continued)*
  impersonality of, 135–136
  labor freedom, 27
  equality, 28
  religion, 22
  slavery, 26
Marriage, 22, 34, 35
  dowry, 23
  markets, 25
  parental approval, 23
Marxists, 7, 8, 91
Masons, 71
Master and slave relations, 41
Master craftsman, 99
  as symbol, 14
Master Plumbers Association, 103
Master–Servant relationship, 37
McCarthy Hearings, 126
McCormack, Cyrus, 96
McKay Gordon, 59
Medford, Massachusetts, 60
Medicine, 21
  and computers, 152
Mercantilism, 27
  wages, 18
Merchants, 18–20
  as commercial class, 28
  British trade policy, 19
  and boycotts, 47
Mergers, 85
Mexican Americans, 135, 141
Middle Classes, 100, 102, 107–108
Middle States:
  and colonial immigration, 26
Migrant Workers, 149
Miners, 135
Minorities, 146, 147
  insular and discreet, 142
Misery index, 159
MMSW. *See* International Union of
    Mine, Mill and Smelter Workers
Mobsters. *See* racketeers
Money:
  debt, 31, 32

Monopolies, 18, 29, 57, 158
Montgomery, David, 67, 68
Morality:
  and slavery, 41
Morgan, Edmund, 21
Morgan, J.P., 85
Morrill Act (1862), 104
Mostel, Zero, 136
Motion Picture Association of
    America, 134
Motorola, 162

N

NAACP. *See* National Association
    for the Advancement of
    Colored People
Nat Turner, 37, 42
Nation at Risk, A, 162
National Association for the
    Advancement of Colored
    People (NAACP), 143
National clubs, 108
National emergency injunctions, 136
National Industrial Recovery Act
    (NIRA), 123, 124
National Labor Relations Act
    (NLRA), 123, 136–140
National Service, 106
Nationalism, 18
Nativism, 102
Natural rights, 21, 31, 48
  and Adam Smith, 30
Navigation Acts, 19
Negative freedom, 4
New Deal, 57, 118, 123, 136
  and Democratic Party, 145
New Orleans, 56
New York City, 34, 102
New York Trade School, 74, 103,
    108, 112
NIRA. *See* National Industrial
    Recovery Act
Nixon, Richard, 144–145

NLRA. *See* National Labor
    Relations Act
No-Strike Clause, 121
Nobility, 15
North, Simeon, 75

O

Occupational Safety Commission,
    147
Ogden v. Saunders (1827), 50
Olson, Mancur, 140
Open-shop, 93, 95, 96,
Opportunity, 46, 99
Organization
    large-scale, 118
Organized Labor, 92
    as percent of labor force, 139
    employment rights, 147
    minorities, 141
Orwell, George, 127
Outwork, 78
Owners, 80
Ozanne, Robert, 90, 96

P

Pacific coast, 73
Page, Satchel, 131
Parental control, 34, 35
Passions:
    mob, 30
Patents, 29
Paternalism, 87–90, 165
Patronage:
    government, 130, 139
Patrons:
    independence, 23, 24
Patroons, 16
Pedagogy:
    child-centered, 107
Peerage, 15
Penn, William, 16
Pension Guarantee Board, 147

Pensions, 90, 94
People v. Fisher, 44
Personnel Policies, 120
Piece Rates, 78, 81, 82
Piecework, 8, 79
Pinkerton Agency, 76
Plantation owners, 38
Player Piano, 149, 153
Plessy v. Ferguson (1896), 64, 110
Pluralism, 147
Plumbing, 72, 102, 106
Pluralism, 145
Pluralists, 125
Poor relief, 27
Population:
    colonial, 23
    and trade, 33
Positive freedom, 4
Powderly, Terrence, 103
Power, 5, 6, 25
Prices, 158
Prison Labor, 42, 45, 64
    China, 149
    Nazi, 42
Private Property:
    and liberty, 31
Privileges and immunities clause, 57
Producerism, 78
Productivity, 81, 82, 83, 150
    gain-sharing, 75
    Slowdown, 162
Professionals, 7, 100
    See also middle classes
Professions, 99, 112
Profits:
    and slavery, 42
Propaganda, 135
Programmers, 156
Progress:
    markets, 27
Progressive era, 92
Progressives, 100, 108
Property:
    and investment, 57

Property *(continued)*
 and strikes, 88
 basis of independence, 55
 governance, 15
 in labor, 68
 land, 14
 ownership and liberty, 142
 rights of, 30
 women, 20
Property rights, 31, 127
 defined, 5
Prostitutes:
 forced labor, 149
Protectionism, 159
Public Health, 64
Public Policy, 69
Public Schools, 104
Pullman, 86–87
Pullman, George, 87–89

Q

Quality circles, 161
Quotas, 146

R

Race:
 and the law, 65
Race relations, 144, 167
 post bellum South, 64
 separate treatment, 55
Race riot, 133
Race to the bottom, 32, 167
Race-Norming, 146
Racketeers, 139
Railroad Brotherhoods, 88, 91
Railroads:
 and management, 80
Rank and status, 24
Racism, 133
Rational basis test, 142
Reagan, Ronald, 159–160
Redistribution, 99

Reich, Robert, 164–165
Relatives. *See* kinship
Religion:
 social control, 21–22
Religion:
 tolerance, 16
Repression, 93, 165
Republic:
 democracy and equality, 28
Republic Steel, 123
Republican:
 ideals, 14
 ideology, 20
 independence, 20
 ideology, 46
Republican Party, 146
Republicanism, 14, 127
 and gender, 21
 landed independence, 21
Reuther, Walter, 128, 129
Reverse Discrimination, 146
Rhetoric, 48, 72, 166
Rickey, Branch, 131–134
Rifkin, Jeremy, 149
 Right to Quit, 45
 Right-to-Work, 136, 140
Rights:
 collective versus individual, 148
 government, 20
 group versus individual, 142
 sale of, 167
 See also natural; civil; property;
  and inalienable
Riots, 144
Robinson, Jackie, 130, 134
Robots, 152
Rockefeller, John D., 84, 104
 family, 94
Roediger, David, 133
Romance, 23
Roosevelt, Franklin, 8, 117–118, 123
Roosevelt, Theodore, 67
Rousseau, Jean-Jacques, 28, 33
Royalties, 18

Rubber, 125
Rules, 120
Runaway Slaves, 42
Russian Revolution, 93
Ruth, Babe, 131

S

Sabotage, 127
Safety, 80
Sales, 78, 79
Salt of the Earth, 134, 137
Savage, Judge John, 45
Scale economies, 91
Schaffner, Jacob, 120
Scientific management, 88, 100
  and competition, 81
Scientific Managers, 120
Seattle, 93
Segregation, 110–111
  in employment, 132
Self-Employment, 84
Self-Interest, 29, 37
Seniority, 91
Sensory Devices, 151
Service Employment, 154
Service work:
  personal, 155
Servility, 14
Servitude, 68
Sewing Machine:
  in shoemaking, 59
Shipbuilding, 93
Shoemakers, 43, 58
  apprenticeship, 59
Shop-floor control, 69, 121, 125
Shop-floor democracy, 126
Silent Majority, 145
60 Minutes, 149
Skill:
  and freedom, 70
  as property, 21
  competition and technology, 58
  education, 160

Skill *(continued)*
  in information age, 155
  investment in, 162
Skilled Workers:
  and independence, 69–74
Slaughterhouse Cases (1873), 56,
    59–60, 63
Slave:
  management, 41
Slave trade, 38
Slavery, 7, 25, 32, 26, 27, 55, 69, 167
  and capitalism, 43
  and industrialization, 42, 43, 47
  and politics, 39
  and recruitment of indentured
    servants, 26
  and wage labor, 43–48
  as complete system, 42
  containment, 40, 43
  education and training, 43
  efficiency of, 40
  expansion of, 37, 38
  fugitives, 39
  in northern states, 38
  in the North, 40
  physical brutality, 41
  rationality, 41
  rationalizations for, 26
  resistance, 37, 42, 43
  reward system, 41
  the courts, 9, 40
  imminent collapse, 40
Smith, Adam, 18, 28–32, 80,
    167
  on fair competition, 46
Snake, the, 163
Snow v. Wheeler (1873), 62
Social Change, 34, 35
Social Contract, 28
  Theory, 37
Social Welfare, 91
Socialism, 107, 141
  discrimination, 142
Socialists, 87

Soil Depletion:
 and slavery, 40, 41
Soldiering, 81
Solidarity, 71, 138, 145
 and ethnic tensions, 133
Sons of Liberty, 47
South Korea, 164
Southern Labor Law:
 post-reconstruction, 64
Southern strategy, 145
Soviet Union, 126
Specialization, 33, 43
Stalin, Joseph, 117, 126, 138
Stampp, Kenneth, 47
Standard Oil, 84
Standardization, 83
 justice and freedom, 120
Stanford, Leland, 104
State paternalism, 90–91
States:
 enforcing rights of master in labor,
  25
States Rights, 39
Status, 15, 35, 36, 37, 58
Statute of Artificers (1563), 17, 18
Steam engine, 75
Steel, 75, 76, 79, 93, 123, 125
Steel Workers Organizing
  Committee, 123
Stein, Herbert, 130
Steinfeld, Robert, 16
Stock options, 90
Strikebreakers, 74, 95
Strikes, 103–104
 conspiracy doctrine, 44–48
 enticing breaches of contract,
  60–61
 violence and intimidation, 61
Subcontracting, 79
Substantive Due Process, 57, 58
Sugar production, 26
Supreme Court, 39, 50, 56–57, 64,
  68, 93, 110, 123, 138, 143, 144
Surveillance, 151

Sweated labor, 78
Symbolic analysts, 164–165
Syndicalism, 127

T

Taft–Hartley, 126, 136–141, 146,
  148
Tailors, 43
Taiwan, 164
Takaki, Ronald, 133
Tariffs, 18, 157
Taxation:
 consent, 19
 representation, 27
Taxes, 18, 160
Taylor, Frederick W., 81–82
Taylorism, 81–83
Teamsters, 137
Technological Progress, 58
Technology, 9, 86, 91, 149, 155, 165
 Orwellian, 6
 skilled labor, 74–77
Telecommunications:
 and trade, 157
Ten footers, 59
Ten-hour Laws, 69
Tenement workers, 74–75
Thirteenth Amendment, 55
Tile, Grate and Mantel Association,
  73, 74
Time and motion studies, 81
Tipping, 80
Tocqueville, Alexis De, 36, 37, 40,
  46, 65
Towns:
 and guilds, 17
Trade, 18
 custom, 25
 logic of, 27
Trade Schools, 62, 74
Transaction costs, 120
Transportation:
 labor markets, 44

Trask v. Parsons (1856), 50–51
Tredegar Iron Company, 47
Trickle-down, 167
Triumph of Contract:
  and slavery, 43
Trumbo, Dalton, 135
Tyack, David, 111
Typing Pools, 154
Tyranny of Majority:
  property, 142
  Southern democracy, 65

U

U.S. Steel, 123
UAW. *See* United Auto Workers
UMW. *See* United Mineworkers
Unalienable. *See* inalienable
Unemployment, 123, 158–159
  German, 164
  Japanese, 163
Union:
  rules, 72, 73
Union Shop, 139
Unionization, 86, 124
Unions, 6, 7, 81, 90
  bread and butter, 66
United Auto Workers (UAW), 119,
  125, 126, 128, 129
United Electrical, Radio and
  Machine Workers Union,
  126
United Mineworkers (UMW), 94
Univac, 150
Upskilling, 76
Urbanization, 34
  and slavery, 42

V

Vagrancy Laws, 64
Veblen, Thorstein, 107
Veysey, Laurence, 104
Vietnam Era, 159

Virginia:
  slave importation, 26
Virginia Company, 16
Vocational Education, 111
Vocational Guidance, 109
Vocational Training, 92
Voice, 123
Volcker, Paul, 159
Vonnegut, Kurt, 149, 153

W

Wage:
  contracts, 69
Wage labor, 8
  and independence, 46
  as compared with slavery, 43–48
  as rental or lease, 45
Wage Slave, 69
Wage Worker:
  interest different from farmers, 48
Wages:
  and education, 112
  and purchasing power, 85–86
  and scientific management, 82
  assignment of, 22
  post–World War I, 158
  programmers, 156
  stagnation and productivity, 150
  steel, 76
  unionization, 112
Wages and Incomes:
  black versus white, 143
Wagner Act. *See* NLRA
Walk-outs, 70
  See also strikes
Walker v. Cronin (1871), 60
Wall St. Journal, 152
  poultry workers, 156
War:
  and labor, 93
War Labor Boards, 93
Warren Court, 145
Warren, Earl, 144

Watts, California, 144
Wealth of Nations, 28
Weavers, 75
Weaving, 150
Welfare, 144
  state, 91
Welfare movement, 90
Welfarism, 87, 97
  See also paternalism
Wells, H.G., 98, 101, 113
West, Julian, 101, 105
White collar labor, 76
Whitney, Eli, 38, 75
Wildcat strike, 127
Wilentz, Sean, 79
Wilson, Woodrow, 95
Wives, 22
Women, 7, 110, 141
  single, 22
  in shoemaking, 59
Women's Auxiliary, 135
Wood, Gordon, 23, 24

Woodward, Calvin, 105
Work ethic:
  and slavery, 37, 38
Worker's Councils, 139
Workers:
  factory or industrial, 7
  two types, 13
Workforce 2000, 162
World War I, 125, 128, 130,
    133–134, 139, 150, 157
World War II, 93, 95–6, 118

Y

Yale, 105
Yellow Dog Contract, 140
Yellow Fever, 56
Yeoman, 14
  See also farmer
Yeoman Farmer, 16, 24, 29,
    99
Young, Arthur, 96

About the Author

A New Yorker now transplanted to Seattle, Daniel Jacoby earned his Ph.D. in economics at the University of Washington. He now works as an associate professor for the very unusual University of Washington–Bothell's Liberal Studies Program, where interdisciplinarity and teaching are especially valued. His apprenticeship in academic scholarship has led him to publish monographs in several academic journals including *Labor History, Industrial Relations,* and the *Journal of Economic History.*

DATE DUE

GAYLORD   PRINTED IN U.S.A.